THE
MEDICARE
ANSWER
BOOK

Other books by Geri Harrington

Never Too Old: A Complete Guide
for the Over-Fifty Adult

Total Warmth: The Complete Guide
to Winter Well-Being

Fireplace Stoves, Hearths and Inserts

The Wood-Burning Stove Book

Grow Your Own Chinese Vegetables

The Salad Book

Summer Garden, Winter Kitchen

The College Cookbook

THE MEDICARE ANSWER BOOK

by Geri Harrington

1817

HARPER & ROW, PUBLISHERS, New York
Cambridge, Philadelphia, San Francisco, London
Mexico City, São Paulo, Sydney

If there have been any changes in Medicare benefits since publication, you may write the publisher, care of Department 524, for a free Medicare Update sheet that will list any major new developments in 1982.

THE MEDICARE ANSWER BOOK. Copyright © 1982 by Don Harrington Associates. All rights reserved. Printed in the United States of America. No part of this book may be used or reproduced in any manner whatsoever without written permission except in the case of brief quotations embodied in critical articles and reviews. For information address Harper & Row, Publishers, Inc., 10 East 53rd Street, New York, N.Y. 10022. Published simultaneously in Canada by Fitzhenry & Whiteside Limited, Toronto.

FIRST EDITION

Designer: C. Linda Dingler

Library of Congress Cataloging in Publication Data

Harrington, Geri.
    The medicare answer book.

    Includes index.
    1. Medicare—Handbooks, manuals, etc.   I. Title.
HD7102.U4H29   1982   344.73'0226   81–48037
                         347.304226   AACR2
    ISBN 0–06–014979–5   83 84 85 86 10 9 8 7 6 5 4 3
    ISBN 0–06–090938–2 (pbk.)   83 84 85 86 10 9 8 7 6 5 4 3

Contents

Appendix

Acknowledgments

My very special thanks are due to Mary McCarthy of the Medicare Claim Office of Connecticut General Life Insurance Company, and to Richard Getrost of the Office of Beneficiary Services of the Health Care Financing Administration, both of whom patiently answered my questions all during the two years of research and writing, read the completed manuscript, cheerfully checked my figures, facts and interpretations, and enriched the writing of the book with their salty comments.

I am deeply indebted also to Louise Bracknell, Staff Director of the Subcommittee on Health and Long-Term Care of the House Select Committee on Aging under Congressman Claude Pepper and to Kathleen Deignan of the Special Committee on Aging of the United States Senate under Senator Lawton Chiles, both of whom spent hours with me discussing the past, present and future of Medicare, and who gave me so much valuable material, in the form of hearing reports, memoranda, releases and letters, that I had to take it back to Connecticut by car instead of by plane as I had originally planned.

Thanks also to Congressman William Ratchford and Senator Lowell Weicker, Jr., who furnished me with material that I could not otherwise have easily obtained. And to Virginia Gray of the Health Care Financing Administration, Betty Assola and Pat Brassel of Blue Cross/Blue Shield of Connecticut, all of whom contributed generously of their time and expertise.

The physicians I interviewed in the course of writing this book prefer to remain anonymous, but I appreciate their sparing me time in a busy day, as well as answering frankly my not-always-tactful questions.

A small army of social workers, HMO staffers, senior citizens and volunteers helped me gather together the questions that form Chapter 22, and guided me as to which areas of Medicare are most confusing and least-well understood. I hope my answers in particular and the text in general will help make a difficult subject matter a little easier to deal with.

Geri Harrington

Wilton, Connecticut

I
MEDICARE—THE BASICS

1

What Is Medicare and How Does It Work?

WHAT IT IS

Medicare is health insurance that you buy from the federal government. Like all health insurance it offers only limited coverage and doesn't pay for many necessary health-care expenses. At present, however, it is by far your best buy, although you probably should also have some private insurance to supplement it. As with any health-insurance policy, it has premiums, deductibles and coinsurance.

WHO IS ELIGIBLE?

Four kinds of people are eligible for Medicare:

1. A person 65 or more years of age who is eligible for social security or survivor benefits, or who is a qualified railroad retirement beneficiary. You can qualify for Medicare when you reach 65 even if you decide not to retire at that time. At present, government employees are not eligible; they have a different health-care insurance plan.

2. A person who is not eligible for social security or railroad retirement benefits but reached age 65 before

1968. Or, who reached 65 after 1967 and has a certain minimum number of quarters of social security coverage.
3. A person who is 65 or older, not eligible under (1) or (2), but wants to enroll voluntarily and can pay the premium for this type of enrollment.
4. A person who is under 65 but has been receiving disability payments for at least 24 months. This includes people with end-stage renal disease (ESRD).

Does this include just about everyone?

If you include the people who fall into category 3, it is available to almost everyone age 65 or over. If you don't, it is estimated that, out of about 25 million persons in that age group, there are about 1 million who are not eligible.

Category 3 allows them to join voluntarily, but the premium is so high that many elderly would find the cost beyond their means. Since voluntary enrollees must enroll in both Medicare Part A (HI) and Medicare Part B (SMI), the premiums (through June 1982) would be $89 and $11, respectively, per month—a total of $1,200 a year. As of July 1, 1982, premiums are scheduled to be $113 and $12.20 respectively (a total of $1,502.40). This is a hefty total and would buy a fairly good health policy if you were younger, but if you are over 65, you can't shop around. If the premiums are beyond your means, maybe you can qualify for Medicaid: the qualifications are stringent but the coverage is better—and free.

HOW DOES ONE ENROLL?

1. When you apply for social security or railroad retirement at the age of 65, you are automatically enrolled in the two parts of Medicare—HI (Hospital Insur-

ance, or Part A) and SMI (Supplementary Medical Insurance, or Part B). SMI is optional and you may ask not to be enrolled in it, but read about it before you decide.

2. If you have taken early retirement, you will be automatically enrolled when you reach 65.
3. If you are not eligible, you can enroll voluntarily when you are 65 but must notify Medicare that you wish to do so. Call your local social security office and ask how to do this.

WHAT IS MEANT BY HI AND SMI?

Medicare is divided into two parts: Medicare Part A, or Hospital Insurance (HI), and Medicare Part B, or Supplementary Medical Insurance (SMI). You pay no premium for HI but you do pay a monthly premium for SMI.

WHAT IS THE DIFFERENCE IN BENEFITS BETWEEN HI AND SMI?

HI (PART A) COVERS:	SMI (PART B) COVERS:
Hospital costs for inpatient services	Doctors' services
Skilled nursing facilities (a special kind of nursing home)	Outpatient hospital services
Home health care	Other health-care services

WHAT DOES HI COST?

For most people eligible for HI, there is no premium. For those who enroll voluntarily (because they aren't eligible any other way), there is a monthly premium (HI Premium); in 1981, it was $89 a month, or $1,068 a year (in 1982, it will go up to $113 a month).

In addition, there are the following costs.

- *Hospital deductible,* for first hospital admission in a single benefit period.
- *Hospital coinsurance,* from the 60th to the 90th day in the hospital in a single benefit period.
- *Hospital coinsurance* for Lifetime Reserve days, 91st to 150th day in the hospital.
- *Blood deductible:* cost of first three pints of blood (unless replaced).
- *Nursing-home (SNF) coinsurance,* from the 21st to the 100th day.

These costs increase each year. The deductible approximates the national average cost of one day's stay in a hospital and the amount changes each year, usually on January 1. The coinsurance from the 61st to the 90th day equals one quarter of the deductible. The coinsurance for the Lifetime Reserve days equals one half of the deductible.

For 1982, the dollar amounts are:

Hospital deductible:	$260
Hospital coinsurance, 61st to 90th day, daily:	65
Hospital coinsurance, 91st through 150th day, daily:	130

Nursing-home coverage in a skilled nursing facility is not subject to a deductible because Medicare does not cover you unless you have first been in the hospital (where you will have paid the hospital deductible). Therefore, the 1st to the 20th day of your stay in an SNF is completely covered by Medicare. Your costs start on the 21st day.

For 1982, the dollar amounts are:

Nursing-home (SNF) coinsurance,
    21st to 100th day, daily: $32.50

WHAT DOES SMI COST?

Enrollment in SMI, or Medicare Part B, requires payment of a monthly premium. This is adjusted on July 1 of each year. As of July 1, 1982, through June 30, 1983, it will be $12.20. In addition, there is a yearly deductible you must pay before coverage begins—$75 in 1982—and there is a 20% coinsurance charge for all bills where the doctor accepts the assignment, and for most other covered services if the provider accepts the assignment. An exception to this is outpatient physician treatment of mental illness, which is covered only to a maximum of $250 in any one year.

The only charge you can anticipate is the deductible, since the 20% coinsurance will vary according to the amount of the bill; whether you must pay even more depends on whether or not the provider accepts the assignment. (We will cover this in detail in Chapter 11.)

WHAT DOESN'T MEDICARE COVER?

After you pay your SMI (Part B) monthly premium, you must still pay:

1. Deductible and coinsurance.
2. Noncovered items and services.
3. Charges exceeding "reasonable charges."

These areas are the ones that create Medicare "gaps" and the ones you try to cover when you buy Medigap insurance (see Chapter 21).

WHY DO PEOPLE FIND MEDICARE CONFUSING?

It is very difficult—sometimes actually impossible—to find out exactly what Medicare will and will not cover. In addition, such limitations as "accepting the assignment" and "medically necessary," and all the various deductibles and coinsurance—as well as the fact that the actual dollar amounts of these are constantly changing—make Medicare very involved and complicated.

Even the experts, the people in each state who administer Medicare, cannot implement changes in the law until they have received detailed explanations (guidelines) from the government that tell them exactly how to do this.

An example of how difficult it is to understand Medicare is the coverage for nursing-home stays. Medicare covers only one kind of nursing home; it is called a skilled nursing facility and is commonly referred to as an SNF. There are very few SNFs in the United States—and most elderly people who need nursing-home care don't qualify for admission to this type. If you are expecting Medicare to take care of you when you are aged and may need long-term nursing-home care, you will probably be disappointed.

MORE ABOUT HI (PART A) COVERAGE

HI, or hospital insurance, covers charges incurred when you are in a hospital, an SNF nursing home or under the care of a home health agency. Coverage in the hospital includes: a semiprivate room, staff nursing care, in-hospital medicines, lab tests, X-rays, operating and recovery rooms and special-care services, anesthesia, rehab services, food, physical therapy, splints, wheelchairs, walkers. But it covers these costs only for 90 days in the hospital in a single benefit period (150 days if you use your once-in-a-lifetime

Reserve days) and up to 100 days in an SNF.

You pay a deductible amount when you first enter the hospital, and after 60 days in the hospital in a single benefit period you pay a daily coinsurance charge. There is no limit to the number of benefit periods you can have but you *must be out of the hospital or nursing home for 60 days before you can start a new period* (see page 27).

You are fully covered for the first 20 days in an SNF but must pay coinsurance from the 21st to the 100th day. After that, Medicare coverage ceases until you start a new benefit period.

You are covered for an unlimited number of home health-care visits for skilled nursing care, physical therapy, speech therapy and part-time home health aide services as well as medical supplies and equipment. Doctor visits are partly covered under SMI (Part B).

Outside of the inadequate coverage for nursing homes, HI is the best part of Medicare. Its weakness is that it does not cover long-term care. If you have a chronic illness or one that lasts a long time, you may never get to start a new benefit period. Under these circumstances, it is possible to use up your Medicare coverage 150 days after you turn 65 and to never be able to get any use out of HI coverage again.

MORE ABOUT SMI (PART B) COVERAGE

SMI covers most "regular" doctors' services but only a very small part of the actual bills, unless the doctor agrees to accept the assignment or unless you belong to an HMO (see Chapter 24). Dentists, chiropractors, optometrists and podiatrists are covered for only a few specified services.

SMI also covers outpatient hospital services, such as outpatient surgery, X-ray and radiation therapy services, limited ambulance service, laboratory services, and some

durable medical equipment and other medical supplies and
equipment.

SINCE I CAN'T DO ANYTHING ABOUT IT, WHY SHOULD I TRY TO UNDERSTAND HOW MEDICARE WORKS?

In the first place, you *can* do something about it if you
think Medicare should cover more than it does. You can
write your congressman whenever there is a Medicare-
related vote coming up in Congress, join senior-citizen organizations that fight for better benefits and, in general,
make your existence as a citizen felt.

In addition, the better you understand Medicare, the
better use you can make of it and the quicker you will
notice when a mistake is made. Coverage is sometimes denied by mistake, errors are made in paying claims, and
other people will give you misinformation. The more you
know, the better the deal you will get from Medicare. If
you understand what Medicare does and does not cover,
you will have fewer unpleasant surprises (thinking you are
covered when you are not) and you will be better able to
judge whether a Medigap policy is or is not worth buying.

2

Medicare Benefits in a Nutshell

We are now ready to take a more detailed look at Medicare benefits. Here we will begin to take note of some of the factors (deductibles, coinsurance, noncovered items) that limit the extent of the benefits. And keep in mind that no benefits are covered unless Medicare says they are "medically necessary" and furnished by providers certified or approved by Medicare. Keep in mind, also, that terms used in Medicare do not always mean what you may think they mean; in this table we will use Medicare's terms and later we will explain exactly what they mean. (Or if you can't wait, look them up in "Medispeak" on page 311.)

Later on we will give you current figures for the actual amounts of the deductibles, coinsurance and premiums, but these are subject to change (the HI deductible, for example, is increased every January 1), and you should check with your social security office if you want to be sure you have the latest figures. Once you are enrolled in the Medicare program, you will be informed by mail of any changes of this sort.

HI (Hospital Insurance)—MEDICARE PART A

As the name implies, this pays some of the costs of hospitalization and related services, such as skilled nursing home facilities and home health care.

SERVICE	MEDICARE PAYS	YOU PAY (IN 1982)
Hospitalization in a single benefit period:		
first 60 days	all but deductible	the deductible: $260.00
61st to 90th day	all but daily coinsurance	daily coinsurance: $65.00
from 91st day on	nothing (unless you use your Lifetime Reserve Days)	all costs
Lifetime reserve days:		
60 additional days of hospitalization you can use once in a lifetime	all but daily coinsurance	daily coinsurance: $130
In a psychiatric hospital:		
190 days of hospitalization in a lifetime	same benefits as for other hospitalization	same costs as for other hospitalization
after 190 days	nothing	all costs

Nursing home (SNF only):		
first 20 days	100%	nothing
21st to 100th day	all but daily coinsurance	daily coinsurance: $32.50
from 100th day on	nothing	all costs
Home health care:		
unlimited home health visits (not including doctor visits)	100%	nothing
custodial care	nothing	all costs
Blood	all but first three pints	first three pints

SMI (Supplementary Medical Insurance)—MEDICARE PART B

As indicated by the name, SMI supplements HI coverage; it helps pay doctor bills, for certain medical equipment and for a few other medical services.

In order to be eligible for SMI coverage and benefits, you must pay a monthly premium of $11 ($12.20 after July 1, 1982) and, once a year, a deductible amount of $75 of your actual medical bills. You must pay these charges in addition to coinsurance and noncovered charges. You do not pay the $75 deductible to Medicare; you simply pay the first $75 of covered Part B charges.

SERVICE	MEDICARE PAYS	YOU PAY
Physicians:		
if they accept the assignment	80% of the bill	20% of the bill
if they do not accept the assignment	80% of the "reasonable charge"	20% of the "reasonable charge" plus any costs over the "reasonable charge"
Chiropractors:		
only for manual manipulation of the spine to correct subluxation	same as other physicians' services	same as other physicians' services

Podiatrists: except for exclusions	same as other physicians' services	same as other physicians' services
Dentists: only for jaw surgery or setting fracture or physicians' (but not dental) services	same as other physicians' services	same as other physicians' services
Optometrists: only for treatment of aphakia	same as other physicians' services	same as other physicians' services
Mental illness: physicians' services	$250 a year; 190 days lifetime maximum	all costs over $250 plus any costs over "reasonable charges"
X rays, diagnostic tests	same as other physicians' services	same as other physicians' services
Ambulance, if covered	same as other physicians' services	same as other physicians' services
Home dialysis for end-stage renal disease	100%	nothing
Durable medical equipment	from 100% to nothing, depending on the item	from nothing to all costs, depending on the item

II
MEDICARE PART A: EXPLAINING HOSPITAL INSURANCE (HI)

3

When You Are in the Hospital

HI, or Medicare Part A, pays for many of the health-care costs incurred when you are in the hospital for the first 90 days of a benefit period (see page 26 for explanation of "benefit period"). It is much more complete than out-of-hospital coverage; for instance, it pays for all drugs taken while hospitalized, whereas out-of-hospital coverage doesn't pay for any drugs except those that cannot be self-administered. (Being squeamish doesn't help; Medicare says you can give yourself your own insulin shots and doesn't cover the cost of insulin.) HI also covers all the medically necessary medical services the hospital usually provides, including staff doctors, interns, X rays, nurses, therapists, laboratory tests and so on. It pays for custodial care, such as meals and baths. It even pays for the little amenities you often find by your bedside, such as talcum powder, mouthwash and towels, if the hospital always provides them free to all patients.

It does not pay private doctor bills, such as those of your own doctor and of consultants he may call in from the outside. Nor does it pay anesthesiologists, podiatrists, and other private physicians. These bills may be partially covered by SMI, or Medicare Part B.

It also does not pay nonmedical costs, such as TV, telephone or a private room (unless medically necessary). It will never pay for private nurses.

If a Medicare beneficiary requests services or accommodations (such as a private room) that are not covered, Medicare does not prevent the beneficiary from having them; it simply will not pay for them. In this case, Medicare will pay for what it usually does and the hospital will bill the beneficiary for the rest.

A beneficiary who does not request such services or accommodations may still find himself in a hospital that provides them automatically. In this case, Medicare has a provision to protect the beneficiary from charges that he was not aware he was incurring. The law specifically requires that the hospital providing luxury items not covered by Medicare and not requested by the patient inform the patient *in advance* that he or she will be charged for these items, and that the cost, or part of the cost, of these items is not covered by Medicare. If the hospital doesn't do this, you have a right to question the propriety of the bill; if it were a medically necessary service, the presumption is that it would have been covered by Medicare. The hospital has no right to arbitrarily bill you for services you neither asked for nor knew were going to cost you money.

Hospital Insurance is the most straightforward and easy-to-understand part of Medicare, but even here it is important to be aware of restrictions and limitations.

THE DEDUCTIBLE: THE FIRST 60 DAYS

As we have seen in "Medicare in a Nutshell," you must pay a deductible the first time you enter a hospital during a benefit period. This is supposed to be equal to the average cost of one day in the hospital, so it goes up every year.

Suppose I Can't Pay the Deductible Right Away?

If you are going into the hospital for an urgently needed operation, you may not immediately be able to put your hands on the more than two hundred dollars you will need to pay the deductible. Most hospitals will take your word that you will pay it eventually, but a few will insist that you must pay on admission or they will not admit you.

You should know that this is unconscionable. There is no excuse for this inasmuch as the hospital has nothing to lose; it will be reimbursed by Medicare if you fail to pay the deductible. Your local senior-citizens group should canvass the nearest hospitals and find out what their policy is in this regard. If they state that they will refuse admission to anyone not prepaying the deductible, you may want to take action to try to change this policy. You could first meet with the head of the hospital and discuss the unfairness of such a prerequisite, reminding him or her of the fact that the hospital runs no risk. If this is not effective, local newspapers and regional magazines might be interested in a factual article about the matter. You will usually find a lack of consistency among hospitals, so you might want to make available to seniors and to the media a comparison of the various hospitals serving your community, pointing up the ones that are more reasonable.

WHOLE BLOOD, AN EXCEPTION TO 100% COVERAGE

Once you have paid your deductible, you will not incur any hospital expenses—with a few exceptions—for the first 60 days of your hospitalization. Medicare will take care of most charges if medically necessary.

One of the exceptions to 100% coverage is whole blood. If you require whole blood, in connection with an operation for instance, you will have to pay for the first three pints yourself. Some states, such as Connecticut, do not allow a charge for whole blood; they pick up the tab. Others do, however, and it is a good idea to know your state's policy. If you prefer, you or a friend, relative or organization may replace the blood used. In that case, you will not be charged. Some hospitals, however, have a policy of not accepting blood from certain outside sources. If you *offer* to have your blood replaced, you do not have to pay for it even if the hospital prefers not to accept your offer. The only exception would be if the replacement blood was not acceptable on health grounds.

Only whole blood is charged for; plasma, gamma globulin and other whole-blood components are covered.

If you choose to pay the whole-blood deductible, you will then be covered for that entire benefit period, even if you require whole blood during a different hospitalization. (You do not have to pay *any* HI deductible again until you start a new benefit period.)

COINSURANCE—THE 61ST THROUGH THE 90TH DAY

After the first 60 days of hospitalization in any one benefit period (and these days need not be consecutive or used up in a single hospital admission), you become liable for what is called "inpatient hospital coinsurance." In other words, you must begin to pay something toward your hospital charges. As of January 1, 1982, the amount is $65 a day. This amount will change every January 1; Medicare will notify you of the new amount if you are already enrolled in Medicare. Except for the $65, Medicare will pick up 100% of most charges, just as it did for the first 60 days.

AFTER THE 90TH DAY

After the 90th day of hospitalization in a single benefit period, your hospitalization coverage ceases (unless you have some Lifetime Reserve days left).

A 90-day hospital stay during a benefit period may sound like good coverage; after all, the average stay for an over-65 hospital patient is 11 days. But not everyone is average; for the senior citizen with a chronic or terminal disease who requires hospitalization for the rest of his or her life, 90 days are not enough. And there are no exceptions. Even if there is nowhere else for you to go, you will not be covered for hospitalization if your coverage has been used up.

The cruelty of this was sharply brought home to me one day when I encountered a woman in the hall of a local hospital where I was visiting a patient. She was crying and looked at the end of her strength. I went up and asked her what the trouble was. She was so upset she could hardly speak but managed to explain that her husband was dying of terminal cancer and had, at the most, two weeks to live. She was badly crippled with arthritis and could not take care of him at home but the hospital had told her his Medicare coverage would cease the following day. They had no money to pay for hospital care themselves and she simply did not know what to do. I suggested she talk to the hospital's social services department and see if they could get her husband into a hospice. Here is an area where the gap in Medicare coverage is clearly inhuman.

Medicare was never designed to provide long-term care. You should think of it as primarily insurance for acute illnesses; that is where it works best. Medigap insurance will not fill this gap; most private health insurance does not offer any coverage for this area. Catastrophic insurance would, but it is available to the over-65 individual only through group insurance. If you have it, be sure not to let it go.

LIFETIME RESERVE DAYS

There is one exception to the fact that Medicare hospital coverage ceases after 90 days in any one benefit period; it is called Lifetime Reserve days and is an option available to you only once in your lifetime—although it may be used over many years.

Lifetime Reserve days are an additional 60 days of hospitalization that Medicare will cover, in addition to any other coverage. These covered days are there for you to call upon whenever you need more than the 90-day coverage. You can use them a few at a time, all at once, all in one benefit period or stretched over several benefit periods. They are yours to use any way you want, but once they are gone, they can never be renewed.

You may be asked, upon being admitted to the hospital, whether or not you will use these reserve days if needed. Since it is impossible to tell at that time how long you will be in the hospital, you may not want to commit yourself. Or you may have second thoughts. Medicare provides for those contingencies. If you state that you wish to use your reserve days, you have up to 90 days *after you have left the hospital* to change your mind.

If you actually use some of your reserve days and then change your mind, you will have to reimburse the hospital, out of your own pocket, for charges incurred after the 90th day of hospitalization. You might want to look at your bill—especially that portion of it you would have to pay—before deciding.

Coinsurance for Lifetime Reserve Days

The coinsurance you must pay for Lifetime Reserve days is twice as much as for the 61st to the 90th day of hospitalization. As of January 1, 1982, it is $130 a day.

WHAT WOULD 150 DAYS IN A HOSPITAL COST YOU?

Although coverage of hospital bills is the best of Medicare benefits, it still leaves a tidy sum for the beneficiary to pay.

With complete Medicare coverage, the cost to you of a 150-day hospital stay in a single benefit period in 1982, not counting your doctor bills or any other medical charges, would be

1st through 60th day, deductible	$ 260
61st through 90th day, at $65.00 daily coinsurance	1,950
91st through 150th day, at $130.00 daily coinsurance (Lifetime Reserve Days)	7,800
Total you pay:	$10,010

In other words, even with Medicare Part A hospital coverage, a 150-day stay in the hospital will cost you over ten thousand dollars. And that is at 1982 rates; if inflation continues and Medicare coverage is not improved, it will be even more in years to come. No wonder enlightened senators and congressmen think the Medicare law should be amended to include a cap on how much out-of-pocket cost a Medicare beneficiary should have to pay.

WHY NOT GO TO THE HOSPITAL WHENEVER YOU DON'T FEEL WELL?

Medicare coverage for the first 60 days of hospitalization is so good that you may wonder why the doctor doesn't put you in the hospital more often. After all, you get all your meals free, and all your medicine, and you don't even have to worry about heating bills. Of course it's not home, but it does have many advantages. If you are crippled with arthritis and can't get out to shop for food or if you are unable to prepare your own meals, hospitalization may seem like a sensible solution.

The answer is simply that Medicare will not cover hospitalization unless it is "medically necessary." You must require the level of care provided in a hospital. If you have a chronic disease that requires intermittent hospitalization, you will be sent home as soon as you no longer need hospital-level care.

HOW IS "MEDICAL NECESSITY" DETERMINED?

All Medicare beneficiaries claiming Medicare coverage are routinely supervised by a Professional Standards Review Organization (PSRO) in their area. This organization decides whether Medicare coverage is justified—whether it is "medically necessary." Your doctor cannot overrule PSRO decisions. See Chapter 20 to learn more about this organization.

WHAT IS A BENEFIT PERIOD?

Medicare Part A (HI) benefits are limited by benefit periods; for instance, you are covered for only 90 days in the hospital *in a single benefit period*. Because of this limitation, you may run out of Medicare hospital coverage within 150 days of turning 65 if you immediately have a 150-day hospital stay and are never able to qualify for a new benefit period. It is obviously very important to know what a benefit period is.

Benefit periods are also called "a spell of illness." The benefit period begins the first day you enter the hospital (day one) and continues until you have been out of the hospital or skilled nursing facility for *60 consecutive days.* (The day of discharge is not counted as a day in the hospital.) It has nothing to do with the calendar but only with the number of days involved. There is no limit on the number of benefit periods you can have in a year or in a lifetime.

How Does the Benefit Period Work?

To understand a benefit period you need to know the various ways in which it is applied. Here are the most important:

1. You must pay the hospital deductible only once during a benefit period. No matter how many times you may be admitted to the hospital—even if the admissions are for different kinds of illnesses—you do not have to pay it twice in one benefit period.

2. Any hospitalization or stay in a skilled nursing facility counts. Even if your stay was not eligible for Medicare coverage, you cannot begin a new benefit period until you have been out of the hospital or SNF for 60 consecutive days.

3. If you are hospitalized, then go into an SNF, then go back into the hospital, you cannot begin a new benefit period unless there were 60 consecutive days when you were out of the SNF before going into the hospital the second time.

4. If you did not receive nursing-home coverage because you did not fulfill the prior-hospitalization requirement, your nursing-home stay (if in an SNF) would still constitute a spell of illness, beginning with the day you were admitted. The fact that you paid all the costs of the nursing home wouldn't make any difference.

How Could the Benefit-Period Provision Lead to Your Losing Coverage?

Let me give an example:

Suppose you enter the hospital a month after your 65th birthday—let us say on January 1st. You stay in the hospital 60 days and are then transferred to a skilled nursing facility. You stay in the skilled nursing facility for 50 days and are then able to go home. After 45 days at home, you again are sent to the hospital where you stay for 50 days. You are sent home again but your condition worsens after 10 days and you return to the hospital. By now, during the two hospitalizations you have used up all your Medicare hospital coverage for a single benefit period, including your Lifetime Reserve days (60 + 40 + 50 = 150 days). But you have not been out of the hospital or SNF for 60 conservative days, so you cannot start a new benefit period.

So by September—less than a year after you turned 65—you have used up your Medicare Part A hospital coverage. If you have a terminal illness and have to remain in the hospital until you die, you will have no Medicare hospital coverage no matter how long you are there.

This is, admittedly, an extreme example but it does happen. Even if it doesn't happen before your 66th birthday, it is increasingly liable to happen as you get older. With life expectancy increasing each year, more and more people will find themselves with chronic illnesses, many of which require intermittent hospitalization so frequent that they may become locked into a benefit period, as in the above example. As the law stands now, the older you are, the more likely you are to exhaust your Medicare hospital coverage.

You may think it extraordinary that you are deserted by your government at a time when you need help most—in the event of a long illness—but that is consistent with the philosophy behind Medicare. If you remember that it is basically meant to cover only short-term acute illness, you will understand that it is a young person's health-insurance plan presented as health care for the aged. Medicare was created by Congress and can be altered by Congress, as we have seen in recent legislation. Whether future changes will be made to provide increased benefits for the elderly or to erode those benefits more than they have already been eroded over the years since 1965 is up to the voter. And the number of voters over 65 is great enough to make the needs of that group felt.

WHAT IS THE COVERAGE FOR MENTAL ILLNESS?

In spite of the fact that 15% to 25% of the elderly have significant mental illnesses, Medicare limits its coverage to 190 days of inpatient psychiatric hospital care during the entire lifetime of a beneficiary. Combined with the even more inadequate Medicare Part B coverage ($250 a year), the total Medicare coverage for mental illness is so inadequate as to be practically nonexistent.

In addition to the 190-day lifetime limitation, Medicare erodes even that benefit by counting hospitalization prior to your 65th birthday, if you are in the hospital when you become 65.

Here is how it works: If you are already in a psychiatric hospital on the day you become 65, all the days of hospitalization—and they need not be consecutive—in the period 150 days before your 65th birthday are *deducted* from the 150 days of Medicare hospital coverage to which you are entitled in a single benefit period.

For example: You turn 65 on June 1 and become eligible for Medicare hospital coverage. You are already in a psychiatric hospital and have been there for 20 days previous to your birthday. In addition, you were hospitalized for 90 days during January, February, March and April. This means you were hospitalized for 110 days in the 150 days before you became 65. The way the Medicare law works, you are now entitled to only 40 more days in the hospital in your first benefit period (40 + 110 = 150). In other words, after your 65th birthday you would lose your Medicare hospital coverage after 40 days of hospitalization unless you could then manage to stay out of the hospital for 60 consecutive days. And you would lose this coverage even though Medicare had not paid one penny for the 110 days of hospitalization prior to your 65th birthday.

You do get one break, though. The days of prior hospitalization are not counted against the 190 days of coverage to which you are limited in your lifetime.

WHAT DO THE EXPERTS THINK OF MEDICARE'S MENTAL HEALTH COVERAGE?

Congressman Claude Pepper, of the Select Committee on Aging of the House of Representatives, has this to say on Medicare coverage of mental illness: "While the elderly constitute only 11 percent of the population . . . more than 25 percent of all suicides are committed by persons over 65. . . . Addressing the gaps in mental health coverage under Medicare is a matter of the highest priority."

Robert Drinan, chairman of the Aging Committee's National Conference on Mental Health and the Elderly, speaking before the American Psychological Association on "Meeting the Mental Health Needs of Older Americans: A Failure in Public Policy," went to even greater length:

"The reality is that those senior citizens who need assistance in the area of mental health are generally invisible. . . . Some of these illnesses—perhaps many—are correctible if they are diagnosed at an early stage. . . . Depression and psychosis increase significantly among people over the age of 65. This is even more so among those over the age of 75. This is a very significant statistic, since members of the over-75 group constitute the fastest-growing segment of the senior population. . . . The American Psychological Association has estimated that 80 percent of senior citizens requiring mental help do not obtain it. Only 2 percent of all patients in private psychiatric care are over 65. Only 4 percent of all persons seen at public outpatient mental health clinics are senior citizens.

"Clearly we are confronting a tragedy of enormous proportions. It is tragic because . . . there are some 100 reversible conditions that mimic senility. . . . Many physicians unfamiliar with geriatric medicine labelled forgetfulness or confusion as indicators of fixed organic brain disease when frequently these symptoms do not indicate anything that serious.

"The limitation of $250 annually and the 20–80 copayment for mental illness [Part B coverage] clearly are built-in acts of discrimination against mental illness.

"Another discrimination exists in present law in that inpatient psychiatric hospital care is limited to 190 days during the entire lifetime of the insured. This clearly should also be changed, so that at least the same coverage is offered to mental illness as to physical illness."

ARE ALL U.S. HOSPITALS COVERED BY MEDICARE?

No, but most are. First of all, the institution must meet Medicare's definition of a hospital. Second, it must qualify by conforming to Medicare regulations, such as keeping records and filing claims as Medicare requires. Third, it must—with three exceptions (see below)—be located in the United States (as defined by Medicare).

It is possible for a hospital to be participating one month and then to lose its status the next (although this doesn't happen very often).

Psychiatric and tuberculosis hospitals may participate, but under slightly different conditions from those of general hospitals.

Christian Science sanatoria are included but "only with respect to services provided by or in such a sanatorium only to the extent and under such conditions, limitations, and requirements as may be provided in regulations." In effect, the same services are covered that would be provided by a general hospital but services that are unique to such a sanatorium would not be covered.

Chances are that any institution not covered by Medicare will notify you upon admission when you routinely present your Medicare card as "health insurance coverage."

HOSPITAL COVERAGE IN A FOREIGN COUNTRY

Medicare coverage is usually not available when you are out of the United States, and Medicare coverage does not usually extend to a foreign hospital.

An exception to this rule is made if you are in the United States but are taken to a foreign hospital in an emergency because it is nearer to, or more accessible from, the site of the emergency than a suitable hospital in the United States. For example, if you are in an automobile accident near the Canadian or Mexican border, it is possible that you can get Medicare coverage for emergency treatment in a Canadian or Mexican hospital. Depending on the arrangement the hospital has with Medicare, Medicare may pay the hospital or may pay you (upon receipt of an itemized hospital bill).

Of course it is assumed that your condition meets Medicare's definition of an "emergency": a potentially life-threatening situation or one that might lead to serious health impairment.

As soon as the emergency has ended, you will no longer be covered for continued treatment if you are in a foreign or nonparticipating hospital. If after the emergency you continue to require hospitalization, you will have to move to a participating United States hospital if you expect to continue to receive Medicare coverage. Generally your attending physician will determine when the emergency is over, but remember that Medicare usually has the last word.

Another exception is in a nonemergency situation when the foreign hospital is the nearest suitable to your home. Medicare coverage is provided under these circumstances "whether or not an emergency existed and without regard to where the illness or accident occurred."

The third exception applies only to travel between Alaska and another state. Under these circumstances, it is conceivable that you may require emergency medical care in Canada. Although you are not in the United States, you will be covered because you are traveling from one state to another. A limitation, however, is that you must be traveling by the most direct route between the two states. If you are on a tour of Canada or otherwise vacationing in Canada, this exception will not apply.

SOME THINGS YOU SHOULD KNOW ABOUT HOSPITAL BILLS

Why Should You Insist on Receiving an Itemized Hospital Bill?

First of all, you are entitled to it under the Patient's Bill of Rights. Second, you are the only one who can pick up certain kinds of billing errors. Everyone makes mistakes but mistakes in hospital billing increase already inflated costs and decrease the amount of Medicare money available. Medicare tries to look over hospital bills but yours is one among many they have to check, and the area in which you are best informed is one in which they cannot make a judgment.

How to Check Your Hospital Bill

You should check it item by item, line for line, charge for charge. Here are some specific areas:

1. Check the spelling of your name, address, admission date and your identification number (usually your Medicare number). If an insurance company is listed (Medicare and private), make sure it is coverage you actually have and that it includes all your coverage.

    Aside from the fact that it is important for this information to be correct, it is also helpful to find a mistake in this basic area; if the hospital makes such a simple mistake, it will not be able to take as strong a position when you discover other mistakes.
2. Check all totals and subtotals.
3. Check cumulative charges—how many days in the hospital at so much a day; how many hours in the operating room.
4. Check specific items; drugs, X rays, electrocardiograms and similar charges you recognize. If you have

kept a journal, you will have a record. If you couldn't, maybe a relative or friend might have done it for you. For a short stay, you may be able to remember.

In checking specific items, take into account that the dates for the charges may not be the same as the dates you received the services; hospitals sometimes put down the date the charge was recorded, rather than the date it was billed. This makes it a little more difficult to check but you may remember that you had one X ray, not three as the bill says; when you had it isn't that important.

Only you know whether you received the services listed on the bill. I have found many errors on hospital bills and most of them were for services not rendered—at least not to the person who was being billed.

Another reason for requiring an itemized bill is to spot unreasonable charges. The *New York Times* reported the story of a woman who spent five months of "persistent telephoning and letter-writing" before the hospital finally broke down and sent her an itemized bill. When she looked it over, she found "she had been charged $26.86 for a teaspoon of cough medicine that costs $2.07 per ounce at the drugstore. There was also a $50.58 charge for two milliliters of a drug that had not even been administered. A spokesman for the hospital said that it was all 'an isolated error,' and that the billing system was being changed."

Errors of this sort in hospital billing are *not* isolated, and you owe it to yourself and to Medicare to catch and correct them.

Hospitals often send bills that ask for payment, without identifying what the bill is for. The only item specified is the amount you are to pay. Politely but firmly refuse to pay any bill that does not state exactly what it is for. If it does tell you but you don't know what the description means, call the business office and ask them to explain it. Maybe you don't know what it is because you never got it.

Do not be intimidated by a form that says "We do not send duplicate bills." If you have never received an itemized bill, you are not asking for a duplicate bill. Simply explain that you have not received anything but a statement and as that does not itemize the charges, you cannot check them and pay the hospital.

Why Does a Hospital Sometimes Dun a Medicare Beneficiary for a Covered Bill

There are two reasons:

1. Even though your hospital bill is completely covered by Medicare and you have nothing to pay out-of-pocket, you may receive a bill from the hospital for the entire cost of your stay. And later on you may receive notices and letters complaining that you have not paid the bill, and threatening to put the matter in the hands of a collection agency. This is due to the hospital computer which makes out the bills but doesn't always check to see if they are covered by Medicare.

   The first time you get a bill, call the business office of the hospital and ask why you are being billed. They may say the bill is just for your records and that you are not expected to pay it. Or they may say it's a mistake. In any case, the computer may keep on its customary billing procedure until payment is made by Medicare; this could take months. Once you have checked and know you are not expected to pay the bill, don't worry about it. It's the problem of the hospital's bookkeeping department, not yours.

2. The other type of bill you may receive is for the de-

ductible and coinsurance. If you have a Medigap policy that pays these charges, you will be surprised that the hospital bills you for them. The reason may be that the hospital has not yet been paid, because the insurance company probably will not pay until after Medicare does. Hospital billing computers don't like to wait for payment and they have a way of billing the patient whenever there is any sort of delay. Here again, this is the hospital's problem, not yours. Make sure your insurance covers what you are being billed for and then forget about it. Eventually the hospital will get paid and the computer will stop bothering you.

UNEXPECTED BILLS

Generally speaking, a hospital is not allowed to charge for most of the medically necessary services you get as an inpatient. Gradually, however, exceptions have crept in. These are especially insidious because you have no control over them, have no way of knowing when you are incurring them, and do not know how much they will cost until you receive the bill. Any time you get a bill from the hospital for the first 60 days of a stay in any one benefit period, for other than convenience and personal comfort items (such as television rental) and the deductible, you have a right to question it. The business office is usually not very forthcoming with explanations but you should persist. Without constant consumer attention, these exceptions could increase rapidly and soon make Medicare coverage even more inadequate.

After the first 60 days, any charge over and above your coinsurance charges should be questioned the same way.

It is obviously neither right nor proper that the consumer should be put in the position of incurring charges about which he or she is not informed in advance. Yet this happens in the hospital every day. In effect, a Medicare patient hands a hospital a blank check when he is admitted.

The most common example of this type of charge is what is called "the physician's component."

The "Physician's Component"

Since the Medicare law went into effect, hospitals are reimbursed for many services that you may assume the hospital itself is paying for. For instance, interns and residents in teaching hospitals are paid for their supposed services rendered to Medicare beneficiaries who may be in their hospital. Reimbursement, however, is not based on actual costs but is determined by negotiation and adjustments of costs between the hospital and Medicare at the end of each year. This is all very complicated and would be of no interest to anyone except perhaps an accountant, were it not for an odd little item called the "physician's component."

The simplest way to describe the physician's component is to give an example. You are in the hospital and your doctor drops in, examines you, looks at your chart and says, "I think I'd like to see some X rays of your chest." You are hardly in a position to argue with him so you smile nervously and maybe ask what he is checking. He may or may not tell you, but in due course a hospital orderly appears with a wheelchair and off you go to the radiologist.

So far so good. You are in the hospital and X rays are covered by Medicare, so you do not have to worry about how much this will cost. Right? Well, not quite.

Medicare will pay for the X-ray film and for the X-ray technicians who load the machine and push the buttons and so on. What Medicare will not entirely pay for is the services of the staff radiologist who reads the X rays. Actually, that's not entirely accurate; when a specific hospital has a specially negotiated contract with Medicare, it can bill Medicare *and the beneficiary* for certain in-hospital doctor services.

This provision of the Medicare law is so confusing that I found even many Medicare people do not fully understand it. They also cannot tell you exactly when it happens. Under the old law the services of interns and residents are specifically exempt (otherwise you would be getting a lot more unexpected bills than you are now), but a proposed new law will allow them to bill the patient under certain circumstance. The physician's component charge can pop up anywhere and the result is a bill you never knowingly approved, didn't expect and, maybe, are unable to pay.

At present the amount involved is usually small—as little as an unauthorized $20 item on a $3,000 bill. But even that $20 of your money could undoubtedly be put to better use. And there's no guarantee that this item will stay small.

The federal government has already committed itself to noninterference in this contract between the hospital and the insurance company: "It is not the function of the health insurance program . . . to determine the arrangement. . . . The provider and the physicians can continue to negotiate all aspects of their arrangement to their mutual satisfaction." Great. But what about the patient's satisfaction? And why does the government give hospitals and physicians a blank check in so critical an area?

In-Hospital Doctor Services You May Be Billed For

It used to be that many medical services, such as that performed by the anesthesiologist during an operation, were administered by doctors on the hospital staff. If you received anesthesia, it was routinely listed as part of your hospital bill and was covered.

Nowadays everyone is a specialist and fewer doctors are "staff." Chances are that your anesthesia will be administered by an outside anesthesiologist who will subsequently send you a not inconsiderable bill for his services. This can come as a shock if you are not expecting it.

Today, unless it is an emergency operation, you will usually meet with the anesthesiologist shortly before the operation. He may even discuss with you what type of anesthesia he recommends and get your feeling about it. For instance, general anesthesia may not be advisable for an elderly person or for one with certain illnesses. There are a variety of options besides general anesthesia and the anesthesiologist will explain them to you and tell you which one he prefers in your case for your particular operation. This is usually a very friendly conversation to reassure and calm the patient and is a great time to bring up "accepting the assignment" (see page 81 for detailed description). Make a note before your interview and keep it in your hand so you don't forget to mention it. Always ask with the positive feeling that the answer will be yes.

Other types of doctors that may not be covered as part of your hospital bill are: radiologists, pathologists, psychiatrists and physical therapists. Since these doctors often perform services for you without getting your consent, it is important to tell your doctor and the hospital that you need to know when you are incurring charges not covered by Medicare Part A. (Medicare Part B may cover part of their charges.) Routine X rays, autopsies and that sort of thing are usually covered.

4

Coverage for Emergency Services

Emergency services are covered by Medicare under both Part A and Part B.

All services furnished in this category must meet Medicare's definition of "emergency," which is: "services immediately necessary to prevent death or serious impairment to health."

INPATIENT AND OUTPATIENT

Emergency services may be delivered on both an inpatient and outpatient basis.

You may, for example, have an emergency that requires hospitalization. A heart attack, an automobile accident, a stroke, would all come in this category. This is inpatient emergency service.

Many emergencies can be dealt with in the emergency room, allowing you to go home directly after treatment. This would be outpatient emergency service. A broken wrist, a bad cut, an asthmatic attack, could fall in this category.

Generally speaking, emergency services, both inpatient and outpatient, that are performed in a hospital are covered under Medicare HI, or Part A. The routine emergency-room charge, for example, is a Part A benefit.

There are some instances, however, when an emergency would lead you to go to your doctor. In my town, for instance, we have a group of orthopedic surgeons who maintain a seven-day-a-week service. If one of the children in the area breaks an arm falling out of a tree or a leg skiing nearby, most parents would take him directly to this doctors' office rather than to the emergency room of the hospital. In this instance, it wouldn't make any difference whether it was an emergency or not; coverage would be the same as any physician's services and would come under Part B (SMI).

If you have an emergency and go to the emergency room of the nearest hospital, but have someone phone your private doctor and ask him to meet you there, you will be covered by both Part A and Part B. Part A will cover the use of the emergency room; Part B will partially cover the services of your physician. You will never see the bill for Part A; you will receive a bill, as usual, from your physician.

In certain areas the local residents have fallen into the habit of using the emergency room as a provider of primary services; instead of going to a doctor, they simply go to the emergency room. In many instances the services they require are not emergency services. Anyone who uses an emergency room for nonemergency services runs the risk of being denied Medicare coverage for those services.

As we have seen in the previous chapter, in the case of an emergency you may be entitled to coverage in a foreign hospital (see page 32). Be sure you do not stay in the hospital once the emergency is over; Medicare coverage will end for a foreign hospital as soon as there is no longer an emergency. It may be that you still require hospitalization, though not on an emergency basis. If so, you may transfer to a hospital in the United States.

AMBULANCES

See "Ambulance Service" in the explanation of Medicare Part B (SMI) benefits, page 98.

5

What You Should Know
About Hospital Reimbursement

The services provided by hospitals to beneficiaries are covered by Medicare payments to the hospitals in what may seem a generous way. No Medicare beneficiary should settle for less care than he or she needs when in the hospital; the beneficiary should know that the hospital is being paid extra for such a patient.

ROUTINE NURSING CARE

Medicare, for example, takes it for granted that an elderly patient will need—*and be given*—more nursing care than the average hospital patient. On this assumption, Medicare pays what it calls "an inpatient routine nursing salary cost differential." This means Medicare automatically *pays for extra care* for an elderly patient. If you are a hospital patient and are not getting even routine attention from the nursing staff, you should remember that the hospital is being paid especially to give you *more* than average routine nursing. You have every right to complain if the staff is impatient or indicates you are making a pest of yourself. This does not mean you should be unreasonably demanding or not try your best to get along with the nursing staff, but it does mean you should be aware that they are being paid extra to take proper care of you and you have a right to extra care. Do not hesitate to ask to talk to the supervisor if the staff is truly unsatisfactory or unpleasant.

VOLUNTEER WORKERS

Many hospitals have an excellent volunteer organization and these unpaid "civilians" can contribute a lot to the pleasantness of a hospital stay. These volunteers sometimes visit patients, take around trolleys with newspapers and magazines, staff hospital gift shops and coffee shops and do office work and paperwork of various kinds. It may interest the Medicare beneficiary to know that, although these volunteers perform these services free, at no cost to the hospital, the hospital is reimbursed by Medicare for any unpaid workers who contribute more than 20 hours a week (except for those from religious orders) and who do jobs that would normally be paid for if there weren't a volunteer to do it for free. This type of reimbursement is made to the hospital under the heading of "operating costs," even though it is not an actual cost in any way.

MALPRACTICE COSTS

Although it does not affect the beneficiary directly (except to increase the cost of the Medicare program), you might like to know that Medicare has a reimbursement provision that helps hospitals pay for malpractice costs—not only insurance but actual losses. This would seem to discourage the hospital from improving the quality of its service in order to reduce malpractice suits. It also costs the taxpayer for valuable civil-service employee time since the Health

Care Financing Administration periodically updates the ratio on which it bases its determination of the amount of these reimbursements, as well as spending time in administering the program.

6

When You Are
in a Nursing Home

This is the area that causes the greatest disappointment
and shock to most Medicare recipients because the coverage is so much less than they expect it to be. In addition,
the benefits you are entitled to are eroded by the way they
are administered; eight out of ten applications for admission to a skilled nursing facility are denied coverage. And,
although you are theoretically covered for up to 100 days,
in practice the average SNF covered stay is only 16 days.

If you still need nursing-home care after Medicare has
stopped paying for it, you may have to pay the costs yourself. How often this happens, and how inadequate Medicare coverage is in this area, is shown by a simple statistic
from a 1978 policy-planning issues paper prepared by the
Federal Trade Commission: "While 25 percent of the
health expenditures of people over 65 goes for nursing
home care, Medicare pays for only a small percentage of
those expenses—3.6 percent." This leaves over 96% of
nursing-home costs to be paid out-of-pocket by Medicare
recipients.

The result is that most people cannot afford to be in a
nursing home without Medicare coverage, unless they pay
until all their resources are gone and they thus become

eligible for Medicaid. With the cost of a stay in a skilled nursing facility running as high as $1,500 a week, it is not surprising to find that only 5% of the elderly are in nursing homes. If more need that level of care—and more than 5% probably do—this means they are being deprived of needed health services.

As we will see later on, a simple and cost-effective solution to this national problem lies in improved home health care. With a proper support system, many people presently in nursing homes could be much more happily, just as effectively and much more cheaply cared for in their own homes.

WHAT IS A NURSING HOME?

What the average person means by "nursing home" is not covered by Medicare. If you read your Medicare handbook carefully, you will see that nowhere does it say it will pay for care in a nursing home. What Medicare will help pay for is care in a "skilled nursing facility." A skilled nursing facility is only one kind of nursing home; other kinds are intermediate care facilities (ICFs) and residential care facilities—and neither of those is covered at all.

WHAT IS AN SNF?

A skilled nursing facility (SNF) is a facility equipped to provide the highest level of health care next to a hospital. Among the services Medicare requires be provided are 24-hour registered nurses for round-the-clock skilled nursing. In addition, a physician or a registered nurse must be on the staff, and a physician must be available at all times for emergencies. An SNF must also have available daily rehabilitation services for the injured, disabled or ill patients in its care.

HOW DO YOU QUALIFY FOR COVERAGE IN AN SNF?

For you to qualify for coverage, it is not enough that you be staying in an SNF; there are three qualifying requirements:

1. You must have been in the hospital for at least three days prior to being admitted to an SNF. Medicare allows 30 days between your discharge from the hospital (counting the day of discharge) and the day you enter the SNF.

2. You must require skilled nursing care or skilled rehabilitation services *on a daily basis.* This does not necessarily mean seven days a week; if the services are available only five days a week and if you use them every day that they are available, you have fulfilled this requirement.

   The care you require must be such that only a registered nurse could provide it. For instance, if you are not ill, only weak or feeble and require help in eating, dressing yourself and so on, it won't help to have a registered nurse perform those services for you when a much less skilled person could do them equally well. Medicare will look at what it is you need and will determine if those needs require a registered nurse. If Medicare thinks a practical nurse could do just as well, it won't pay for your stay in the nursing home even though it is a skilled nursing facility and you are being attended by skilled nurses. And your doctor has nothing to say about it. He may not agree with Medicare's ruling but he will be helpless to change it.

   If Medicare decides that you no longer require skilled nursing care, you will be given a minimum of 24 hours' notice before your Medicare coverage terminates. After that, you may remain in the nursing home at your own expense but you will not be eligible for Medicare coverage unless your medical condition changes.

3. You must be entering the SNF for treatment for the same illness for which you were hospitalized. In other words, if you break a hip after leaving the hospital and then require rehabilitation therapy (but you have recovered from the illness for which you were hospitalized), you would not be eligible for Medicare coverage for SNF care for your broken hip. Of course, if the doctor put you in the hospital because of your hip, you could—after three days—then be covered in an SNF.

I have not counted the fact that SNF care must be medically necessary and must be so certified by your physician because that applies to all Medicare benefits.

HOW CAN YOU FIND AN SNF?

In many states, not easily. Your doctor will know which nursing homes are SNFs, but there may not be one in your area.

In a 1978 study of private health insurance to supplement Medicare, the Federal Trade Commission found that the kind of nursing home that qualifies for Medicare coverage is in short supply. "Availability of Medicare-approved SNF care varies widely from State to State; in some regions it is almost impossible to obtain. . . . As of July 1975, the number of certified SNF beds per 1,000 Medicare enrollees varied from 1.4 in Oklahoma, 2.2 in Arkansas and 2.6 in Louisiana, to 22.9 in New York, 37.9 in Connecticut and 40.8 in California. In Arizona (the state with the fastest-growing elderly population) there were only 19 Medicare-certified SNFs. Nor has the number of SNFs increased appreciably since then."

In areas where there are no separate facilities that qualify as SNFs, Medicare will sometimes recognize part of a hospital as a skilled nursing facility. Your doctor will know if this is the case.

WHAT IS AN INTERMEDIATE CARE FACILITY?

An intermediate care facility, often referred to as an ICF, is a nursing home that takes care of the ill but does not generally provide the level of care provided by an SNF. It may be that you still need nursing care but not quite the daily skilled nursing care of the SNF. It may have licensed practical nurses rather than registered nurses and the director may not be either a registered nurse or a physician.

It may be hard for you to tell whether a nursing home is an SNF or an ICF—an important distinction since ICFs are not usually covered by Medicare—because ICFs often provide regular nursing and rehabilitative services for those who need it. Primarily, however, they take care of patients who need some medical services but not on a daily basis. If there is no SNF available in the area, part of the ICF may function as one and may be covered by Medicare as if it were one, if it meets Medicare requirements. If you are entering a nursing home on the assumption that your stay will be covered by Medicare, ask before you go in. You may think you are so ill that Medicare will surely cover you but if you go into a nursing home not covered by Medicare, you will not be covered.

WHAT IS A RESIDENTIAL CARE FACILITY?

Most nursing homes fall into this category. A residential care facility is the kind of institution that assumes you are functionally independent. Most people in this type of facility could easily be taken care of in their own homes if home health care were provided. If you are somewhat absent-minded but otherwise in good health, a facility of this type that provides monitoring as well as custodial care would probably suit you. This kind of nursing home provides all meals, frees you from housekeeping chores and provides social opportunities. It is never covered by Medicare.

MEDICARE BENEFITS IN AN SNF

There is no deductible to pay when you enter an SNF and Medicare will pay all covered costs for the first 20 days if you qualify.

From the 21st to the 100th day, Medicare will pay all costs except for the coinsurance amount that you must pay. For 1982, the coinsurance payment is $32.50 a day.

After the First 100 Days

After a stay of 100 days in any one benefit period in a skilled nursing facility, Medicare coverage ceases. Unless you are out of the nursing home and have no hospitalization for 60 consecutive days, you will not be eligible for any more Medicare hospital or nursing-home coverage.

If you do meet the 60-day requirement and are again hospitalized, you can begin a new benefit period and receive benefits again.

In a Christian Science Sanatorium

If you are in a Christian Science sanatorium for skilled nursing care, the coinsurance starts on the first day and lasts for 30 days (day 1 to day 30); there are no fully covered days. Since this type of facility may also be covered as a hospital, your status must be made clear.

MAY MY DOCTOR VISIT ME WHEN I AM IN AN SNF?

Your family doctor (or any other doctor you choose) may visit you in a skilled nursing facility but for only a limited number of visits (usually one to three a month), depending on your condition. His bill will not be covered under Medicare HI (Part A) but under SMI (Part B) as usual. If, however, he comes more often than the number of times Medicare has established as a reasonable number of visits for your illness, Medicare may refuse coverage of the "excess" visits.

If this should happen, it is possible that your doctor may be able to explain why extra visits were necessary—perhaps your condition worsened—and may be able to persuade Medicare to change its denial of coverage and pay its share of the bill.

MAY I STAY IN A SKILLED NURSING FACILITY AS LONG AS I DON'T FEEL WELL—UP TO 100 DAYS?

How you feel has very little to do with the length of your stay. The PSRO (see Chapter 20) will determine whether it is "medically necessary" for you to be in the SNF. If the PSRO decides you no longer need that level of care, you will be informed that Medicare coverage will no longer be available.

If this should happen, you will usually be given 24 hours to decide whether to move to a cheaper nursing home or to pay the costs of the SNF yourself. In such an eventuality, consider the possibility of home health care; even if you have to pay some of the costs, it will probably be cheaper than a nursing home.

7

How Medicare Covers
Home Health Care

This is another area of Medicare that beneficiaries find confusing. The problem is that you need to know not only what Medicare will pay for, but also what the requirements are in order for you to qualify for coverage.

Let us consider three different situations:

1. You are so ill you require around-the-clock skilled nursing, but you prefer to stay home rather than go to the hospital.
2. You have a chronic condition so that you cannot take care of your personal needs—meals, housecleaning, bathing and dressing—but you can have someone come in and help you and you are then able to stay at home.
3. You are not so ill as to be in the hospital but you do need intermittent skilled nursing care if you are to stay at home.

Of the three above situations, Medicare will cover costs for only example number 3. Let us see what this means in the day-to-day situation.

WHO QUALIFIES?

In order to qualify for Medicare coverage for home health care services, your physician must certify that you are confined to your home by your illness and that you require intermittent nursing care or other therapeutic services, such as physical or speech therapy.

Intermittent Nursing Care

Intermittent—as opposed to daily—nursing care can be as seldom as once every 60 days. However, that is the outside limit and you would be more likely to qualify if you required this kind of service somewhat more often.

If you require an occasional injection—such as a single gamma globulin or flu shot—that would not count as intermittent nursing and would not be covered. Ideally, the need for nursing care on a regular, but not daily, basis should be able to be predicted by your doctor and be specified in the plan he writes up for your home nursing care.

If you usually require only intermittent care but temporarily require a short period of intensive skilled nursing care, Medicare will cover up to eight hours a day, five days a week, but only if there is some reason why you cannot be hospitalized for this period (such as a shortage of beds which prevents immediate hospitalization), and only for a short time. This is strictly an exception.

Confined to Home

Another condition for coverage is that you must be confined to your home, but this isn't quite as strict a limitation as it sounds. "Confined to your home" means—in

Medicare's terms—that your illness limits your ability to leave your home; it does not mean that you must be bed-ridden. It also does not mean that you may not leave your home at all. For instance, if you require the use of equipment that is available only in the hospital (such as certain physical therapy equipment or hydrotherapy), you will be covered for these services and you will be permitted to leave home and go to the hospital as an outpatient to get them. However, Medicare will not cover the cost of transportation from your home to the hospital, even if you have to go by ambulance.

You are also allowed to walk around outside a little—to a chair on the lawn, for instance—and may even go out to get a haircut or go to the dentist. It is presumed that none of this activity will be easy for you, and if it is, you will soon find that you are no longer eligible for home health care coverage.

WHAT SERVICES ARE COVERED?

Covered services include any and all of the following:

1. part-time intermittent skilled nursing care
2. physical therapy
3. speech therapy
4. occupational therapy
5. home health aides
6. social services
7. medical supplies and appliances

Let us see what these services include.

Skilled Nursing Care

While this term usually refers only to care provided by a registered nurse, in the case of home health care it also applies to services provided under the supervision of a registered nurse, a licensed practical nurse (LPN) or a licensed vocational nurse.

Physical, Speech and Occupational Therapy

These services must be provided by or under the supervision of a therapist. There are very specific guidelines regulating the therapists and their treatment, but this need not concern you since from your standpoint they act as quality control.

A special note about occupational therapy: This is a confusing area because the rules keep changing. Recent legislation added occupational therapy to speech and physical therapy as a qualifying factor. In other words, you could qualify for home health aid if you needed occupational therapy on a regular basis. Subsequently the law was rescinded and now, if that is your only medical problem, it will not qualify you for home health care.

However, if you are already receiving home health care and if it includes occupational therapy, you will be covered by Medicare even if you no longer need other care. For instance, if you qualified for home health care because you needed physical therapy and you also needed occupational therapy, you would still be covered even if you no longer needed physical therapy. In other words, while the need for occupational therapy will not qualify you initially, it is grounds for continued coverage.

Since this is an unstable area of Medicare coverage, keep an eye on it; it may change again. If it is important to you, write your congressman when any changes in Medicare are contemplated.

Home Health Aides

The services provided by home health aides are the closest Medicare ever gets to covering custodial care. Although their services must be ordered by your doctor and supervised by a nurse or therapist, they are concerned primarily with your personal care. Among the things a home health aide will do for you are: help you get in and out of bed; help you take your medicine; help you bathe and brush your teeth; help you learn new ways to do old household tasks if your illness or injury makes the old ways impractical.

A home health aide does not sleep in.

Social Services

Covered social services are only those defined as "medical." The home health agency will know which social workers are covered by Medicare and will not send you ones who are not. Psychologists are not covered.

Medical Supplies and Appliances

These are usually items used by the nurses or therapists (from Band-Aids to catheters) or loaned to you (such as wheelchairs or hospital beds). They do not include medicine you can take yourself—aspirin, prescription drugs and so on.

WHAT IS A HOME HEALTH AGENCY?

To qualify for Medicare coverage for home health care, you must obtain the covered services through something called a home health agency. (You cannot, for instance, hire a neighbor as your home health aide.) This may be either a public or a private organization (some are nationwide and run by insurance companies) but it must meet specific Medicare requirements. The home health agency provides all the personnel (except for physicians) and may go outside its own staff if you require services that it does not have.

The availability of home health agencies varies widely; your doctor or local social worker will know which ones there are in your area.

HOW MUCH WILL HOME HEALTH CARE COST?

Nothing for covered services. Medicare pays 100 percent of covered home health care costs. There is no deductible or coinsurance for you to pay and no home health agency is allowed to bill you for anything. If you get a bill from a home health agency, send it to Medicare explaining what it is; it is against the law for the agency to bill you.

There are no claim forms for you to file. The agency bills Medicare directly and you never see a bill.

WHAT IS THE LIMITATION ON HOME HEALTH CARE COVERAGE?

Unlike hospital coverage, home health care coverage is not expressed in number of days covered. Until recently there was a limited number of visits covered, but that law was changed on July 1, 1981, to allow an unlimited number of visits. It may, however, be changed again or changed back, so check with Medicare if you need home health care to be sure you are still entitled to unlimited visits. Home health care coverage ceases when the treatment no longer improves your condition or when you get well.

WHAT "UNLIMITED VISITS" MEANS

Medicare doesn't really give you a blank check when it says it will cover an unlimited number of visits; the visits must be certified by your doctor as medically necessary and Medicare must agree. Medicare has a rule of thumb for various illnesses and will quickly notice if you have had more home health care visits than they think your condition warrants.

SERVICES MEDICARE WILL NOT COVER

Covered home health care services are similar to the services you would receive in the hospital. A service you would not receive in the hospital will usually not be covered as a home health service. An example of this is a private registered nurse; this service would not be covered in the hospital nor at home.

Home health care that is solely custodial is not covered; that is why coverage ceases if it no longer contributes to improving your health.

8

How to Save $9,750 on Hospital Bills in a Single Benefit Period

Now that you know all about Medicare Part A (HI) benefits, let's see how you can make the most of them. (If you don't know all about them, go back and read the previous chapters.)

As we have seen, Medicare Part A (HI) has good hospital coverage over the short haul, but an extended hospital stay will end up costing you a considerable sum of money. And if some members of Congress have their way, it will become much, much more expensive in the near future. I have looked carefully at the limitations and think I have found a way around some of these costs, *if your illness allows* you to follow the proposed course of action. If you think you are in for an extended illness that will require long-term skilled nursing care, read this chapter carefully and then talk it over with your doctor; you will need his full and informed cooperation in order to make it work.

Incidentally, I have gone over it with Medicare personnel and they say it is entirely practical, providing the patient qualifies.

YOUR COSTS FOR A 150-DAY HOSPITAL STAY

As we have seen earlier, even with complete Medicare coverage your *minimum* out-of-pocket costs for hospital services, not including private physician or consulting charges, comfort items and charges for "physician's component" billed to you by the hospital, will be $10,010 for 150 days. And that's as of January 1, 1982. By 1983, it may be higher. It adds up this way:

1st to 60th day, deductible of $260:	$ 260
61st to 90th day, 30 days at $65 a day:	1,950
90th to 150th day, 60 days at $130 a day:	7,800
Total you pay:	$10,010

If you stay in the hospital for 150 days in a single benefit period, there is no way, unless you qualify for Medicaid, that it will cost you a penny less than the $10,010 total. And in addition, you will have used up all your 60 Lifetime Reserve days.

If you qualify, however, and if your doctor works with you, you can hold your costs to $260—a savings of $9,750.

HOW TO CUT $10,010 IN HOSPITAL BILLS TO $260

You must follow this schedule exactly.

1. Upon admission to the hospital, you automically owe $260, the deductible. This entitles you to 100% Medicare coverage (for covered services) for the next 60 days. You can't get around the cost of the deductible, but the 60-day coverage it gives you is the best part of the deal, so stay in the hospital the full 60 days.
2. If you were to stay beyond 60 days, you would incur

charges of $65 a day in coinsurance. To avoid this, *leave the hospital on the 60th day.* You may be able to do this because, with an extended illness, a point is usually reached where the patient still requires skilled nursing care on a daily basis but does not require all the equipment and technology available in a hospital. To get the care you still require, move to a skilled nursing facility. There is no deductible to pay upon admission, and Medicare will pay 100% of the covered charges for the first 20 days of your stay. So you now have 80 days of an extended illness, but you have paid out only $260.

3. On the 20th day, you have to leave the nursing home or you will begin to incur coinsurance charges of $32.50 a day. Make arrangements through a home health agency, with your doctor writing the necessary plan and prescriptions, and go home. The support system available to you through home health care will be paid for by Medicare, 100% for all covered charges. At present you are entitled to unlimited health-care visits, so home health care might work out fairly well.

At this point you have now saved $9,750. Here's how:

1st to 60th day in hospital, deductible:	$260
20 days in SNF:	free
home health care, unlimited visits:	free
Total out-of-pocket cost:	$260

It has cost $260 dollars instead of $10,010, so you have saved $9,750. And you have not even used up a single one of your 60 Lifetime Reserve days. In addition, you may now have qualified (60 days out of the SNF) to start a new benefit period, in which case you can do this all over again.

This is not to say that you will not have additional medical and health-care expenses. You will still have part of your doctor bills, and when at home, you will have to pay for your own medicine (except if given to you by your doctor or the home health agency) and to pay part of any durable medical equipment, such as a hospital bed, that you may decide to buy or rent. Sometimes you can save this last cost by getting it free on loan from the home health-care agency. The only items that would have been covered if you had stayed in the hospital or SNF are the cost of your medicine and food.

Obviously, this particular plan will work only with an illness that lends itself to shifting from the hospital to the nursing home to home health care at strategic times. But once you understand the principle behind it, you can adapt it to various circumstances and still realize a considerable savings in out-of-pocket cost. One of the really important things about understanding this plan is that it shows you that you can be creative in using Medicare benefits. Don't expect your doctor to figure these things out for you; make it your business to learn all about Medicare yourself.

III

MEDICARE PART B: EXPLAINING SUPPLEMENTARY MEDICAL INSURANCE (SMI)

9

How Does Part A
Differ from Part B?

It would be much better if the beneficiary were not concerned with the difference between these two parts of Medicare; the administration of it could still go on behind the scenes just as it does now, but it would not be so confusing for the person who has to use it. However, since that is not the case, you may as well grit your teeth and concentrate; it's not nearly so hard as Medicare sometimes makes it sound.

Put simply, Part A pays for hospitalization (in a hospital or an SNF) and for home health care, and Part B pays for everything else that is covered. That is why Part B is called "supplementary" medical insurance; it is intended to supplement your Part A coverage. The "medical" refers to the fact that the lion's share of the coverage goes to physicians of various kinds.

Here are some specific ways Part B insurance is different:

- It is optional rather than automatic. You can decide not to have it.
- It requires payment of a monthly premium.

- It has a deductible amount that you must pay before coverage starts.
- With a few exceptions, it pays, at most, 80% of the "reasonable" or "allowable" charges of most covered services.
- It has an "assignment" system.
- If the provider does not accept the assignment, you must file a claim with Medicare for the charges.
- You have a little more control over Part B costs.
- It is administered by a different carrier from Part A. For instance, in Connecticut Part A is administered by Blue Cross and other private insurance companies, and Part B by Connecticut General Life Insurance.

10

How Do You Get
Medicare Part B (SMI) Coverage?

Since Medicare Part B (SMI) is optional (you can decide not to have it), the rules for eligibility and enrollment are somewhat different from those for Medicare Part A (HI).

WHO IS ELIGIBLE?

Two groups of persons are eligible for Medicare Part B (SMI) insurance:

1. Persons entitled to Medicare Part A (HI).
2. Persons not eligible for Part A but who have chosen to enroll voluntarily (by paying a monthly premium). In this case, however, you cannot choose; you must take both.

HOW DOES ONE ENROLL?

If You Are Eligible for Medicare Part A (HI)

Since 1972, anyone eligible for Part A is automatically enrolled in Part B as soon as he or she becomes eligible for Part A. Most of the time this means that on your 65th birthday you will automatically be enrolled in Part A and

Part B, unless you inform social security that you do not want this to happen.

Since Part B is voluntary, you may elect not to have it. In this case, if you notify Medicare before your automatic coverage begins, you will not have to pay the first premium. If you do not notify them in time, you will not only have to pay the first month's premium but you will also be considered as having enrolled and then dropped out. If you subsequently decide to re-enroll, you will have to pay a higher premium as a penalty for dropping out.

If You Are Voluntarily Enrolled in Medicare Part A (HI)

If you are not automatically eligible for Medicare Part A (HI), but elect to join it by voluntarily paying a monthly premium, you must also enroll in Part B. The law does not give you a choice. If you do not enroll in Part B, you will lose your Part A coverage. If at any time you fail to pay your Part B premium within the grace period, you will lose your Part A coverage automatically. You pay the same premium for Part B as does any person enrolled in the program.

WHEN DOES ONE ENROLL?

Enrollment in Medicare Part B is limited to certain specific enrollment periods. I should mention here that this is another unstable area in the Medicare law. For a few short months in 1981 there was open enrollment, with no limitations, for Part B. The law soon changed back and now you can enroll only during specific times.

If you are eligible for Part A and want Part B, you will be automatically enrolled (on your 65th birthday, if you are receiving social security benefits).

If you are not automatically enrolled, it is a little more complicated. You must write and ask for enrollment; do so as soon as possible within the three-month period before your 65th birthday. The enrollment period begins with the third month preceding the one in which you are eligible and is considered to have ended three months after the month in which you become eligible. Since the month in which you become eligible is counted, this means that the initial enrollment period is seven months.

When you enroll affects how soon your coverage starts. If you enroll in the three months prior to the month of eligibility, coverage starts as soon as you become eligible; for instance, on your 65th birthday. If you wait until the month in which you turn 65, your coverage begins the following month. If you wait until the last of the seven-month period, coverage begins from two to three months after you have enrolled, depending on how long you waited to enroll.

For example, suppose your 65th birthday falls during the month of April:

IF YOU ENROLL:	YOUR COVERAGE BEGINS:
In January	April 1
In February	April 1
In March	April 1
In April	May 1
In May	July 1
In June	September 1
In July	October 1

WHY IS EARLY ENROLLMENT IMPORTANT?

It is important to enroll early in Part B Medicare for two reasons: you may otherwise find yourself without health insurance, and you will have to pay a higher premium if you enroll after you first become eligible.

HOW COULD I FIND MYSELF WITHOUT HEALTH INSURANCE?

Many private health insurance policies terminate at age 65. In the above example, if your 65th birthday was April 1st and you waited until July 1st to enroll in Medicare Part B, your group or other health insurance would probably cease April 1st and you would not have any health-care coverage until October 1st. During this period any medical bills and similar expenses you might incur would not be covered and you would have to pay them yourself. In addition, because you would not have had continuous insurance coverage, you might have a waiting period before your new Medigap insurance—which you would probably have in addition to Medicare—would cover existing or previous conditions. In some extreme cases, you might never again be able to get Medigap coverage for some of those conditions.

PENALTY FOR LATE ENROLLMENT

If you enroll late or if you terminate your insurance and then re-enroll at a later date, your monthly premium will be higher than if you had enrolled when you were first eligible.

The penalty is 10% for each year in which you could have enrolled but did not. For example, if you are two years past your initial enrollment period, the penalty is an additional 20%, and so on. Since this increased premium must be paid for the rest of your life (if you wish to continue coverage in Medicare Part B insurance), you should avoid it if at all possible.

HOW TO TERMINATE MEDICARE PART B INSURANCE

There are two ways you can terminate your Medicare Part B insurance. First, you can send in a written notice to Medicare. If you would be automatically enrolled on your 65th birthday and do not wish to be, send in the notice *before* coverage begins and you will avoid having to pay the first month's premium.

The second way to terminate your Medicare Part B insurance is simply not to pay your premium. If you enroll at some later date, it will be deemed a re-enrollment and the penalty provision will apply.

SUPPOSE I FORGET TO PAY THE PREMIUM?

Since failure to pay the premium will result in automatic termination of your Medicare Part B insurance, it is very important for you to have a good system of payment. This is no problem if you are receiving social security pension or annuity benefits because the premium will be automatically deducted from your monthly check. However, if you do not receive benefits or if you usually do but for some reason do not in a given month (as in the case where your income exceeds the allowable earnings limitation), you have to remember to send in your premium directly. You are allowed a grace period of up to 90 days after the month in which the premium is due. In special circumstances, you may extend the grace period for another 90 days. These circumstances include physical or mental incapacity or if you mistakenly believed payment had been made when it had not (perhaps your check went astray). Always get in touch with your social security office as soon as you realize you have not paid your premium.

SUPPOSE I CONTINUE WORKING AFTER AGE 65 AND MY EMPLOYER'S GROUP INSURANCE PLAN COVERS ME. DO I STILL NEED MEDICARE PART B?

If your insurance covers everything that Medicare Part B covers, you probably do not need it, but this is highly unlikely. If you do not enroll at the age of 65, you will be subject to the penalty described above when you do enroll. If you decide to enroll, keep in mind that if you do not retire and therefore are not receiving social security benefits, your enrollment is not automatic and must be applied for in writing.

HOW DO PART B PREMIUMS WORK?

Part B premiums are either deducted from benefits you are receiving or sent in as direct payment by you. If you are paying through the direct-payment method, you will receive a premium notice every three months complete with a card and an envelope to make it easier to pay. If you have enrolled in Medicare voluntarily, you will be billed monthly.

WILL MY MEDICARE PART B PREMIUM HELP ME MEET MY COINSURANCE OR DEDUCTIBLE?

No. Just as private insurance premiums do not help meet coinsurance or deductibles when you file a claim, SMI premiums must be paid whether you make a claim or not; your deductibles and coinsurance come into use when you make a claim.

HOW MUCH IS THE PREMIUM?

The monthly premium has risen from $3 in 1968 to $11 in June 1982. It will be increased on July 1, 1982. If you wish to know when the premium will be increased, the formula is simple. Your premium will increase any year after the year in which the social security benefits have been increased. Social security benefits were increased in July 1981, so premiums will be increased July 1982 to $12.20.

SUPPOSE I AM ELIGIBLE FOR MEDICARE BECAUSE I AM DISABLED. ARE THE RULES AND REGULATIONS THE SAME?

Most of the rules and regulations apply to all beneficiaries. There is, however, one obvious difference. Since you may become disabled at any age, your enrollment period is not connected to your 65th birthday. You are eligible for Medicare after 24 months of disability, so in your case the 25th month is the equivalent of a senior reaching age 65. A disabled person's initial enrollment period (during which he or she can enroll without penalty) begins on the first day of the third month before the 25th month for which he or she has been receiving disability benefits.

After you have become eligible, enrollment periods and penalties for late enrollment apply.

WILL I GET MEDICARE IF I TAKE EARLY RETIREMENT?

Your eligibility for Medicare begins with your 65th birthday no matter when you retire.

SUPPOSE I TERMINATE MY PART B COVERAGE. HOW SOON WILL IT END?

Although you pay premiums monthly, termination of coverage will not take place until the last day of the quarter following the quarter in which you notified Medicare in writing that you wished to terminate.

If you terminate coverage by ceasing to pay your premiums, coverage will cease at the end of the grace period (90 days).

THE DEDUCTIBLE

In addition to the monthly premium there is a deductible. Generally speaking, the deductible applies to most services covered by Part B, and you must pay the deductible before you start receiving Medicare coverage. The amount of the deductible as of December 1981 is $75.

Since there are no benefit periods under Part B, you must meet this deductible only once in any calendar year. As soon as you have met it, your Part B coverage begins. This system is similar to automobile and homeowner's insurance where, for example, the first $100 of any claim is deducted from what the insurance company pays.

THE COINSURANCE

Once you have met your deductible for the year, your Part B medical insurance will start helping you pay your bills. Here is an area where you must understand the system or you will be unpleasantly surprised by your medical expenses.

Theoretically, after your deductible has been met, Medicare pays 80% of your medical expenses and you pay coinsurance of 20%. In practice, Medicare pays about one third of your bills. You can, however, improve the payment percentage considerably if you understand the rules and work within them.

11

What Part B Pays for
Physicians' Services

As we have seen, Medicare Part B, or Supplementary Medical Insurance (SMI), covers some of the health-care expenses not picked up by Part A. These include physicians' services, X rays and diagnostic tests, home dialysis, certain medical equipment (called "durable medical equipment") and limited ambulance service.

The most important covered service under Medicare Part B (SMI) is partial payment of doctor bills. The Medicare beneficiary is much more involved with, and much more in control of, doctor bills than hospital bills. You usually feel comparatively helpless when you are hospitalized, and charges mount up without any specific knowledge on your part. Because of extensive Medicare coverage in the first 60 days of hospitalization, most beneficiaries do not concern themselves with hospital bills. Doctor bills are different because they are usually incurred on a visit-by-visit basis and deal with individuals rather than an institution. Often, when more than one doctor is involved, you may freely choose your own doctor; whereas there is often no choice among hospitals.

In describing its coverage of medical services, the Medicare handbook says, "medical insurance (SMI) will pay 80% of the reasonable charges for any additional covered services you receive during the rest of the year" after you have met your deductible. That statement is strictly accurate and totally incomprehensible, unless you clearly understand what is meant by "covered services," and "reasonable charges."

COVERED SERVICES

Covered services means those services that are deemed "medically necessary" by Medicare and that Medicare has agreed to pay for. Many things you might think would certainly be considered medically necessary are not included in the Medicare definition of that term. For instance, food may be medically necessary to sustain life, but Medicare does not pay for food (except when you are in an institution). Hearing aids and eyeglasses may be medically necessary but Medicare does not pay for them. Dental services may be medically necessary to prevent you from losing all your teeth, but Medicare does not pay for them. It is essential that you know or be able to look up the various categories Medicare will and will not cover; you cannot determine on the basis of logic alone whether you are covered. Even your doctor cannot always tell you whether Medicare will cover a service he deems medically necessary; his decision may be overruled by Medicare or the PSRO (see Chapter 20).

In the following pages we will try to be as specific as possible as to which services are covered and which are not, and will give you useful tips on ways to get better coverage.

REASONABLE CHARGES

"Reasonable charges" are charges Medicare establishes for every medical service it covers: doctor office visits, lab tests, X rays and so on. Unfortunately, the determination of a "reasonable charge" is arrived at in such a way that the amount Medicare allows is always out-of-date and behind the rate of inflation. Even if it were up-to-the-minute, the nature of the formula is such that its "reasonableness" is open to question. Medicare recognizes this as a fact and is trying to change the term "reasonable charge" to "allowable charge," which is more accurate since it is the amount Medicare allows, whether it is reasonable or not. For a detailed explanation of how a "reasonable charge" is arrived at, see Chapter 19.

DO MEDICARE REASONABLE CHARGES VARY?

Medicare charges vary both geographically and from doctor to doctor, due to the way they are figured. For instance, the Health Care Financing Administration issues guidelines each year for the local carriers in the form of an operating manual. The prevailing charge is only one of several factors that determine the allowable charge. In addition, the doctor's customary charge is considered, and the prevailing charges cannot rise beyond the amount allowed by an economic index formula.

A look at the 1978 *Directory of Prevailing Charges* shows, for instance, that the prevailing charge for an initial comprehensive office visit would range from $25.00 to $40.70 in Connecticut and from $61.07 to $67.96 in California. The prevailing charge for insertion of a pacemaker in Connecticut would range from $800 to $1,600, and in Arizona from $850 to $900. The range within the state is partly due to the difference between high- and low-income areas, as well as to the difference in fees charged by the general practitioner as compared with the specialist. Generally, the prevailing charge for a procedure is higher if it is done by a specialist; which would seem to indicate that you would do better going to a general practitioner if it is a procedure that he or she could handle equally well. On the other hand, it sometimes happens that the prevailing charge for a very minor procedure is actually cheaper when done by the specialist—perhaps because he or she thinks of it as easy.

The geographical difference in reasonable charges can create a better or worse situation for the Medicare beneficiary. In a nationwide study by the Federal Trade Commission, the conclusion was that "in California Medicare beneficiaries bear a greater share of the physician's charges than elderly people in most of the country, because fees are higher and Part B carriers' reasonable charge reductions are greater." In other words, the study concluded you pay more of a doctor's bill in California, even when he accepts the assignment, because his bill is not only higher to begin with but, in addition, Medicare pays less of it.

The formula for arriving at the reasonable or allowable charge is so complicated that the instructions are given to carriers in the form of a thick, bound book. Doctors are unhappy with the way a customary charge is determined; they feel some of the regulations are inequitable. For instance, a new doctor moving into the area, with no previous fee schedule in that area, can start out charging higher prices and being allowed higher reasonable charges than some of the doctors who have been practicing there for some time. This is due to regulations governing increases in the amount Medicare can reimburse for doctors' services. Any increase in Medicare reimbursement must be justified, by increasing costs or change of status (as from general practitioner to board-certified specialist) if it is to change Medicare's determination of his customary charge. The new doctor can establish his customary charges at any level he wishes. Medicare will not accept this schedule outright because it will be tempered by comparison with the prevailing charges, but the doctor new to the area will still benefit to some extent from higher reasonable charges allowed.

The only way to determine what Medicare will allow a particular doctor in the way of a reasonable charge is to call Medicare and ask. You may not want to bother with small charges, but any major medical expenditure certainly should be checked out unless the amount you spend for your health-care costs is unimportant to you.

The important thing you need to know for now is that Medicare *will not pay the actual bill* (from your doctor or medical supply store) but will only pay 80% of what it determines is the reasonable charge. The reasonable charge may be less than half of the actual bill, in which case you will have to pay 20% coinsurance (20% of the reasonable charge) plus any amount over the reasonable charge, unless the doctor or other provider agrees to accept the assignment.

ACCEPTING THE ASSIGNMENT

If the doctor or any other provider of medical services agrees to accept the assignment, it means he or she will accept Medicare's reasonable charge as the basis for payment. Medicare will then pay 80% of the amount, you will pay 20%, and the provider will consider the bill paid in full. For example, you have an operation and the surgeon bills you $1,200. Medicare determines the reasonable charge for that operation by that surgeon to be $800. Here is how it would work out:

If the Surgeon Does Not Accept the Assignment	Medicare Pays	You Pay
Medicare pays 80% of $800 (the reasonable charge)	$640	
You pay 20% of $800		$160
You pay the amount of the bill over the reasonable charge ($1,200 minus $800)		400
Total payment to surgeon	$640	$560

If the Surgeon Agrees to Accept the Assignment	Medicare Pays	You Pay
Medicare pays 80% of $800	$640	
You pay 20% of $800		$160
Total payment to surgeon	$640	$160

In other words, in this example you save $400 in out-of-pocket costs if the surgeon agrees to accept the assignment. Over a period of time, this kind of savings can amount to thousands of dollars that you would otherwise have to pay yourself.

If the doctor or other provider accepts the assignment, it does not mean you will not have to pay anything; you will still have to pay the coinsurance of 20% of the reasonable charge. What you save is the amount of the bill over and above the reasonable charge. In our example the surgeon accepted $800 as the total amount of his bill and did not ask for payment of the $1,200, his original bill.

FILING A CLAIM ON ASSIGNMENT

If the doctor or other provider accepts the assignment, his or her office will send in the claim. Medicare will send payment directly to the doctor and the doctor's bill will show when Medicare payment has been received and will show the balance that you owe and should pay the doctor yourself. In addition, you will receive a statement from Medicare containing complete information as to the amount of the bill, the amount Medicare decided was reasonable, the amount Medicare paid and the amount you have to pay. See the discussion of the "Explanation of Benefits" form, Chapter 17. In Connecticut, Medicare pays, on the average, within two weeks of receiving the claim form.

WHEN CAN THE DOCTOR BILL YOU FOR MORE THAN THE 20% COINSURANCE?

Even if the doctor accepts the assignment, there are some instances when he or she will bill you for more than the 20% of Medicare's reasonable cost:

If You Have Not Met the Deductible

Medicare will not pay the first $75 of your medical bills in any one calendar year. Until you have paid this deductible, the amount owing will have to be paid by you to the provider. For example, if you had not met your deductible, the surgeon's bill we examined above would look like this:

IF THE SURGEON AGREES TO ACCEPT THE ASSIGNMENT AND YOU HAVE NOT YET MET ANY OF YOUR DEDUCTIBLE:	MEDICARE PAYS	YOU PAY
You pay $75 deductible		$ 75
You pay 20% of $800		160
Medicare pays 80% of $800, less the $75 deductible	$565	
Total payment to surgeon	$565	$235

Once you have met (paid) the deductible, you will not have to pay it again until the next calendar year. The calendar year runs from January 1 to December 31.

If the first bill you receive after December 31 is only for a reasonable charge of $25, for example, the entire $25 will be counted against the $75 deductible. You will have to pay the $25 out of your own pocket and Medicare will credit $25 against the deductible, so you will then have $50 more to pay ($25 + $50 = $75 deductible). In other words, you accumulate credits against the deductible, paying your medical bills yourself until you have paid $75 worth for that calendar year.

If you do not have $75 worth of covered medical bills in a year (say you have only $50 in medical bills), you cannot carry over a credit (in this case $25) to the following year. This is a change in the law; you used to be able to carry over an unused portion of your deductible under certain circumstances. A change in the law has done away with the so-called Carry-Over Rule and you lose any unused portion of the deductible. No matter what you have done with your deductible the previous year, it will not affect the next year. A new deductible goes into effect each January 1.

Suppose I Have a Bill in Another State?

People sometimes worry that medical costs incurred in a state other than the one in which they usually file their Medicare claims (see Chapter 16) will not be properly credited against their deductible. All claims go to a central office in Maryland and are put on the computer under your account number. The computer keeps track and notifies Medicare, each time you file a claim, as to what your deductible status is. It's a good idea to always check your Explanation of Medicare Benefits form to see if it is correct but this is an area in which you will not generally find errors.

If You Have Noncovered Services

Medicare will not pay anything on a bill for services it does not cover. This may include services provided by a doctor who has agreed to accept the assignment. His accepting the assignment will not benefit you where noncovered services are concerned; you will have to pay the full amount of the bill for them out-of-pocket. Flu shots, vitamin B_{12} shots, and routine physical examinations are all examples of noncovered services for which Medicare does not pay. If your doctor suggests a course of treatment or tests, ask if it is covered by Medicare and if not, how much it will cost. You should know what costs you are incurring if you are going to have to pay the whole bill yourself; maybe there is a different, less expensive treatment available.

WILL MOST DOCTORS ACCEPT THE ASSIGNMENT?

In Maine, Vermont, New Hampshire and Massachusetts, between 85% and 95% of the doctors accept the assignment. In Connecticut, also a New England state, less than half as many doctors will accept the assignment. The difference is thought to be mostly the difference in the Medigap health plans available. I encountered another factor, in interviewing doctors in areas with a low acceptance rate, that arises out of a basic attitude toward the Medicare program. Fairfield, the most affluent of the Connecticut counties, has the poorest record of doctors accepting the assignment. The reason, as one doctor put it: "I don't think someone living in a million-dollar house on the beach in Westport should ask me to accept the assignment." Since, under the present rules, accepting the assignment means the doctor will often end up getting paid less than his usual fee, what he was saying is why should he take money out of his own pocket for someone who is obviously richer than he is. I asked if that meant he favored a means test for Medicare beneficiaries. He thought a minute and said yes. He clearly thought of Medicare as a welfare program, rather than a benefit the person had earned by paying into the system all his working years. He did not think of Medicare as health insurance that, like any insurance, is used more by some policy holders than by others. When I suggested that health care was a right in every other industrialized nation in the world, many much smaller and poorer than the United States, he shrugged his shoulders and indicated many things were different in this country and that's just the way it was.

Part of the resentment that many doctors feel toward Medicare might disappear if the program were administered the way it is in countries with a national health plan, where all participating doctors are reimbursed the same amount, according to an established fee schedule. A schedule of fees is set up and all doctors must abide by that when serving beneficiaries. If a person chooses, as in England, to go to a doctor outside of the plan, the fees are whatever the doctor chooses to charge. The point is that no one need buy expensive medical care unless they want to, and no doctor need feel that he is being underpaid (because Medicare may allow him less than a no-better-qualified doctor just because of extraneous factors, such as when the two doctors moved into the area).

Another unpopular aspect of Medicare's method of determining reasonable charges has to do with the number of such procedures that particular doctor has performed during the year. If, by chance, he last performed that particular procedure three years ago, or not often enough to have established an up-to-date customary charge, Medicare would use the 50th (instead of the 75th) percentile as the basis for establishing the prevailing charge. This will mean he will be allowed proportionally less of his actual charge for a service than other doctors in the area. This is clearly not equitable and a doctor affected by this regulation is bound to be less inclined to accept the assignment. Since assignments are accepted on an item-by-item basis, the result might be that he will never perform that procedure for any of his Medicare patients.

HOW TO INCREASE YOUR CHANCES OF GETTING A DOCTOR TO ACCEPT THE ASSIGNMENT

Ask him. No doctor is going to offer; you must ask. And ask as if you expect the answer to be yes. This means looking the doctor in the eye and speaking in a positive manner. If you look down at your hands, speak in a very low voice and twist your hands while asking, you increase the chance that the answer will be no. Assertiveness, not aggressiveness, is what is called for. I have been told over and over again by doctors in areas with low assignment-acceptance rates that they will accept the assignment *if asked*. And I have also been told by several doctors that they find that wealthy patients, or patients who can afford to pay their own medical bills, usually do not ask for this coverage. This attitude toward Medicare is quite different from that in England, where a study showed that Britons who could afford to pay for their own medical bills tended to use private physicians for minor complaints but used the National Health Plan for major expenses. Apparently we as a nation still feel that we should somehow take care of ourselves if we possibly can and that our government has no obligation to take care of its citizens, unless they are automobile or aircraft manufacturers, oil-producing companies and other large corporations. It is ironic that the independent spirit of the American frontier seems to live on only in the American citizen and not in special-interest groups and captains of industry.

What If the Doctor Says No?

If the doctor says he or she will not accept the assignment, you have two choices: you can go to another doctor or you can pay, out of your own pocket, whatever Medicare does not pay. Find out what Medicare will pay and then decide.

If the doctor turns you down once, ask again next time. It's possible that he or she will accept the assignment for one service and not for another.

If the doctor uses as an excuse the fact that he belongs to a group, don't believe it; most doctors in a group are free to accept the assignment whenever they wish.

If you believe the doctor may think you are affluent and you are not, explain a bit about your circumstances and why it is necessary for you to ask. You may always dress up a little when you go to the doctor, giving him an exaggerated idea of your circumstances. Or you may be in a profession that people think of as glamorous and well-paid. If your circumstances are modest, do not hesitate to say so. You aren't asking for charity; you are just trying to take advantage of something you have earned the right to have.

What If He Still Says No?

If he still says no and you would rather not go to another doctor, ask if he will lower his fee for you just this once. Many doctors think that Medicare would frown on their having special fees for special patients; this is not the case. The Medicare law defines a "customary charge" as the charge a physician usually and most frequently charges *the majority* of his patients for a specific service. As long as a physician charges the majority of his patients this fee, he is free to charge less to other patients who cannot pay his usual charge. Conversely he is also free to charge patients more than his customary charge if he thinks they are affluent.

In the event a physician charges less, Medicare will pay the allowable charge as long as that is not more than what is actually being charged. In other words, Medicare will not pay the doctor more than he is charging, even if he is charging less than the reasonable charge. Also, if the doctor bills more than his customary charge, Medicare will not, of course, pay more than what it has determined as the reasonable charge.

What If the Doctor or Other Provider Absolutely Refuses to Accept the Assignment?

In this case, it is very important that you understand how little Medicare will cover and how to make the most of it.

First, you might want to consider trying to find a provider who will accept the assignment. In the case of your family doctor you may not want to make a change, but in the case of a surgeon, whom you may never have even met, you should consider that there is often more than one good doctor in various specialties and that it will make no difference whether you go to one or the other. In the same spirit, if you are making a major purchase such as a hospital bed, you may be able to shop around until you find a supplier who will work with you. You usually have to ask doctors in person but you can ask a supplier over the phone.

HOW TO FIND OUT HOW MUCH IT WILL COST YOU

If the provider will not accept the assignment, you still do not have to buy a pig in a poke. Ask what the charge for the service or item will be. Then phone Medicare, give them the name of the provider, describe the service or item and ask what their reasonable or allowable charge for it is. Since Medicare has a different allowable charge for each doctor and supplier who performs a specific service, the only way you can tell how much they allow is to ask in a specific instance.

For example: For a hernia operation, Medicare may allow $350 for Doctor A who charges $500; $300 for Doctor B who charges $400 and $50 for Doctor C who charges $375. Assuming that none of them will accept the assignment, you would have to pay more out of your own pocket to the doctor who charges the least. Here is how it works out in this example:

	DOCTOR A	DOCTOR B	DOCTOR C
Doctor's Charge	$500	$400	$375
Medicare Allowable Charge	350	300	50
Medicare Pays 80%	280	240	40
You Pay	70	60	10
Amount Over Allowable	150	100	325
Your Total Out-of-Pocket Costs	$220	$160	$335

Because Medicare allows a higher reasonable charge for Doctor A, his surgery will cost you less than Doctor C's.

Note that these are imaginary figures and will vary from doctor to doctor and from locality to locality; Medicare will not always allow the amounts shown here but may allow more or less. The only way to know what Medicare will allow is to ask them.

Incidentally, in the event that all three doctors had *accepted* the assignment, you would only pay the amount shown in line 4: $70 to Doctor A, $60 to Doctor B or $10 to Doctor C. You can see how accepting the assignment radically changes your share of the cost.

12

How to Get More Medicare
Money for Doctor Bills

The better you understand how Medicare works, the more likely you are to be able to get maximum benefits. On the other hand, if you do not understand Medicare, you are liable to shortchange yourself. Medicare people are usually very helpful but they can only work with the information you give them and they cannot be at your side to advise you that one course of action will work better than another. In this chapter I will suggest some specific ways you can improve your Medicare benefits; even if some of the rules change, understanding how these methods work may help you to use Medicare more creatively and to your benefit.

HOW TO INCREASE MEDICARE PAYMENTS FOR EYE-DOCTOR BILLS

Once you understand the sort of thing Medicare will and will not pay for, you can be a more intelligent medical-care consumer.

You now know that Medicare will not pay for routine eye examinations for eyeglasses, nor for the eyeglasses themselves. So you do not make an appointment with your ophthalmologist "because I think I need new glasses." Instead, you tell the nurse you want an appointment because you are having trouble with your eyes. Describe specific symptoms, if possible. Your eyes may be watering a lot; you may see black specks; you may be getting headaches more often and associate their occurrence with eyestrain. Whatever has called your attention to your eyes and made you decide to see the doctor is what you should describe. After all, who are you to diagnose your problem as a need for new glasses? Stick to describing your symptoms and leave the diagnosis to the doctor.

If it does turn out that you need new glasses, ask the nurse to be sure to break the amount of the bill down and bill you a separate charge for the prescription for the glasses. If the bill is written out properly, Medicare will be happy to pay part of the bill for finding out what was wrong. The charge for writing the prescription—which Medicare won't pay—will be a small part of the total bill.

WHEN YOU SHOULD GO TO AN OPHTHALMOLOGIST RATHER THAN AN OPTICIAN

If you think you need new glasses (although, as we have just noted, you should not assume that), you may be inclined to go to an optician for a new prescription.

Many people get their glasses in the optical department of large department stores or in discount optical stores, and many of these offer an excellent service at somewhat lower prices than you will be charged by an ophthalmologist. Unfortunately, the lower price may actually cost a Medicare beneficiary more because he or she will have to pay 100% of the bill, whereas Medicare may pick up part of the bill from an ophthalmologist.

If the ophthalmologist agrees to accept the assignment, you are almost certain to be better off paying 20% of his bill, plus the extra for the prescription, than paying 100% of the optician's bill. And as a bonus, you will get a more complete examination from an ophthalmologist, which is an important consideration for an elderly person.

HOW TO PAY LESS FOR AN OPERATION

Even with Medicare coverage you will have to pay part of the cost of an operation. Here's how to reduce that cost.

Shop around. Ask your doctor to recommend more than one surgeon and call their offices to find out their fees for your operation. Then call Medicare to find out the allowable or reasonable charge for each surgeon for that operation. With these two figures you can determine how much your share of the bill will be if the surgeon doesn't accept the assignment.

If your doctor has accepted the assignment, the surgeon is much more likely to. So figure it both ways to see what works out best for you (the assignment plus the amount of the reasonable charge for each surgeon). When you ask the surgeon to accept the assignment, tell him your doctor has already agreed to (if he has). Now, using all these figures, make a table like the one on page 90. You will then see which surgeon is the better "buy."

HOW TO GET YOUR MEDICARE BENEFIT FASTER

Money in your hand is better than money in Medicare's hand and it's beneficial to you to get your claims paid as quickly as possible. To some extent, this is within your control; the faster you send in your claims, the faster you will receive your benefit payment from Medicare. Send in your claims as soon as you get your bills. Do not allow bills to accumulate with the intention of sending in a bunch all at once.

HOW TO SAVE MONEY ON A CHIROPRACTOR'S BILL

If you go to a chiropractor for manual correction of a spinal subluxation, Medicare will pay 80% of the reasonable charge for this procedure. The only problem is that the need for this procedure must be determined by taking an X ray. Medicare will not pay for the X ray if the chiropractor takes it; but it will pay 80% of the reasonable charge if a radiologist or regular physician takes it. Get your family doctor to take it and let the chiropractor check it out. That way both the X ray and the procedure will be partially covered by Medicare.

HOW TO GET MEDICARE TO PAY 100% OF YOUR INPATIENT RADIOLOGIST'S BILL

When you are in the hospital, Medicare will pay 100% of the bill of any radiologist or pathologist who accepts the assignment for all his patients. Shop around until you find one in this category.

HOW TIMING CAN INCREASE YOUR BENEFITS

As we saw earlier, Medicare updates its reasonable charges on July 1 of each year. Since health-care bills and doctors' charges keep going up, the reasonable charge will invariably be larger after July 1 than before July 1 for exactly the same service or procedure.

Let us look at three sets of figures to see what this could mean to you.

In example one, let us assume you are scheduled in June for a nonemergency operation that the surgeon says will cost $950. You check with Medicare and they tell you that for that operation performed by that particular surgeon, the reasonable charge (of which they will pay 80%) is

$500. If the surgeon refuses to accept the assignment, your costs would be:

EXAMPLE ONE: JUNE	MEDICARE PAYS	YOU PAY
80% of $500	$400	
20% of $500		$100
the difference between the reasonable charge ($500) and the surgeon's bill ($950)		450
Total paid	$400	$550

Of the original $950 bill, you will pay more than Medicare ($550 compared with $400).

If the doctor accepts the assignment, things work out much better for you.

EXAMPLE TWO: JUNE	MEDICARE PAYS	YOU PAY
80% of $500	$400	
20% of $500		$100
Total paid	$400	$100

You do better, but the $450 you don't pay is $450 the surgeon isn't making on the operation. Even if his charges are on the high side, it may be difficult to convince him to settle for the smaller amount—especially if he has more work than he can handle.

On the other hand, he may be a nice guy and need just a little sweetener to agree to accept the assignment. You hope so, so you ask if there would be any harm in putting the operation off until after July 1. If he says that would be fine, wait until then and then check with Medicare. You will probably find that the reasonable charge has been increased; it may have gone up, for example, to $650. In that case, this is what would happen if he agreed to accept the assignment:

EXAMPLE THREE: JULY	MEDICARE PAYS	YOU PAY
80% of $650	$520	
20% of $650		$130
Total paid	$520	$130

It will cost you only $30 more than it would have in July, but the doctor will get $150 more—and that just might make the difference in his accepting the assignment.

So, whenever you can, put off elective surgery until after July 1. But get a quotation on the doctor's fee before July 1, if possible—although actually doctors don't usually increase bills according to Medicare's schedule because they do better increasing them at the beginning of the calendar year.

OTHER WAYS TO INCREASE YOUR BENEFITS

Elsewhere in this book you will find a number of other suggestions for increasing your benefits, such as: how to buy medical equipment with 100% Medicare coverage, how to save money on hospital bills, how to improve your odds with a second opinion on surgery, and why you should freely appeal your claims. You will find these suggestions in the chapter that covers that particular Medicare area.

13

Other Services Part B
(SMI) Pays For

In the previous pages we have discussed coverage of physician's bills in considerable detail because that is where most of Medicare Part B money goes. Most health-care costs under Part B are either actual doctor bills or charges that are doctor-related, such as tests, X rays and medical equipment. Even home health care requires a doctor to activate it if it is to be covered. In the following pages, we will look at these related areas of coverage.

AMBULANCE SERVICE

Medicare Part B provides limited coverage of ambulance service. The first limitation is Medicare's definition of "ambulance." It can be a boat or a plane, as well as a specially designed automobile, but it must be used primarily for transporting the ill or the injured, and must include certain equipment and meet certain other specified requirements.

It must be medically necessary; the use of any other vehicle must be contraindicated by your condition. If you could travel by private auto without endangering your health, you will not be covered for transportation by ambulance. Even if no automobile is available, even if an ambulance is the only form of transportation around, you still will not be covered if you do not meet this requirement. Lack of other suitable transportation is not an acceptable reason for ambulance use.

How Far May the Ambulance Take You?

The ambulance is partially covered only if it takes you to the nearest hospital or skilled nursing facility that has the equipment you need. This generally means local transportation.

If you or your doctor want the ambulance to take you to an institution that is not the nearest appropriate one, Medicare will partially cover the cost; it will pay the same amount it would have paid if you had gone to the nearest facility.

Where Can the Ambulance Take You?

Ambulance service is partially covered for:

1. Travel from your home to the hospital.
2. Travel from the hospital to your home.
3. Travel from one hospital to another, when medically necessary.
4. Travel back and forth from one hospital to another for special treatment (CAT scan, special therapy, etc.), providing all requirements for such transportation are met.

Noncovered Ambulance Service

Ambulance service will not be covered if it is used merely for convenience or because no other transportation is available. It will not be covered if used for purely personal reasons; for instance, if you want the services of a particular physician who is in a different hospital or in one that is not the nearest appropriate facility. It is not covered if you are in a foreign hospital because of an emergency and want to transfer to a U.S. hospital when the emergency is over. The reason for the transfer in this last instance would be financial rather than medical, because you would probably be losing your Medicare coverage (due to no longer needing emergency care) in the foreign hospital and would want to transfer to a U.S. hospital where you would get Medicare coverage. While you will have to pay the cost of transferring by ambulance, it will probably be far less than the cost of staying in the foreign hospital at your own expense.

Amount of Reimbursement

For all practical purposes, you can assume that Medicare will pay approximately 80% of the reasonable cost of covered ambulance services. (The actual formula Medicare uses is somewhat more complicated than this so it may work out to slightly more or less than 80%.) This leaves the 20% coinsurance as your share of the bill. If your Medicare reimbursement differs substantially from this, phone and ask why.

HOME HEALTH CARE

Until recently, home health care was covered under both Medicare Part A and Part B, and administered under Part A. With the passing of the law that eliminated the restriction of number of visits, home health care was put under Medicare Part A, where we have discussed it in detail. And at present you are entitled to unlimited home health-care visits. However, since this area has been subject to a number of recent changes, keep an eye on it in case further ones are forthcoming.

The only part of home health care that is pertinent to a discussion of Medicare Part B (SMI) concerns visits by physicians.

Your family doctor's or other physician's visits to your home when you are under home health-care coverage are counted and covered in exactly the same way as an office visit or a visit to a patient in a hospital or nursing home. And just like those visits, they are subject to Medicare's criterion of "medically necessary."

Generally, Medicare does not examine each and every visit; it assumes a certain number of visits are normal—the number depending on the nature of your illness—and only looks into the situation if your doctor comes more frequently than your illness would seem to warrant. In the event that your health has changed and actually requires more frequent visits, Medicare may deem them medically necessary and grant coverage, even though they exceed the average number usually allowed. The patient who is fond of her doctor and is comforted by having him drop in frequently for a visit may find coverage disallowed for "excess" visits.

OTHER PHYSICIANS

Until recently, dentists, chiropractors and other doctors were not defined as physicians for the purposes of Medicare coverage; that has recently been changed and now they are accorded the status of physicians but not full physician coverage. You should be aware of the limitations or you will be unpleasantly surprised to find you are liable for the entire bill from these doctors.

Chiropractors

Although so-called medical doctors are gradually accepting the validity of some chiropractic treatments, Medicare will cover part of only one. Medicare will partially cover manual manipulation to correct a subluxation of the spine that has been demonstrated necessary by X ray.

If the chiropractor performs any other services, they will not be covered by Medicare. These services may include services usually performed by a physician, such as X rays, tests, the writing of prescriptions, general routine examinations and so forth; Medicare will not cover any of these if performed by a chiropractor even if they would have been covered if performed by a "medical" doctor. It is especially important to note that Medicare requires the proof, through an X ray, that the condition exists in order for you to qualify for coverage of the subluxation, but will not pay for the X ray if the chiropractor takes it.

Dentists

Medicare will not pay for most of the services for which you usually go to a dentist: filling cavities, fitting bridges and dentures, correcting a faulty bite or improving the health of your gums.

Dental services covered by Medicare used to be confined to certain specific surgery related to the jaw, and to the reduction of fractures of the jaw and facial bones, to the extent to which a dentist would normally be involved. That coverage has been extended, as of July 1, 1981, so that services that would be covered if performed by a medical doctor will now be covered if performed by a dentist. This extended coverage is an important breakthrough since it means that oral infections and some gum diseases are now covered when the dentist treats them. Since an oral infection can be serious and can require costly treatment, this is a significant new benefit.

In addition, a dentist may order hospitalization for a patient who requires certain types of dental procedures and

Medicare coverage will apply just as with any hospitalization. Hospital coverage is also provided for dental services when the patient's condition warrants it, even though the initial reason for hospitalization may have been nondental. For example, if you are hospitalized for a heart attack and it then becomes necessary to extract all your teeth, Medicare may accept the fact that your heart condition makes the extraction sufficiently hazardous to your health to warrant continued hospitalization for the duration of the extractions. In this example, however, while the hospitalization would be covered under Medicare Part A (HI), the extraction, or dentist's services, would not be covered under either Part A or Part B. If the dentist was needed to reduce a jaw fracture instead of to extract teeth, his services would be partially covered by Medicare.

There are a few other instances in which dental services such as tooth extraction would be covered, but these are rare and difficult to determine ahead of time. If your dentist recommends a procedure, ask whether it would be covered by Medicare. If by any chance the dentist is not sure, phone Medicare and describe exactly what the procedure will be and why it is needed and you will probably get a clear yes or no as to coverage. Be sure to fully describe what is contemplated since, for example, tooth extractions by themselves are not covered, but tooth extractions in connection with radiation treatments would be covered.

If you are in a covered nursing home (SNF) that has a dental clinic or facilities for a visiting dentist, the routine dental services you receive there will not be covered any more than they would be if you went to the dentist's office. If the nursing home provides dental services to all its patients as routinely as it provides food and nursing care, it probably would be covered, but I know of no nursing home that does so.

Podiatrists

As people get older, they tend to have more trouble with their feet and to seek the services of a podiatrist. Technically, Medicare covers the services of a podiatrist but the exclusions, or noncovered services, are numerous.

Noncovered Services

1. Treatment for flat feet and prescriptions for special shoes or insoles or other corrective devices.
2. Routine foot care—including foot baths, massage, nail and cuticle cutting (even if the patient is unable to do it), removing corns and calluses, prescriptions for creams and lotions—is not usually covered, but it is covered under certain circumstances, such as in the case of diabetic ulcers or infections.
3. Foot exercise treatments not accepted as medically effective.
4. Orthopedic shoes and doctor visits for the purpose of determining what type of shoes or for prescribing or fitting such shoes.

Covered Services

1. A new benefit recently added to coverage is treatment of plantar warts (warts that form on the soles of the feet). This was previously a noncovered service.
2. Fungal and other infections of feet and toenails that could not be treated by a nonprofessional or do not come under the heading of routine foot care.
2. Special shoes, if they are attached to a leg brace (which is also covered).
4. Foot care normally considered routine but performed

in the case of diabetes or severe circulatory disease, or similarly serious problems with the legs or feet.
5. Treatment for fungal diseases or foot infections.

If you require the care of a podiatrist and are not sure whether it will be covered, talk it over with your family doctor. It may be that he can prescribe it as a medically necessary treatment. This will not automatically insure Medicare coverage but it may make the difference in a borderline case.

Optometrists

There is only one kind of service performed by an optometrist that is covered by Medicare: treatment for aphakia. This is a new benefit which was not available before July 1, 1981.

Aphakia is the absence of the natural lens of the eye. This condition may be congenital or the lens may have been removed in the course of a cataract operation or other eye surgery. Natural lenses are often replaced by either temporary postsurgical lenses or by permanent lenses, but they may also be compensated for by special cataract eyeglasses. All such replacements, including cataract eyeglasses, are covered by Medicare. Both contact lenses and eyeglasses can be covered, but not prescription sunglasses. Glasses and contact lenses for other conditions are not covered.

Christian Science Practitioners

The services of Christian Science practitioners are not covered. Generally speaking, no one outside the standard medical professions is considered a physician by Medicare's definition.

Radiologists and Pathologists

Services of these physicians are covered by Medicare in the same way as other physicians' services, so long as you are out of the hospital.

For in-hospital patients, there has been a change in coverage. Before July 1981, your Medicare Handbook would have stated that Medicare would pay 100% of the reasonable charges "by doctors for radiology services [such as X rays] and pathology services [such as blood and urine] tests you receive as an inpatient in a participating or otherwise qualified hospital."

In addition, the Handbook would have instructed you, "if you do receive doctor bills for these services, send them in . . . for *full* payment of the reasonable charges, even though you have not met the $75 deductible." In other words, these charges were paid 100% and you did not even have to pay the deductible.

At present, Medicare will pay only if the doctor accepts the assignment for *all physicians' services furnished by him for all hospital inpatients enrolled under Medicare.* If the physician refuses to accept the assignment for all these patients, he can bill whatever he pleases, and Medicare will deal with it just as it does with any other doctor bill.

Theoretically, this was done to improve the situation for the patient. Before this amendment, Medicare had assumed that radiologists and pathologists would combine their billings with those of the hospital and be reimbursed by Medicare along with the hospital's bills. It was found, however, that, instead, these physicians frequently billed the patient directly. As a result, Medicare was paying twice for these services: once to the hospital that counted the physicians as a staff cost and once to the beneficiary who submitted this bill along with other doctor bills.

Unfortunately, you have no way of knowing which doctors fulfill this requirement so you have no way of knowing whether you are incurring bills from the radiologists and pathologists who perform services for you. This is another gray area; you may be running up bills, entirely beyond your control and without your informed consent, that you are in no position to pay. You might, perhaps, want to discuss this with your doctor when you are hospitalized from now on; perhaps he can assign you to a doctor who is covered 100%.

Plastic Surgeons

Plastic surgeons are covered but not all the services they perform are. You are not covered for any sort of cosmetic surgery: face lifts, tummy tucks or any other surgery for which the sole objective is to improve your appearance. However, you are covered if plastic surgery is needed to restore function, correct a malformation or to repair damage from an accident (such as a severe burn). If the surgery incidentally improves your appearance, that does not nullify coverage as long as the original purpose fell in a covered category.

Acupuncturists

Medicare does not pay for acupuncture.

OUTPATIENT SURGERY

In an effort to reduce costly hospitalization, Medicare has added a new benefit: outpatient surgery for specified procedures is now covered. Many minor operations and surgical procedures do not require hospitalization; they can be performed in a short time and the patient can go home soon after. In recognition of this, Medicare is drawing up a list of surgical procedures that it will cover when performed in a walk-in surgical center or in a doctor's office equipped for these procedures.

If the surgeon does not accept the assignment, Medicare will pay 80% of the reasonable charge. If the surgeon does accept the assignment, Medicare gives you a further break; it will pay 100% of the doctor's reasonable charge and you will not have to pay anything—not even the usual 20%. This provides considerable incentive for the beneficiary to have whatever he can done on an outpatient basis. If your doctor recommends minor surgery, be sure to ask whether it falls in this category and, if so, whether he would prefer to do the operation himself or to recommend an outpatient surgical facility. Be sure to ask, also, whoever performs the surgery to accept the assignment.

Since this is a comparatively new benefit, your doctor may not be aware of it, so it is important for you to know it exists.

OUTPATIENT PHYSICAL THERAPY

This is another benefit for which coverage has been improved. Until now, physical therapy provided by a practicing physical therapist has been covered by Medicare only to the extent of $100 a year. Starting January 1, 1982, this has been raised to $500 a year. Remember that your deductible and coinsurance apply to these charges. For instance, if you had no other medical bills that year, $75 would be deducted from the $500 and $425 would be partially covered.

Not all physical therapy is covered, however. Check with your doctor (who must establish the need for it) and with the home health agency, or whoever provides it, as to whether your treatment is covered and under what circumstances coverage might end. An example of when coverage might end is the point at which Medicare would determine that further therapy would not improve your condition.

PNEUMOCOCCAL VACCINE INJECTIONS

As a general rule, Medicare does not pay for preventive medicine, and most shots, such as flu shots, fall into this category. Since July 1, 1981, however, an exception has been made for pneumococcal vaccine. Because 90% of the deaths attributed to pneumonia occur in the over-65 age group, Medicare will now cover shots to prevent this disease. Furthermore, costs associated with the vaccine and its administration will be covered 100% and will not be subject to the deductible or coinsurance.

MEDICAL EQUIPMENT

In addition to the services provided by individuals (doctors, nurses, social workers), Medicare will pay for certain types of equipment needed in connection with an illness. This is a very important area and much more complicated than you might think, so I have given it its own chapter.

If you have occasion to use any medical equipment, see Chapter 14.

14

Durable Medical Equipment:
What It Is and When It Is Covered

WHAT IS DURABLE MEDICAL EQUIPMENT?

Durable medical equipment is, by Medicare's definition, medically necessary equipment that has a proven therapeutic value or effect and is durable rather than disposable. A guide to whether or not medical equipment meets the criterion of "durable" is to ask whether it is the kind of item that can be rented. Surgical leggings, for example, are sold, not rented, as are incontinence pads, lambswool bed coverings and surgical stockings; none of these, therefore, would be considered durable even though they are undoubtedly medically necessary under certain circumstances.

Durable medical equipment can be as small as a pair of crutches or as large as a hospital bed. If it is too elaborate or complicated to use, coverage may be denied on the grounds that it is inappropriate for use at home. This is especially true of technical equipment that should be operated or at least supervised by a trained technician and that is considered dangerous or difficult for a layman to operate.

Medicare also will not pay for a deluxe version of medically necessary durable equipment if the simpler version will do. Even when coverage is extended to the basic item, all unnecessary or "frill" devices will be prorated and denied. It is possible, for instance, to get a heating pad with several special features, but Medicare will pay only on the basis of the cost of an ordinary heating pad and you will have to pay the difference.

Another type of item that is not covered is anything that could be considered custodial—that is useful in terms of personal comfort or convenience but not "medically necessary." Here we cross a fine line because many of the items denied coverage on this basis are ones I would expect to be included. For example, devices to help people in and out of bathtubs or up and down from toilet seats are not covered. Medicare is not entirely consistent on this point since it does cover power-operated wheelchairs "if the patient's condition is such that a wheelchair is medically necessary, and the patient is unable to operate the wheelchair manually." An electrically operated hospital bed (when change of position is medically necessary) is allowed under much the same conditions, as are various kinds of seat lifts. Why grab bars are denied, when many elderly people would have trouble taking sitz baths or other forms of treatment at home without the aid of a grab bar to help extricate themselves, is a question no one I talked to was able to answer. It does seem that items that are obviously not frivolous, such as grab bars, should be covered—but they are not, and you should be aware of it.

HOW IS THE COST OF DURABLE MEDICAL EQUIPMENT COVERED?

If the equipment satisfies their definition, Medicare will cover up to 80% of the reasonable cost, providing you buy or rent it from a provider whom Medicare finds acceptable. Medicare, theoretically, does not allow you a choice; it decides which is more economical.

HOW IS THE EQUIPMENT OBTAINED?

There are three ways Medicare says you may obtain durable medical equipment: rental, outright purchase or lease-purchase. It used to be that the beneficiary was free to decide which method was more satisfactory, but the law was changed in 1977 so that now Medicare has more of a say in the matter. This means that before you arrange for the purchase or rental of any durable medical equipment, you should first check with Medicare to find out how they want you to handle it. However, this law has *never been implemented,* so in practice you may find the choice is up to you. Ask Medicare in case the guidelines have finally come through.

Medicare's decision to rent or buy is usually made on the basis of predicted length of use; equipment that is to be used over a long period of time might cost less if purchased outright rather than rented. If Medicare determines that purchase would be more economical than rental, it will recommend that you purchase the equipment, either outright or on a lease-purchase arrangement. If this would create undue hardship on the beneficiary, however, the law gives Medicare the leeway to allow the equipment to be rented.

Medicare is supposed to tell you as soon as possible how to obtain the equipment and how much it will be covered for. In addition, Medicare will tell you how it will reimburse the supplier and is supposed to work out payments that the supplier finds "equitable, economical and feasible," especially in the case of lease-purchase agreements.

In some instances, electrically operated wheelchairs for example, Medicare will base its coverage on the lowest charge at which the item is available in that locality. In most instances, however, it is not necessary to shop around to find the item at that price. Medicare will tell you how much they will allow and you can then see if the supplier will agree to that price. This is, in effect, asking the supplier to accept the assignment; otherwise you will have to pay not only the 20% that Medicare does not pay, but also the amount over and above the "reasonable charge" on which Medicare bases its 80% coverage.

Fortunately, most suppliers who are accepted by Medicare are used to dealing with it and know the limitations and rules better than you possibly could. They will often be able to answer your questions and will advise you and will be inclined to accept the assignment. It wouldn't be a bad idea, however, to check with others who have purchased similar items from the supplier to see whether there have been any complaints or difficulties.

Outright Purchase—the Disadvantages

If you are allowed the option of purchasing the equipment outright and decide to do so, you should be aware that you are running a risk of being stuck with part of the cost in the event that the equipment is no longer "medically necessary." To give an extreme example, suppose you purchase a hospital bed outright and the person for whom it was obtained dies a month later. In that case, the bed would be ruled no longer necessary and Medicare coverage would end. Since Medicare often reimburses through monthly payments, you would have been paid for only one month and the family or estate of the deceased would have to somehow make the remaining payment. Usually length of use is estimated by a physician or by Medicare, but since neither has a crystal ball, the medical necessity may end long before their estimate and long before all Medicare payments have been made. You could be liable for a thousand dollars or more on a large purchase.

Rental

If Medicare determines that rental payments are more practical or will cost less in the long run than outright purchase—as for instance in the case of an expensive item that will not be medically necessary for a long period—and if, under these circumstances, the beneficiary goes ahead and buys the item outright anyhow, Medicare will pay the rental charges up to a point. However, as soon as Medicare has paid what it would have paid for outright purchase, it will discontinue payments of any sort.

If, on the other hand, the beneficiary changes his or her mind and decides to purchase an item that has been rented until then, contrary to Medicare's recommendation to purchase, Medicare will deduct whatever it has paid to date in rental payments from its coverage for purchase. If you should find yourself in this position, try to work out a deal with the carrier so that he applies what you have already paid in rental charges to the selling price. It is even better if you can arrive at such an arrangement when you make the rental agreement in the first place.

In the event that the patient's condition changes so that Medicare changes its mind and opts for a purchase rather than the rental that has been going on, Medicare will cover all the costs on an 80% basis.

SUPPLIES NEEDED FOR DURABLE MEDICAL EQUIPMENT

Drugs and biologicals, such as oxygen, that are used with the equipment are covered if the equipment is covered. Parts that may need replacement, such as hoses or mouthpieces, are covered only if the beneficiary owns the equipment outright or is in the process of purchasing it. Medicare feels that rental equipment should be furnished with these items by the supplier without cost. Do not assume, however, that the supplier has automatically agreed to this arrangement; get it in writing. If you do not, you may find yourself regularly billed for items you should not have to pay for, without any Medicare coverage to pick up part of the cost.

Repairs

Here again, Medicare will help pay for repairs for equipment you own or are purchasing. Rental equipment is supposed to be repaired free of charge by the supplier. Get an agreement to this effect in writing.

Maintenance

What Medicare calls "routine periodic servicing"—including cleaning and regulating—is not covered. The rationale here is that the patient or someone connected with him or her ought to be able to perform these necessary tasks with the help of the owner's manual. It is assumed that hiring someone else to do the servicing and maintenance is a matter of convenience and not necessity, and Medicare firmly believes in discouraging that sort of thing.

Considering how owner's manuals and instructions for the assembly, use, servicing and maintenance of anything—from a wood stove or a bicycle to an IPPB machine—are common subjects for jokes and cartoons and funny anecdotes, this seems highly unrealistic on the part of Medicare. In addition, it certainly does not take into account the kind of person on whom this burden may fall.

Many a bedridden husband is taken care of by an arthritic, half-blind spouse, who is barely able to manage preparing a meal and dealing with minimal housework. To expect this person to clean and adjust an IPPB machine or some other piece of equipment is totally unrealistic. Probably the district nurse often fills the gap and tries to help out, but health-care personnel are often short on time, have all they can do to attend to their proper duties and truly cannot stop to be maintenance men.

A possible out may be found in the exception to this rule; when the maintenance is extensive and requires the services of a trained technician, Medicare gets around the rule by calling this kind of maintenance "repair." As we have seen, repairs are covered to some extent.

HOW TO ESTABLISH "UNDUE HARDSHIP"

If Medicare determines that an expensive piece of durable medical equipment should be bought outright, but you cannot afford it, you can plead undue hardship and ask Medicare to allow you to rent it.

To do this, you must notify Medicare, in writing, that the deductible or coinsurance amounts you would have to pay are beyond your means and that you haven't been able to make an arrangement with the supplier to pay on the installment plan. Naturally, you must also state that you are not on Medicaid (which would take care of these payments for you).

Medicare will check to make sure that the supplier doesn't usually offer installment payment plans, and if he does not, will give you three months' leeway during which to make partial payments, as if on the installment plan. This three-month provision actually amounts to a nine-month installment plan because of Medicare's method which it calls "interim rental payments."

INTERIM RENTAL PAYMENTS

It is often necessary to obtain durable medical equipment before it can be determined how Medicare wants the transaction handled—in other words, before Medicare tells you whether to rent or purchase. Because of this, you should file your claim for reimbursement as soon as possible to allow Medicare time to look into the matter and decide. While Medicare is deciding on purchase vs. rental, it will pay an "interim rental payment" for a maximum of six months from the beginning of your rental or purchase. If you are slow in filing this claim, you will use up part of this six months without being reimbursed. However, if the delay in filing the claim wasn't your fault, you may be given an extension to more than six months.

You do not lose coverage on the purchase price because of these interim rental payments; Medicare does not normally deduct them from what it will pay in purchase payments.

HOW TO SAVE MONEY WITH USED DURABLE MEDICAL EQUIPMENT

You can often save money by buying used durable medical euqipment; it may be a little shabby but still be in excellent working condition. Also, because of the nature of this equipment, it may have been used for a very short time but still have to be sold as "used."

Medicare encourages the purchase of this used equipment because it costs less than a new item. If the cost of the equipment is at least 25% less than what Medicare would allow for the item purchased new, Medicare will waive the coinsurance (the 20% you would usually have to pay) and will pay 100% of the cost. (You must have met your deductible to get the full benefit of this arrangement.) This is a good deal and makes sense.

In order to get full Medicare coverage of a used item, you must buy from a supplier who will give you certain assurances of quality: the same warranty as if the item were new, assurances that it has been completely reconditioned and is in good working order and an understanding that he will not mark up repair and maintenance costs beyond his usual charges. Most suppliers who handle items of this type are used to working with Medicare and are set up to comply with these requirements, but you should ask when making arrangements with them, since it may be some time before Medicare gets around to looking at your claim.

If you have the opportunity to purchase this kind of equipment from a friend or other private person, you might prefer that to getting it from a supplier. Often, under these circumstances, you will know for a fact how much use the item has had and how it has been taken care of. Medicare recognizes that this may be a good way to get used equipment and allows you to do it, providing you meet the above requirements. Obviously, however, a private person cannot give you the same warranty as a store, so Medicare requires instead that you say you have examined the equipment and believe it is in good working order and will last for as long as you expect to need it.

DISPOSING OF DURABLE MEDICAL EQUIPMENT

The fact that you've purchased the equipment and been partially reimbursed for it by Medicare does not mean that you are not free to sell it once you no longer need it. Nor does it prejudice your situation in the event that you need that kind of equipment again in the future; you can get Medicare coverage for it again if your medical situation again requires it.

WHY SHOULD YOU ASK THE PROVIDER OF DURABLE MEDICAL EQUIPMENT TO ACCEPT THE ASSIGNMENT?

There are two main reasons why you should ask the provider of durable medical equipment to accept the assignment. The first is the obvious one: you save money.

As with doctor bills, any provider who accepts the assignment agrees to settle for Medicare's decision as to what his bill should be, the so-called reasonable or allowable charge. Once he has agreed to that, Medicare will pay 80% of his bill and you will have to pay only 20%. If he refuses to accept the assignment, you will have to pay the 20% of the reasonable charge plus however much his bill is over and above the reasonable charge. If, for instance, his bill is $2,000, and Medicare says the reasonable charge is $1,500, Medicare will pay 80% of $1,500, or $1,200. You will have to pay $300 (the remaining 20%) plus $500 (the amount over the reasonable charge), or a total of $800. If the gap between the provider's bill and Medicare's reasonable charge is high enough, you may end up paying more than Medicare does. Your only protection is to find a supplier who will accept the assignment. If this is not possible, be sure you try to find out from Medicare what they consider the reasonable charge for this item so that you can determine how much you are going to have to pay out of your own pocket.

Another reason for asking the provider to accept the assignment is that you then do not have to worry about whether the provider is trying to sell you an item with features that Medicare will decide are not medically necessary and will not cover. There is no way you yourself can be sure this will not happen since it depends to some extent on whether Medicare agrees with your physician that your condition requires some of these extra features (as in an electrically operated hospital bed). If the provider agrees to accept the assignment, it is his problem. He has agreed to accept what Medicare sets as the cost of the item and it is his hard luck if he has sold or rented you an unnecessarily deluxe version of the equipment.

GETTING SPECIFIC: DURABLE MEDICAL EQUIPMENT NOT COVERED

All of the above discussion of durable medical equipment is academic if you do not know whether an item you need is covered by Medicare. We have seen Medicare's definition of this type of equipment but let us look at it again. It is equipment that is primarily and customarily used to serve a medical purpose and would generally not be used in the absence of illness or injury. Furthermore, it must be able to withstand repeated use (durable). And last but by no means least, it must be appropriate for use in the home (although it may also be used in hospitals and nursing homes).

To give you a better idea of what items are covered or not covered, let us look at an excerpt from a Medicare Screening List that gives a list of specific items for which Medicare carriers are told to *deny* coverage, which begins on page 122.

If you glance over the list, a pattern will soon become clear and you will be able to anticipate the kind of items for which you would not be covered. Broadly speaking, unless the equipment is generally recognized as medically necessary, it will not be covered. The fact that so-called comfort or convenience items may be essential for daily care, or may help the patient stay at home rather than go to a hospital, is unimportant.

Another category of items to avoid is deluxe versions of medically necessary pieces of equipment. For instance, even when ordinary heating pads are covered, more complicated and expensive versions are covered only to the extent that the ordinary heating pad would be covered. This seems reasonable in most cases, but where the extra features would make the patient able to be more independent, it seems shortsighted not to extend coverage for them.

Occasionally, it seems to me, the denial usurps the physician's prerogative. Percussors, for example, are denied on the grounds that they are not generally recommended for use in treatment of patients in the Medicare age group. It seems to me that the attending physician, rather than Medicare, should be the one to make this determination, especially since, in this example, some leading specialists do recommend them. So "not generally recommended" means that sometimes it is recommended—yet Medicare does not cover the cost even in that eventuality. It is also an illogical basis on which to deny coverage since the "Medicare age group" can include disabled young adults. While it is true that, on the whole, the majority of Medicare recipients are elderly, no allowance seems to be made for those who are not.

In addition, it is often precisely the elderly who require percussion. If they have a respiratory problem, they may be too weak to clear the mucus from their lungs without help, and percussion, combined with IPPB and other therapy, may make a big difference in their condition. The physician, with his personal knowledge of the patient, should be the one to make the judgment.

Another item that falls in this category, although its use is not so clearly medical, is air conditioning. There is no question that an efficient air-conditioning unit makes life more bearable for people with allergies, and in the case of severe asthma may defuse a life-threatening situation. It is seldom possible for asthmatics to remove themselves from their homes at the peak of the hay-fever season, for instance, but staying in an air-conditioned room during those few weeks might reduce the dangers of a severe attack or attacks.

Some specialists feel that the cooling, as well as the filtering, function of air conditioners is very helpful in treating certain respiratory problems and put those patients in specially cooled hospital rooms whenever possible.

I called Medicare to see if, in practice, they allowed exceptions to some of these denials. They said no, they couldn't because the guidelines came from Baltimore and had to be strictly adhered to, with no room for discretion on the state level. I asked what if the attending physician said the equipment was absolutely necessary. The answer, with a sigh, was, "Oh, the physicians say all of the durable medical equipment we list is medically necessary, but that doesn't cut any ice if it is listed as 'to be denied.'"

*Medical Equipment Not Covered**

ITEM	REASON DENIED
Action Bath hydro massage	primarily used to soothe and comfort rather than for therapeutic purposes
Adjust-A-Bed	a comfort or convenience item
Aero Massage	primarily used to soothe and comfort, rather than for therapeutic purposes
Aero-Pulse Surgical Leggings	not reusable
air cleaners	not medical; environmental control equipment
air conditioners	not medical; environmental control equipment
air-fluidized bed	inappropriate for home use
American Bidet Toilet Seat	not medical; hygienic equipment

*This list is adapted from the *Medicare Carriers Manual*, HIM-14.

Medical Equipment Not Covered (*cont'd*)

ITEM	REASON DENIED
American Sonoid Heat and Massage Foam Cushion Pad	not considered generally therapeutically effective
Aqua-Whirl	primarily to soothe and comfort rather than for therapeutic purposes
Aquamatic K-Pad	payment limited to amount payable for ordinary heating pad
Aquamatic K-Termia	inappropriate for home use
Aquasage Portable Whirlpool	primarily to soothe and comfort rather than for therapeutic purposes
Arteriosonde	may be partially covered
Astromatic Bed	a comfort or convenience item
Astropedic bed	a comfort or convenience item
Autolift	a convenience item
automatic blood pressure	may be partially covered
Autosfig	physician's instrument
Auto-Tilt Chair	not considered generally therapeutically effective
bathtub lifts	a convenience item
bathtub seats	a comfort or convenience item
Bead bed	inappropriate for home use
Beautyrest Adjustable Bed	a comfort or convenience item
bed baths (home type)	hygienic, rather than medical equipment
bedboards	not primarily medical
bed lifter	not primarily medical
beds—lounge (power or manual)	a comfort or convenience item
beds—oscillating	inappropriate for home use
Bell & Howell Language Master	educational, rather than medical, equipment

Medical Equipment Not Covered (*cont'd*)

ITEM	REASON DENIED
Bidet Toilet Seat	hygienic, rather than medical, equipment
Blood Glucose Analyzer— reflectance colorimeter	inappropriate for home use
Braille teaching texts	educational, rather than medical, equipment
Burke Bed Elevator	a convenience item
Burke Electric Portable Commode Erector	a convenience item
Burke Toilet Seat Erector	a convenience item
carafes	a convenience item
catheters	not reusable
Cheney Safety Bath Lift	a convenience item
circulator	inappropriate for home use
Communic-Aid	a convenience item
Cos-Medic Automasseur	a comfort item
dehumidifiers	not medical; environmental control equipment
Den-Mat	payment limited to amount payable for an ordinary hospital bed mattress
Diapulse machine	inappropriate for home use
diathermy machines	inappropriate for home use
disposable sheets and bags	not reusable
Dual King Bed	a comfort or convenience item
Ease-O-Matic Bed Spring	a comfort or convenience item
Eaton-E-Z Bath	a comfort or convenience item
elastic stockings	not reusable
Electra-Rest Bed	a comfort or convenience item
electric air cleaners	not medical; environmental control equipment
electrostatic machines	not medical; environmental control equipment

ITEM	REASON DENIED
elevators	a convenience item
emesis basins	a convenience item
esophageal dilator	physician's instrument
exercise equipment`	not primarily medical in nature
Exercycle	not primarily medical in nature
face masks (surgical)	not reusable
Gatchboard	not primarily medical
grab bars	not primarily medical
Hand-D-Jet	primarily used to soothe and comfort, rather than for therapeutic pusposes
heating and cooling plants	not medical; environmental control equipment
Honeywell Air Purifier	not medical; environmental control equipment
humidifiers	not medical; environmental control equipment
Hydrocollator Heating Unit	serves no clearly identifiable medical purpose
Hydrocollator Steam Packs	payment limited to amount payable for ordinary heating pad
Hydro-Jet Whirlpool Bath	primarily to soothe and comfort, rather than for therapeutic purposes
incontinence pads	not reusable
irrigating kit	not reusable
ITI Mechanical percussor	not generally recommended for use in treatment of patients in Medicare age group

Medical Equipment Not Covered (*cont'd*)

ITEM	REASON DENIED
Jacuzzi portable whirlpool	primarily used to soothe and comfort, rather than for therapeutic purposes
Jobst Stockings and Support Hose	not reusable
lambswool pads	not reusable
Lattoflex Spring-Base	a comfort or convenience item
LC-3 Oxygen System	not appropriate for home use
Lib-O-Cycle	not primarily medical in nature
Lymphedema Pumps (segmental therapy type)	inappropriate for home use
Magic-Dailey Bedpan	payment limited to amount payable for ordinary bedpan
massage devices	comfort and convenience items
Medcolator	inappropriate for home use
Medco-Minalator	inappropriate for home use
Medco-Therm Muscle Stimulator	inappropriate for home use
Micronaire Environmental Control	not medical equipment; environmental control equipment
Mobile Monomatic Sanitation System	inappropriate for home use
Moore Wheel	a convenience item
Muscle Stimulator Burdick MS-300	inappropriate for home use
Myoflex Muscle Stimulator	no demonstrable therapeutic effect
Niagara Massage pillow	a comfort or convenience item
Niagara Thermo-Cyclopad	not generally accepted as therapeutically effective
Nolan bath chair	a comfort or convenience item

ITEM	REASON DENIED
Oakes Controller Unit	self-help, institutional type equipment
oscillating beds	inappropriate for home use
overbed tables	a convenience item
paraffin bath units (portable)	not essential to paraffin heat therapy
paraffin bath units (standard)	inappropriate for home use
parallel bars	primarily for institutional use
percussors	not generally recommended for use in treatment of patients in Medicare age group
portable room heaters	not medical; environmental control equipment
Pressure Gradient Fabric Supports	not reusable
pressure leotards	not reusable
pulse tachometer	not reasonable or necessary
raised toilet seats	a convenience item
safety grab bars	a convenience item
sauna baths	not medical in nature
spare deionization supply tanks	a convenience or precautionary item
spare tanks of oxygen	a convenience or precautionary item
spectrowave machine	inappropriate for home use
speech teaching	educational, rather than medical, equipment
Stairglide	a convenience item
stairway elevators	a convenience item
standing table	a convenience item
Superpulse machine	inappropriate for home use
Surgi-bed	inappropriate for home use

Medical Equipment Not Covered (*cont'd*)

ITEM	REASON DENIED
surgical leggings	not reusable
telephone arms	a convenience item
therapeutic fomentation device	payment limited to amount payable for an ordinary heating pad
Translit chair	institutional equipment
treadmill exerciser	not primarily medical in nature
tub chairs	a comfort or convenience item

LIMITATIONS

Even the durable medical equipment that is covered is often subject to ifs, buts and maybes. Roll-about chairs, for instance, are defined in detail to ensure that coverage does not apply to an office, desk or secretarial chair. This is done by going so far as to specify: "Coverage is limited to those roll-about chairs having casters of at least 5 inches in diameter and specifically designed to meet the needs of the ill." Mattresses are covered "only where hospital bed is medically necessary. (Separate charge for replacement mattress should not be allowed where hospital bed with mattress is rented.)"

Hospital beds themselves are carefully spelled out. They are covered if a patient is bed-confined (by Medicare's definition) and has a condition necessitating positioning the body in a way that would not be feasible in any ordinary bed. Even electric controls are covered under certain specified conditions, but the variable-height feature, found in beds in hospitals for the convenience of nurses and others working with in-bed patients, is considered without medical relevance and is dismissed as a convenience feature. Since convenience items are not covered, a bed with these adjustments would be subject to a reduction in coverage for those features. Even this is not simple, however, since a bed with these features *will* be covered if no other type of bed is available in the locality.

What denial of coverage of many of these items points up most clearly is the sharp line drawn between necessary medical and custodial or extended care. Many of these items would make it possible for an elderly person to stay at home, rather than requiring care in a nursing home. Since home health care is far less costly to everyone concerned, including the federal government, it would seem sensible to encourage the use of any equipment that furthered that end. Unfortunately that is not the guiding philosophy behind Medicare, and people are forced into institutions for want of a little common sense in writing the law.

Among the many ways of cutting health-care costs, that of keeping people at home as long as possible is recognized as one of the best. We are far behind other industrial nations in implementing laws in this area. Even Denmark—not nearly so rich a country as the United States—goes to considerable lengths to keep its elderly independent as long as possible. If an elderly Dane cannot manage in his or her home because of being confined to a wheelchair that cannot be maneuvered over doorsills, and that prevents the patient from reaching the sink or stove to prepare food, the government will, at its own expense, remodel the apartment—removing sills, lowering sink, stove and counters, and making other changes that adapt the apartment to the capabilities of a person in a wheelchair. Medicare has a long way to go before it even begins to approach the health care to which citizens of all other industrialized nations are automatically entitled.

15

Why You Should Get
a Second Opinion on Surgery

IS YOUR OPERATION REALLY NECESSARY?

It may come as a surprise to you that that may be a matter of opinion. As a noted cardiologist once told me, "Medicine is an art, not a science." Two equally good doctors may hold opposing views on the necessity for surgery or other forms of treatment. Also some doctors may be much more conservative than others. For instance, it has recently been found in studies of women who have undergone surgery for breast cancer that the results are equally good with far less radical surgery. More and more surgeons are tending toward removing less and less in the case of breast cancer. Some surgeons, in fact, are now considering whether removal of just the cancerous tissue, without disturbing the rest of the breast, might not be sufficient. Yet even today, not all surgeons accept this evidence. In this respect, British doctors have been far ahead of American medicine, since this is much closer to the British approach to this disease.

With so much uncertainty within the profession, it is no wonder if the average person is confused about making a decision regarding a suggested operation. If professionals do not agree, or if professionals are sometimes not trust-worthy, how is the prospective patient to make up his or her mind?

THE FACTS ABOUT UNNECESSARY SURGERY

Today most of us are somewhat sophisticated in our ap-proach to medical care; we have often been told by the medical profession itself that medicine is an art, not a sci-ence. So we have finally come to realize that doctors, like other human beings, are subject to errors in diagnosis, and we have learned that there can be an honest difference of opinion even among leading specialists.

What we find difficult to accept is the dismaying fact that doctors, like garage mechanics, plumbers and other people, come in all shapes, sizes and degrees of honesty. Not many of the less-than-scrupulous medicine men are as brazen or as obvious as the surgeon who sat at his desk across from the patient who had just arrived for a consul-tation and, without an examination of either the patient, the X rays, or the patient's records, pronounced his opinion that the patient was in urgent need of an appendectomy. Most of us would immediately be alerted by such unpro-fessional conduct, but there are many more subtle dishon-esties that we are not able to recognize. We must turn for help to the profession itself, to police the dishonest as well as to confirm the diagnosis of the honest and conscientious.

If you are of the old school, you may be shocked at the idea that a surgeon would operate for other than medical reasons. Unfortunately, it is now a matter of record that millions of unnecessary operations are performed each year.

A congressional subcommittee led by former Represent-ative John E. Moss, Democrat of California, found in an intensive investigation into surgery performed in 1974 that

2.4 million unnecessary operations had been performed in that year alone. And that, as a result of these operations, 11,900 patients died. In addition, the operations cost the patients 4 billion dollars. In a recent update the government estimated that about one third of all operations performed in any given year are unnecessary and should not have been done.

In 1978, the Subcommittee on Oversight and Investigations of the Committee on Interstate and Foreign Commerce of the House of Representatives issued a report, *Surgical Performance, Necessity and Quality.* The report stated: "Unnecessary surgery remains a major national problem which requires urgent and accelerated attention. . . ."

WHAT IS BEHIND UNNECESSARY SURGERY?

In an article in a January 1981 issue, the *New York Times* characterized unnecessary surgery as "frivolous surgery." But it is necessary to examine the motives behind this kind of surgery to see how frivolous it truly is. There are a number of reasons for deliberately performing frivolous surgery.

The Profit Motive

The most common reason for unnecessary surgery is the high profit that can be realized from it. The whole medical profession may benefit from the profits of unnecessary surgery: the surgeon through his fee, the hospital through utilization of its services, the anesthetist through his fee, the laboratory through preoperative testing, the pharmaceutical companies through use of their products, the medical supply houses through increased sales of expensive equipment, perhaps even the family doctor if he gets a "kickback."

The Utilization Motive

Whenever services are examined today, one of the criteria as to whether or not they are needed is utilization: how much these services are being used. For a hospital, for example, a simple test of utilization is what percentage of its beds are being filled. If a hospital routinely has a high percentage of unused beds, that hospital may be declared redundant and denied outside funding. Committees called Utilization Review Committees have been set up to determine when hospitals, nursing homes and similar facilities are being underutilized. The idea is to prevent hospitals being built where and when they are not needed and to encourage better and more efficient use of existing facilities; the aim is to keep down or reduce health-care costs.

Doctors, also, are looked at in terms of utilization, and an effort is constantly being made to determine whether we have a shortage or a glut of doctors. Recently it was determined that our medical schools were turning out far too many surgeons and New York State, for one, put its medical schools on notice that more general-practice physicians and fewer surgeons were to be produced. The present tendency toward specialization among medical-school students is directly related to the fact that specialists have higher incomes than general practitioners.

Unnecessary operations make it appear that there is a need for more surgeons (more operations—more surgeons), as well as making work for all of them. The surgeon glut would be even more obvious if only necessary operations were performed.

The Need-to-Practice Motive

Surgery, like any other skill, requires a certain amount of practice. In medical school, practice is first acquired by performing autopsies. There is a limit, however, to the surgical skills that can be acquired on a corpse. Open-heart surgery, for example, is a team skill that can be acquired only by working on a living person with an experienced team. The importance of practice is so great that candidates for open-heart or bypass surgery are advised by the Inter-Society Commission for Heart Disease Resources to choose only a hospital that performs an average of at least four such operations a week. This recommendation is due in part to the fact that this type of surgery, more than most others, requires a team effort. Any team needs to work together as often as possible if it is to do its best. A surgical team that routinely performs a minimum of four open-heart operations a week soon begins to work as one entity, and in case of an emergency, each member of the team knows exactly what part his skills play and how to mesh with teammates. The Society feels also that it is not enough that a team may have performed a number of such operations in previous years; it stresses the importance of continually exercising those skills in order to maintain them. Just as even a well-developed muscle atrophies if it is not used, surgical team skills lose their fine edge if they are not called on regularly.

Not all operations are as demanding as open-heart surgery, but all require a certain amount of practice, both to develop skills and to maintain them. With the surgeon glut, a physician may find himself performing comparatively few operations of certain types over a period of time. Because of this, young surgeons may be overzealous in deciding on the necessity for an operation for which they need a bit more practice, and older surgeons may feel they are not getting enough practice to keep their hand in. In a way this is perhaps less reprehensible than the profit motive but it is just as unfortunate for the patient who is subjected to an unnecessary procedure.

HOW THE SECOND-OPINION CONCEPT CAME ABOUT

Just as much unnecessary surgery is done to create greater costs (and therefore greater profits), the Department of Health and Human Services seeks to cut down on surgery in order to reduce health-care costs. The problem of how to cut down on unnecessary operations was a sticky one until the government came up with a simple solution: let the doctors check on one another.

Medicare did this by informing people that it would pay for a second opinion whenever a beneficiary was told an operation was needed. A second opinion is also covered and encouraged by Medicare for major nonsurgical therapeutic or diagnostic procedures. This includes such procedures as cardiac catherization and gastroscopy.

THE THIRD OPINION

In the event that the second opinion is different from the first, Medicare will cover a third opinion to resolve the situation. This is very helpful to a patient who finds him- or herself in a dilemma because two highly respected surgeons disagree as to the need for a procedure.

HOW TO FIND A DOCTOR FOR A SECOND OR THIRD OPINION

If getting a second opinion is suggested by your family doctor, he will probably be able to suggest someone else for you to talk to. If, however, you have initiated the idea of a second opinion, you may prefer to talk to a physician in another area or even someone who you know is probably not acquainted with the surgeons in your area. Since the surgeon giving the second opinion will not be the one performing the operation, you can assume that you will get disinterested advice. In any case, you will be going for a second opinion because surgery has already been recommended.

In the event that you want to talk to someone other than the doctor suggested by your doctor, you can obtain names from county medical societies or get a list of referral doctors from your local social security or Medicaid office. You may also get a name by dialing 1–800–638–6833, which is the free national Medicare number. If you live in Maryland (where the office is located), the toll-free number is 1–800–492–6603.

HOW GETTING THE SECOND OPINION WORKS

It is very simple. If you are told that surgery or a major nonsurgical procedure is needed, say you would like to have a second opinion. It is now such a common and accepted request that no doctor should be surprised or offended by it. If he or she is, you are better off with another doctor.

If the two opinions differ, ask for a third.

Submit all such bills to Medicare, explaining what they are for.

HAS THE SECOND-OPINION PROGRAM CUT DOWN ON THE NUMBER OF OPERATIONS?

In New York City the Storeworkers Security Plan, which covers about 12,000 union workers in such stores as Bloomingdale's and Gimbel's, has made second opinions for surgery mandatory for its membership for the past eight years. Eleanor Tilson, vice-president and administrator of the plan, reports:

Since 1972, 2,300 members and dependents have gone for the required second-opinion consultation. Twenty-two percent, or

506 persons, were informed by a board-certified specialist that surgery was unnecessary. A follow-up study, done more than a year later, showed that 18% still had not undergone surgery, and their problems were under medical control.

The arithmetic of cost savings is indisputable. Hospital and surgical bills for 400 men, women and children were eliminated. So were disability payments to members. What cannot be estimated in dollars and cents is the savings in anguish and trauma to the 400 who avoided unnecessary, and potentially life-threatening, surgery.

Employers, union trustees and members all recognize that the mandatory requirement is an important element in the success of the program. The patients are relieved of the need to suggest to the doctor of record that they would like to get a second opinion. They state, without fear, reluctance or embarrassment, that their medical coverage requires a pre-surgical consultation.

It should also be noted that recommendations for elective surgery dropped considerably once the program was introduced.... District Council 37 [another union], covering some 100,000 municipal workers and their families and the Building Service Employees Union, with some 60,000 members, also report that they have found their programs to be cost effective.

In another example, the Massachusetts Medicaid program, which requires second opinions for specified surgical proceedings, has found that it has reduced the number of operations by 20% over previous years.

New York Blue Cross and Blue Shield, in an effort to encourage its members to get second opinions, offered a policy with 100% coverage of the cost of the second opinion. It subsequently did an inconclusive study to determine whether this policy had cut down on the number of operations and, for some reason, decided it did not. Eleanor Tilson of the Storeworkers Security Plan says of this conclusion, "The validity of the study done by Blue Cross must be seriously questioned. In a four-year period, only 1,700, of the hundreds of thousands of their New York subscribers, took advantage of the second-opinion option."

In interpreting statistics concerning the reduction in the number of operations due to the second-opinion option, you must also take into account the fact that many surgeons are more reluctant to propose surgery when they know that the patient will be getting another opinion. Dr. Eugene McCarty of Cornell Medical School found that not only did surgery decrease but the operations that were performed were done so less expensively.

HOW TO MAKE THE MOST OF A SECOND OPINION

Most doctors are not very good about explaining medical procedures to patients, so it is up to the patient to ask the right questions. If you get a second opinion, you have at least two chances to find out as much as possible about the surgeons' thinking. It is important for you to understand the situation as well as possible because you should be the one making the decision about your body and what is done to it, and to do so intelligently, you need as much information as possible.

Be sure to ask at least the following questions of each doctor:

1. Exactly what is my condition?
2. What do you think is the best way to treat it?
3. Even if you think that is the best treatment, are there any other possible treatments?
4. Is the treatment you are recommending in any way experimental? (Medicare may not cover it.)
5. What benefits can I hope to realize from this treatment?
6. What possible side effects might I have from this treatment?
7. What are the risks associated with this treatment?

8. What percentage of success has usually occurred with this treatment?
9. What might be the result of my failing to go through with this treatment?

Do not hesitate to probe further if you do not feel any of the answers are detailed enough. Do not settle for medical language and terms that you as a layman cannot understand. English-speaking doctors are capable of explaining any medical condition, prognosis or treatment in English anyone can understand. Sometimes they use obscure medical terms as an ego-trip; sometimes they honestly forget that you haven't been through medical school. Do not hesitate to ask; even the greatest surgeon calls the plumber or the auto mechanic or the roofer when he has a problem in their area. You are going to a surgeon because he is an expert, not because he is an exalted being, and you have a right to know exactly what you are getting yourself into. Just as you shouldn't let an auto mechanic do anything he pleases to your car, you shouldn't let a doctor do anything he pleases to your body. If you require clear and detailed explanations every step of the way, you protect yourself to some extent. An informed patient is always more difficult to mistreat.

THE BOTTOM LINE

There are many benefits to be derived from a second opinion, but by far the greatest is the fact that it may result in your not having to have an operation after all.

IV
MEDICARE
CLAIMS EXPLAINED

16

How to File
· a Medicare Claim

One of the things Medicare beneficiaries dread most is filling out the claim forms. Actually, the forms are a lot easier to decipher than the instructions for knitting a scarf or putting together a bicycle or a chain saw. In fact, you will find they are really almost as simple as putting down your name, address and Medicare number. In this chapter you will learn exactly how to fill out all the forms you will encounter.

HOW TO FILE CLAIMS FOR MEDICARE PART A (HI)

Part A claims are filed by the provider of the services: the hospital, the SNF or the home health-care agency. Medicare pays the institution or agency directly, so you are not involved at all in the procedure. Because of this system, it is not necessary for you to ask providers that are covered by Part A to accept the assignment; that is all taken care of under a contract between the provider and Medicare.

All you have to do to file a Part A claim is to sign the claim form the supplier provides as proof that those services were rendered to you. If you are receiving the services over an extended period of time, you need sign only once and the provider will use that as a blanket signature.

If you are unable to sign the forms, you may authorize someone to sign for you. The person should sign his or her name, instead of yours, and explain why you are unable to sign.

There is, however, one circumstance in which you may become involved: in the event of denial of payment. If payment is denied, you may not understand why or may disagree with the denial. If so, you have a right to question the decision. The procedure to follow if you do not agree with the denial is described in Chapter 18.

HOW TO FILE CLAIMS FOR MEDICARE PART B (SMI)

If the Doctor or Other Provider Accepts the Assignment

Among the advantages of having the provider accept the assignment is the fact that, in that case, the provider files the claim forms for you. All you have to do is sign them. Payment is then made directly to the provider and you receive an Explanation of Medicare Benefits form (see illustration, page 172), which tells you the reasonable or allowable charge, how much Medicare has paid, and how much of your deductible you have met. *This is not a bill;* the doctor or other provider will send you a bill. See Chapter 17 for more details.

You do not need to know which form the provider should fill out; each provider will have a supply of the correct forms on hand and will take the responsibility for correctly submitting the claims (although, as we will see, your help is sometimes useful after the claim has been processed.)

If the Doctor or Other Provider Does Not Accept the Assignment

In this case, you will have to file a claim in order to get Medicare's payment for its part of the bills. A new easy-to-follow form (HCFA-1490S) has been designed by the Health Care Financing Administration and is the one you will probably be given. If you have filed claims in previous years, you may have used an old form. Do not think you have the wrong form because it is not the one you are used to. As long as it has the number HCFA-1490S at the top or bottom, it is correct. If you have a supply of the old forms in your Medicare file, discard them as soon as you get the new forms.

HCFA-1490S—PATIENT'S REQUEST FOR MEDICARE PAYMENT

This is the only form you will ever be responsible for filling out. If the doctor or other provider accepts the assignment, he or she will send in a different form (HCFA-1500) and you will be asked to sign it before you leave the office. Very occasionally, the provider will not accept the assignment but will fill out HCFA-1500 and give it to you to sign and mail. If this is done, be sure you ask the doctor's secretary exactly what you should do and where you should send the form. This is not a problem with HCFA-1490S because the address where you should send the form is printed right on the form.

HCFA-1490S is very easy to understand. Here are line-by-line instructions for filling it out.

LINE 1:   Put down your name exactly as it is shown on your red, white and blue Medicare Card (Health Insurance Card).

LINE 2:   Copy off your claim number. Look at the card to make sure you are putting down the correct number and be sure to

Form Approved
OMB No. 0938-0008

PATIENT'S REQUEST FOR MEDICARE PAYMENT

IMPORTANT— SEE OTHER SIDE FOR INSTRUCTIONS

PLEASE TYPE OR PRINT INFORMATION   MEDICAL INSURANCE BENEFITS SOCIAL SECURITY ACT

NOTICE: Anyone who misrepresents or falsifies essential information requested by this form may upon conviction be subject to fine and imprisonment under Federal Law. No Part B Medicare benefits may be paid unless this form is received as required by existing law and regulations (20 CFR 422.510).

1   Name of Beneficiary From Health Insurance Card

(First)   (Middle)   (Last)

SEND COMPLETED FORM TO:

When completed, send this form to:
Connecticut General Life Insurance Company
Medicare Claim Office
100 Barnes Road
Wallingford, Connecticut 06492

2   Claim Number From Health Insurance Card

☐ Male
☐ Female

3   Patient's Mailing Address (City, State, Zip Code)
Check here if this is a new address ⟶ ☐

(Street or P.O. Box—Include Apartment number)

(City)   (State)   (Zip)

3b   Telephone Number
(Include Area Code)

4   Describe The Illness or Injury for Which Patient Received Treatment

4b   Was illness or injury connected with employment?

☐ Yes
☐ No

If any medical expenses will be or could be paid by your private insurance organization, State Agency, (Medicaid), or the VA complete block 5 below.

5   Name and Address of other insurance, State Agency (Medicaid), or VA office

Policy or Medical
Assistance Number

NOTE: If you DO NOT want payment information on this claim released put an (x) here ⟶ ☐

I authorize Any Holder of Medical or Other Information About Me to Release to the Social Security Administration and Health Care Financing Administration or Its Intermediaries or Carriers any Information Needed for This or a Related Medicare Claim. I Permit a copy of this Authorization to be Used in Place of the Original, and Request Payment of Medical Insurance Benefits to Me.

6   Signature of Patient (If patient is unable to sign, see Block 6 on other side.)

6b   Date Signed

IMPORTANT!

ATTACH ITEMIZED BILLS FROM YOUR DOCTOR(S)
OR SUPPLIER(S) TO THE BACK OF THIS FORM.

HCFA-1490S (6-80)   Department of Health and Human Services—Health Care Financing Administration

Form 1490S is the only claim form you will ever need to fill out. If the provider accepts the assignment, you will not need to do even this form.

HOW TO FILL OUT THIS MEDICARE FORM

Medicare will pay you directly when you complete this form and attach an itemized bill from your doctor or supplier. Your bill does not have to be paid before you submit this claim for payment, but you MUST attach an itemized bill in order for Medicare to process this claim.

FOLLOW THESE INSTRUCTIONS CAREFULLY:

A. Completion of this form.

Block 1. Print your name **exactly** as it is shown on your Medicare Card.

Block 2. Print your Health Insurance Claim Number including the letter at the end **exactly** as it is shown on your Medicare card.

Blocks 3 through 5. Complete the information in these Blocks as Requested.

Block 6. Be sure to sign your name. If you cannot write your name, make an (X) mark. Then have a witness sign his or her name and address in Block 6 too.

If you are completing this form for another Medicare patient you should write (By) and sign your name and address in Block 6.   You also should show your relationship to the patient and briefly explain why the patient cannot sign.

Block 6b. Print the date you completed this form.

B. Each itemized bill MUST show all of the following information:

- Date of each service.

- Place of each service   —Doctor's Office   —Independent Laboratory
                         —Outpatient Hospital   —Nursing Home
                         —Patient's Home   —Inpatient Hospital

- Description of each surgical or medical service or supply furnished.

- Charge for EACH service.

- Doctor's or supplier's name and address. Many times a bill will show the name of Several doctors or suppliers. IT IS VERY IMPORTANT THE ONE WHO TREATED YOU BE IDENTIFIED. Simply circle his/her name on the bill.

- It is helpful if the diagnosis is also shown. If not, be sure you have completed block 4 of this form.

- Mark out any services for which you have already filed a Medicare claim.

- If the patient is deceased please contact your Social Security office for instructions on how to file a claim.

COLLECTION AND USE OF MEDICARE INFORMATION

We are authorized by the Health Care Financing Administration to ask you for information needed in the administration of the Medicare program. Authority to collect information is in section 205(a), 1872 and 1875 of the Social Security Act, as amended

The information we obtain to complete your Medicare claim is used to identify you and to determine your eligibility. It is also used to decide if the services and supplies you received are covered by Medicare and to insure that proper payment is made.

The information may also be given to other providers of services, carriers, intermediaries, medical review boards, and other organizations as necessary to administer the Medicare program. For example, it may be necessary to disclose information about the Medicare benefits you have used to a hospital or doctor.

With one exception, which is discussed below, there are no penalties under social security law for refusing to supply information. However, failure to furnish information regarding the medical services rendered or the amount charged would prevent payment of the claim. Failure to furnish any other information, such as name or claim number, would delay payment of the claim.

It is mandatory that you tell us if you are being treated for a work related injury so we can determine whether worker's compensation will pay for the treatment. Section 1877 (a) (3) of the Social Security Act provides Criminal penalties for withholding this information.   ☆ U.S. G.P.O. 1981-724-226

The back of Form 1490S contains useful information you should read to familiarize yourself with the kind of information needed.

include the letter at the end of the number.

Many people put the wrong number in this space. In fact, at one time Medicare gave a sample number in an instruction booklet to show how to fill out the form. So many people used the number given in the sample form that it took months to straighten out the claims.

LINE 3:   Put down your address. The box the arrow points to is to be used only if your address has changed since the last time you filed a claim.

LINE 3b: Be sure to include the area code when putting down your phone number.

LINE 4:   Do not be intimidated by this line. Not only doesn't Medicare expect you to describe your illness in medical language, they would really prefer you didn't. Just write down the sort of thing you would tell the doctor. For example, you can write, "I had pains in my chest," or "I felt very dizzy the day before." If you have a chronic condition you know about and it is the reason you incurred the medical bills, it's all right to put down "arthritis" or "diabetes," or some other simple description. But do not attempt to give the diagnosis; it's much better to put down the symptoms.

Aside from anything else, you may get better coverage by leaving this to your doctor. His description of why you went to him may be phrased in such a way that he knows Medicare will approve the benefits; whereas if you try to be too explicit you may talk yourself out of benefits and have to pay the whole bill yourself.

This is especially obvious when it comes to describing why you went to an ophthalmologist, for instance. Do not ever put down, "I needed new glasses." Unless you rae a qualified ophthalmologist and have examined yourself, you cannot possibly know that. Put down the symptoms that made you think so, such as "My eyes were blurring," "I had a problem with my eyes watering all the time," "I kept getting headaches." That way you will have to pay only for the doctor's writing the prescription, not for the time he spent diagnosing your problem (always providing, of course, that he fills out his bill correctly).

An example of how easily you may make a mistake by trying to sound "professional" is the occasion when you might put down "myopia" or some such medical term. Medicare would have no choice but to disallow the bill since that is not a covered item. If the doctor's bill gives the necessary information, it's perfectly all right for you to leave this section blank. As a general rule, I would suggested you do that unless the doctor's bill is very vague or unless you think putting down a symptom will help you get better coverage.

LINE 4b: The purpose of this question is to deter-
                  mine whether your claim should be paid
                  by some agency other than Medicare. If,
                  for instance, your illness is covered by
                  workmen's compensation, your claim
                  should be paid by them rather than by
                  Medicare.

LINE 5:   This is fairly clear and spells out what is
                  wanted. Take the information off your
                  insurance policy or identification card.
                  It should be filled out only if you live in
                  a state, such as Connecticut, where
                  there is a "piggyback" insurance ar-
                  rangement between Medicare and some
                  Medigap insurance company. (In Con-
                  necticut it is Blue Cross.) In this case,
                  you will save yourself the trouble of hav-
                  ing to file the claim with the Medigap
                  company. As soon as Medicare has pro-
                  cessed your claim, it will send a copy of
                  its Explanation of Benefits form to the
                  insurance company for you. Not only
                  does this speed up payment of the claim,
                  it also saves you paperwork. Doctors
                  who accept the assignment like this ar-
                  rangement because they get the 20% co-
                  insurance directly from the insurance
                  company—often much faster than they
                  may get it from the patient—and the
                  whole payment process is made much
                  less painful. Do not, however, choose
                  your Medigap policy solely because of a
                  piggyback clause; compare all the other
                  benefits and make sure you are getting

the best deal all around. Saving you time and bother may not be worth poorer Medigap coverage, if that should prove to be the case.

LINE 5, "Note": If you check the box with the arrow, saying you do not want payment information on this claim released, no one will be able to find out what Medicare is paying you. If you check this box, Medicare cannot release information to an insurance company and will not be able to piggyback your claim. Do not check the box unless you have some special reason.

LINE 6: Sign your name and put in the date on which you filled out the form. If you cannot sign your name, it is acceptable to put a sign (usually an "X") in front of the signature of someone who acts as a witness that you made the mark. The witness should then sign and print his or her name and address.

If you are too ill to fill out the form, someone else can do it for you. In that case, that person would be the one to fill out the form. In addition, the person filling out the form for you should write "By" followed by their signature and address, and a note as to their relationship to you and why you cannot sign it yourself.

Putting in the date isn't much help if you then put the form aside and forget to mail it for a week or so. Always try to fill out and mail claim forms promptly;

the date is an important reference in case of a question or appeal, and you make it meaningless if you do not mail the claim soon after you have filled it out.

The authorization in line 6 is not optional. The minute you sign the claim form you give Medicare access to your private medical records. I don't see how this can be avoided, however, since Medicare needs to see these records in order to "develop a claim," as they call the process of getting more information to determine whether or not to cover an item. Hospital records are often examined by Medicare in developing claims and it would probably be impractical for them to have to obtain your permission each time this was necessary. You can only hope that security is good and that signing this blanket release does not make your personal health records too easily accessible to private parties.

If you or someone acting on your behalf does not sign the claim form, it cannot be processed.

HOW DO YOU FILE A CLAIM IF YOU DON'T KNOW WHICH SERVICES ARE COVERED?

If you're not sure what is covered, file *all* your health-care bills as claims, no matter what they are. The Medicare people will sort them out and pay what they think you are entitled to. They may miss some items or misinterpret a bill, but you will still be better off than if you hadn't sent in the claim at all. If it is something like a bill for drugs or medicines (not covered), the worst that will happen is that they won't pay anything, but it is still best to send in any bills you are not sure of; maybe they will turn out to be covered.

WHEN TO FILE A CLAIM

The best time to file a claim is as soon as possible. Do not let claims accumulate and, especially, try not to send in a bunch of claims at the end of the year. Many people collect bills all year and then get nervous as the year is coming to an end and send them all in in December.

SUPPOSE YOU HAVE MORE THAN ONE BILL?

Theoretically you can attach all your bills to one claim form. In practice, this might be difficult unless your bills are all in connection with the same illness. If you attach an opthalmologist's bill for blurred vision together with a bill from the doctor who set your broken wrist, you will have trouble filling out line 4 (and possibly 4b and 5 also) so that it is clear.

If your bills are detailed and clearly describe the condition for which they were incurred, you could just leave this part of the questionnaire blank and let Medicare get what it needs from the bills themselves.

CLARIFYING THE DOCTOR'S BILL

If you go to a doctor who belongs to a group, his name will be listed along with all the others in the group at the top of the bill. To save Medicare time, circle the name of the doctor who took care of you.

WHEN NOT TO SEND YOUR CLAIMS TO YOUR MEDICARE OFFICE

If you are traveling and incur out-of-state charges or if your doctor sends you to a lab in a nearby state, you should not submit claims for payment of these bills to your state's Medicare office. Each state office processes only bills incurred within the state, so you should send the claim to the Medicare office in the state in which it was incurred. See Appendix A for a list of Medicare offices in each state.

TWO REASONS CLAIMS MAY BE DENIED

There are many reasons why claims are denied, but there are two common areas in particular that sometimes cause confusion.

Preventive Medicine Not Covered

Keep in mind that Medicare does not pay for preventive medicine, and avoid any description of a treatment that could be interpreted this way. A doctor's office visit that was solely for the purpose of getting a flu shot (not covered) would not be covered at all. You would be wise to set up the visit for something that is bothering you and get the flu shot at that time; in this way, the visit will be covered and the only item denied will be the charge for the shot. Many doctors have their nurses perform routine services, such as shots, on specified days at specified times; the charge is minimal. If the shot is all you need, take advantage of this arrangement and keep down your out-of-pocket costs.

Incidentally, if you go for shots frequently, it will do no good to have a cooperative doctor who tries to combine shots with a covered diagnosis; Medicare checks too-frequent visits to determine whether they are medically necessary and might easily deny coverage if they determine that such frequent doctor visits are medically unnecessary. With medically necessary shots that could not be self-administered, you will not have a problem, but Medicare does not make allowances for personal squeamishness—insulin shots are considered able to be self-administered, for example.

An exception is made for pneumoccocal vaccine, which has recently been added to covered services.

Appropriate Treatment

Another area that is confusing to the beneficiary is the denial of a claim because Medicare decides it is not for appropriate treatment. In a recent newsletter, Medicare SMI gives an example: "If a claim is received for an office visit, a chest x-ray and an electrocardiogram, and the claim shows the diagnosis of arthritis, the chest x-ray and the electrocardiogram charges would be denied. A diagnosis of arthritis *only* does not necessarily substantiate those services, and they would therefore be considered noncovered services. However, if our office receives an identical claim to the above, except that the diagnosis or complaint is shown as angina or hypertension, etc. . . . then the chest x-ray and electrocardiogram charges would be supported." Doctors who are familiar with Medicare rulings and have a number of patients who are Medicare beneficiaries usually know how to cope with this.

Sometimes the beneficiary is stuck in the middle between Medicare and the provider. For example, some hospitals routinely require preadmission X rays, electrocardiograms and certain tests. These are not required because they are necessary for the illness for which the patient is being admitted; rather they are routine and are for the protection of the hospital against a liability suit and to ascertain that the patient will be able to undergo surgery or whatever else may take place in the hospital. If you are going into the hospital for cataract surgery and the hospital requires a chest X ray and an electrocardiogram, Medicare will deny the claim and you will have to pay for those yourself. Ironically, because of the more lenient restrictions on hospitals, these charges would be covered if they are incurred *after* admission but if the hospital requires them as a condition of admission, you will have no Medicare coverage for these costs.

YOUR OWN RECORDS

You should keep a record of all communications you have with Medicare or any other insurance agency or company. Send copies of bills to Medicare, rather than the actual bills. Keep copies of all the claim forms you submit. Have a folder in which you put all your Explanation of Benefits forms that you receive from Medicare (see page 344).

It's easy to have a copy made; your local library or Senior Center will probably be able to do it for you, and the cost is nominal.

Date everything: the forms and letters you send in, and the date you receive forms and letters from Medicare and your doctor, hospital, etc.

CHECK EVERYTHING

Never take it for granted that a bill or claim is correct; most of the time it will be, but not invariably. If you think a doctor's bill is incorrect or does not give a true picture, question it and ask if it could be more detailed or why it was done the way it was. In the case of "super bills" (see page 163), this is less of a problem.

THE CLAIM FORM AND YOUR DEDUCTIBLE

You don't have to worry about your deductible in connection with the claim form. All claims, no matter where you file them (and you may have filed in several different states), go to the central computer in Maryland. The computer automatically keeps track of how much of your deductible you have met and the Explanation of Medicare Benefits form tells you your current status. It's not a bad idea to also keep track yourself and make sure the computer is correct.

HOW THE DEDUCTIBLE AFFECTS PAYMENT OF YOUR CLAIM

1. *If you have not met any of your deductible and your doctor does not accept the assignment,* you must pay the deductible, the 20% coinsurance of the reasonable charge and the difference between the doctor's fee and the reasonable charge. For example:

    Your doctor's bill is $450. Medicare decides the reasonable charge is $350. Medicare deducts the $75 deductible from the $350. Medicare then pays 80% of $275 ($350 less $75) or $220. You must pay 20% of $275, or $55 (your coinsurance). In addition, you must pay the $75 deductible and the amount over the reasonable charge of $100 ($450 minus $350).

    Your share of the bill looks like this:

20% coinsurance:	$ 55
deductible:	75
amount over reasonable charge:	100
Total you pay:	$230

2. *If you have met all of your deductible and your doctor accepts the assignment,* you pay only the 20% coinsurance. In the above example that would be $55.

3. *If you have met all of your deductible but your doctor will not accept the assignment,* you would pay the 20% coinsurance plus the amount over the reasonable charge ($55 plus $100, or $155).

WHAT IF YOUR PART B BILLS FOR THE YEAR ARE LESS THAN THE DEDUCTIBLE?

If your Part B bills are less than deductible, you will not be reimbursed by Medicare for any part of your claims. Medicare does not begin to pay until you have paid out or met the amount of the deductible. A new deductible begins each January 1, so you will pay at least $75 a year of your covered bills even if all physicians and suppliers accept the assignment. In addition you will also, of course, have to pay 100% of items not covered by Medicare.

PAY PROVIDERS PROMPTLY

If the doctor accepts the assignment, Medicare will send their share of his bill directly to his or her office. If, however, the doctor does not accept the assignment, Medicare will send the payment to you. It is then up to you to pay the doctor. Be prompt in paying at least the amount Medicare has sent you. If you are very short of cash, there may be a temptation to use that money to pay for prescription drugs or some other expensive but uncovered item. Resist it if at all possible; it will only become more difficult to pay the doctor bill when the money is gone. Of course, don't hesitate to point out to the doctor, when you are asking him to accept the assignment, that he is sure to get his money if it comes direct from Medicare. You might mention, also, that assignment claims are processed faster than nonassignment claims, so he will not only get his money for sure, he will get it faster.

DO NOT HESITATE TO ASK QUESTIONS

Medicare personnel are very good about answering questions. If you do not understand something and there is no one else to ask, do not hesitate to call Medicare. There will be an 800 (free) phone number for the office in your state, so just call the 800 information operator and ask what it is. Keep it handy and use it when you have a question. (See Appendix B for toll-free Medicare numbers.)

Incidentally, do not think you are being brushed off because the person at the Medicare office asks you to call someone else. Medicare is very complicated and personnel often know about either Part A or Part B, but not both. In addition, there are some questions for which they will refer you to your local social security office. You will soon get to know the people in these three areas. If you have a question about a specific claim, you will usually be referred to one of the staff who works with the computer and who can quickly look up your case; have your claim form and Explanation of Benefits form handy so that you can give her the information she needs.

IS THERE A TIME LIMIT ON FILING CLAIMS?

It is always best to file claims as soon as possible; you will get paid that much sooner and you will be able to check the payment while the service is still fresh in your mind. It also helps ease the load on Medicare and makes it easier to check with the doctor or other provider if there is any question concerning the claim.

It is possible, in spite of the generous amount of time

Medicare allows in which to file claims, to file so late that the claims will be disallowed. Weltha Buxton, a volunteer Medicare assistance counselor in Clearwater, Florida, tells of her experience with Medicare beneficiaries: "They come to us and they will open a shoebox and say, 'Here are my claims,' and spread them all over the desk. Or they have a suitcase or a Publix's bag full of claims, and you have to go through all of those. Sometimes you throw out more than three-quarters because they are outdated. . . . I think there were over $600 in expired bills she could have been reimbursed for had she been better informed. . . . So many people don't know they can even file for Medicare."

Medicare recognizes that it is not always possible to file claims promptly and the law allows considerable leeway. It is possible, however, to wait so long to file your claim that it is disallowed on the grounds that it was filed too late.

In effect you are allowed one to two years, but in the language of Medicare a claim will not be honored later than "December of the calendar year following the year" in which the services were supplied. For example, if you incurred charges from January 1981 to September 1981, you would have until December 1982 to file for them.

There is an exception to this, similar to the old carry-over rule, that states that services you receive in the last three months of the year are considered as having been furnished in the following year. For example, charges incurred from October 1980 to December 1980 would not be outdated until December 1982—as if they had been incurred in 1981.

If you have a question about the time limit on a specific bill, check with your local social security office to make sure you do not wait too long to file your claim.

Sometimes a claim is filed late through no fault of yours but due to an error on the part of Medicare. If that happens, you will not be penalized and your claim will be processed for payment.

SUPER BILLS

In an effort to avoid the problem of slow claim processing due to incomplete information, some doctors are now using "super bills." These are printed forms that contain checklists of the services most commonly provided by the doctor. Each doctor or group of doctors prepares a form that fits their practice, so the forms are not standardized throughout the profession.

Upon completion of an office visit, for example, the doctor checks the boxes on the form that indicate what he has done—X rays, diagnosis—and writes opposite the box the charge for that service. These forms are then sent to Medicare for claim processing. You will be given a copy of the bill for that visit.

A well-designed super bill not only saves the doctor's time—there is much less to write up—but also improves communication between the doctor and Medicare, and facilitates processing of claims. Of course, mistakes and inadequate information can still creep in, but it's a step in the right direction. Not all doctors have these forms and you will probably not find them among surgeons.

HOW TO FILE A CLAIM IN CASE OF DEATH OF THE BENEFICIARY

The filing of Medicare claims for a beneficiary who has died used to be very difficult and unwieldy. For one thing, you could not file the claim unless you had already paid the bill. Since April 1981 the procedure has been simplified and you may file a claim for an unpaid bill.

If the physician or other provider agrees to accept the assignment (and you can ask even though the beneficiary has died), you do not have to do anything. The provider will file the claim as usual.

SCOTCH TAPE TO YOUR INSURANCE FORM ALONG THIS EDGE — NO STAPLES PLEASE

PHYSICIAN'S
STATEMENT FOR
INSURANCE FORMS

SEE REVERSE
SIDE FOR
INSTRUCTIONS

PLEASE COMPLETE   PATIENT DATA

MR. MS.
MRS. DR.
MISS

LAST   FIRST

BILL TO:

STREET

CITY   STATE   ZIP

☐ OFFICE VISIT	☐ CBC	☐ MONO TEST	☐ SCHOOL EXAMINATION
☐ OFFICE VISIT (EXTENDED)	☐ WBC	☐ THROAT CULTURE	☐ COLLEGE EXAMINATION
☐ OFFICE VISIT (BRIEF)	☐ DIFFERENTIAL SMEAR	☐ URINE CULTURE	☐ HOME VISIT
☐ CONSULTATION	☐ HGB/HCT/RBC	☐ HEMOCCULT	☐ NURSING HOME VISIT
☐ COMPREHENSIVE EXAMINATION	☐ SEDIMENTATION RATE	☐ GRAM STAIN	☐ NORWALK HOSPITAL EMERGENCY ROOM
☐ ELECTROCARDIOGRAM	☐ BLOOD PREPARATION	☐ MONILIA CULTURE	☐ NORWALK HOSPITAL AMBULATORY CARE
☐ ELECTROCARDIOGRAM RHYTHM STRIP	☐ URINE PREPARATION	☐ VAGINAL SMEAR	☐ SUTURE REMOVAL
☐ CHEST X-RAY (PA)	☐ MISCELLANEOUS PREPARATION	☐ LUMBAR PUNCTURE	☐ COLLAR / SPLINT / RIB BELT
☐ CHEST X-RAY PA - LATERAL	☐ PULMONARY FUNCTION TEST	☐ ARTHROCENTESIS	☐ AFTER HOURS
☐ SIGMOIDOSCOPY	☐ PPD	☐ CHEMOTHERAPY	☐
☐ SIGMOIDOSCOPY WITH BIOPSY	☐ INJECTION	☐	☐
☐ URINALYSIS	☐		

☐ IF CHECKED, GLASS COLUMBIA MED. LAB WILL RENDER SEPARATE STATEMENT

TOTAL FEE $

AMT. PAID $

DIAGNOSIS:

DATE

PHYSICIAN'S SIGNATURE

ACCEPT ASSIGNMENT ☐ YES ☐ NO   THIS IS YOUR ONLY COPY FOR INSURANCE AND INCOME TAX PURPOSES.

DATE	FAMILY MEMBER	DESCRIPTION	CHARGE	PAYMENT	ADJ. CREDITS	CURRENT BALANCE	PREVIOUS BALANCE		NAME

This is your RECEIPT for this amount
This is a STATEMENT of your account to date

ATTENDING PHYSICIANS STATEMENT
AMA CURRENT PROCEDURAL TERMINOLOGY

90020 Initial Comp. History And Physical Examination

90050 Limited Exam Evaluation or Treatment, Same or New Illness

90030 Injection ☐ I.M. ☐ Subcut ☐ I.V.

90000-90024 Office Visit-New Patient

90030-90090 Office Visit-Established Patient

90100-90170 Home Visits-New/Established Patient

90200-90285 Hospital Visits New/Established Patient

90400-90470 Custodial Care New/Established Patient

90500-90570 Emergency Room Service New/Established Patient

90600-90630 Consultations

PATIENT   ☐ MALE ☐ FEMALE

ADDRESS

CITY   STATE   ZIP

RELATIONSHIP   BIRTHDATE

SUBSCRIBER OR POLICY HOLDER

INSURANCE CARRIER   ☐ MEDICARE ☐ MEDICAID

NUMBER

HOSPITAL   ☐ IN PATIENT ☐ OUT PATIENT

Date Symptoms Appeared Or Accidents Occurred   Mo.   Day   Yr.

Disability ☐ Accident ☐ Pregnancy
Related To ☐ Industrial ☐ Other

DATES: From ____ To ____
OK to Return to Work ____

NEXT APPOINTMENT ____ AT ____ AM PM

SS 247-17-4771

RAYMOND J. JONES, M.D.
2800 FALLS AVENUE   PHONE: AD 3-3363
ANYTOWN, U.S.A.

03288

AUTHORIZATION TO RELEASE INFORMATION: I hereby authorize the undersigned Physician to release any information acquired in the course of my examination or treatment.
Signed (Patient, or Parent if Minor) ____ Date ____

Place of Service ☐ Office ☐ Hospital ☐ Emergency Room ☐ Other

Diagnosis or Symptoms ____

Other Service Rendered ____

Referring Physician ____ Date of Referral ____

Doctors Signature ____

Please keep this record to use for income tax purposes and for any benefits from your insurance carrier.

Litho in USA   FORM 25-MCO1   OFFICE SYSTEMS WATERLOO, IOWA   69-12-0505

Control-o-fax®

Two examples of Super Bills. These new kinds of bills take the place of itemized bills and are accepted by Medicare and most insurance companies.

If the physician or other provider refuses to accept the assignment, this is the procedure for you to follow:

1. Fill out claim form HCFA-1490S (see instructions) as usual and sign your name in the space provided for the beneficiary's name (line 6), explaining why you are signing instead of the beneficiary (death).
2. Get and attach a signed statement from the physician or other provider saying that they refuse to accept the assignment. (A signed 1500 form, checked "Non-assigned," will also suffice.)
3. Write up, sign and attach the following statement:
   "I have assumed the legal obligation to pay (put in name of physician or other provider on the bill) for services furnished (put in the name of the beneficiary who has died) on (put in the date or dates the services were rendered, as shown on the bill). I hereby claim any Medicare benefits due for these services."
4. Attach items 1, 2, 3 and the bill (which should name the beneficiary and identify you as the person the provider expects to pay the bill), and send it all in to Medicare.

If you prefer, you can get a copy (or make a copy of the one in this book) of a form Medicare has designed to make all this easier. The form is called "Unassigned Payment for Deceased Beneficiary," and contains the statement you should sign indicating that you accept legal liability to pay the bills, and the statement the doctor (or other provider) should sign saying he will not accept the assignment. Remember, you do not have to file any claim if the provider agrees to accept the assignment.

If you follow this procedure, Medicare will send the check for the claim payment to you; you, in turn, must pay the bills for which you have claimed benefits. This procedure makes you legally liable to do so, and, from this point

NONASSIGNED PAYMENT FOR DECEASED BENEFICIARY

Deceased Beneficiary:
HIC:

This form should be completed when:

1. The bill(s) has not been paid; and
2. The physician or supplier refuses to accept Medicare assignment of benefits.

The individual who assumes legal obligation to pay for services rendered a deceased beneficiary, should complete Statement I and the Physician/Supplier should complete Statement II.

I. CLAIMANT'S STATEMENT

I have assumed the legal obligation to pay _____ for services
                                              PHYSICIAN/SUPPLIER NAME
furnished _____ on _____ . I
              BENEFICIARY'S NAME   DATE(S) OF SERVICE
hereby claim any Medicare benefits due for these services.

_____
SIGNATURE OF CLAIMANT

II PHYSICIAN/SUPPLIERS' STATEMENT

I _____ will not accept assignment for the services furnished to
      PHYSICIAN/SUPPLIERS NAME
_____ on _____ .
    BENEFICIARY'S NAME   DATE(S) OF SERVICE

_____
PHYSICIAN/SUPPLIERS SIGNATURE

The signed statement by the physician refusing to accept assignment is needed because the Law requires that the physician be given the first opportunity to claim the payment when the bill is unpaid. He may do so at any time before payment is made to a person who assumed a legal obligation to pay the bill. However, once payment is made to a person, the government has no further obligation with respect to the services involved and the physician can, therefore, no longer qualify for payment.

on, the providers will look to you for payment and will dun you if it is not forthcoming. Do not undertake this obligation unless you are prepared to pay the amount of the coinsurance (20% of the reasonable charge) plus any amount over the reasonable charge. (Since you file these claims only when the provider refuses to accept the assignment, you should take it for granted that the actual bill will be for more than the reasonable charge.)

If no one agrees to accept the legal liability for the deceased beneficiary, the provider may try to collect from the estate. If there is no estate and no way of collecting from the beneficiary's property, the provider can always accept the assignment and settle for what Medicare allows.

SHOULD YOU PAY TO HAVE YOUR CLAIM FORMS FILLED OUT?

Many people feel helpless when confronted with a form to fill out—even so simple a one as the Medicare claim form. As Senator Lawton Chiles, chairman of the Committee on Aging, once commented: "The burden of filling out Medicare forms is an almost impossible one for way too many senior citizens. It has also caused many doctors to simply discourage Medicare business. . . . When Congress enacted Medicare in 1965, it did not foresee the day when forms would be so complicated that the average older American would have trouble filing them."

To simplify this task, HCFA has now developed simpler forms that almost anyone will be able to understand and fill out. I understand that some doctors still make a fuss about the "paperwork," and a few actually go so far as to charge for filling out forms.

Doctors who charge for filling out forms are perhaps not the sort of doctor you want to go to, unless there are other advantages. I have interviewed many doctors and all have assured me that the paperwork is, as one of them put it, "no big deal." Another said, "I don't know why some doctors complain about the forms. It isn't really a problem. I have to have a competent girl filling out insurance forms anyway, so Medicare is just one more—and a very simple one compared to some."

Friends in Florida and California have sent me ads for so-called Medicare assistance bureaus that offer to fill out Medicare forms for you for an annual fee of $50 or a percentage of your Medicare reimbursement.

One Florida business advertises that it will file up to three Medicare claims a year for $25 a year for an individual, $35 for a family. They will process additional bills for $1 a bill. Prior claims are processed for 10% of the money collected. A similar service in California advertises that it will file all your claims for one year, including requests for review of questionable claim settlements and representation at hearings, for a yearly fee of $120 for an individual and $220 for a family. Prior claims will be processed by this company for 25% of the amount collected.

The advertising and brochures for these services emphasize the difficulty in filling out these forms. One service claims you have to be "an attorney, doctor, CPA, insurance agent, and mathematician to fill out Medicare claim forms. . . . " This just isn't so and you may be pleasantly surprised if you just get up the courage to try to fill out the form all by yourself (and with the help of the instructions in this book, if you have any questions). If you cannot find a social worker or friend and you are still puzzled about what information a line on the form calls for, just phone the Medicare office and they will help. More and more free services are available—sometimes your local hospital will answer Medicare questions one day a week, sometimes your senior center will have someone who can help you—so you should not have to pay for this kind of help.

Don't give up on the forms until you have tried to fill one out; it is really the easiest form you will ever have to deal with. With the form in front of you, follow the step-by-step instructions in this book. Don't look ahead; just do it one line at a time. If you still find it too confusing, ask a social worker or friend to help you. Then make a copy of the filled-out form and keep it as a model to follow for your next claim. Whatever you do, don't go to a service that offers to do it for you for a fee; you get too little money back to waste any of it.

TWO WAYS TO INCREASE THE AMOUNT OF YOUR BENEFITS

It is important for you to learn a little bit about how a doctor's bill should be made out; it can mean a sizable difference in Medicare coverage because it can affect the size of the reasonable charge.

One of the most important things you can do is make sure the bill is fully itemized. If you see that it has a general description, think about the services you received; maybe Medicare will not know they were provided just from the general description. If Medicare does not know they were provided, it will not cover them.

Here are two examples:

1. If an ophthalmologist's bill says "complete eye examination," Medicare will assume the examination included eye refraction. Since eye refraction is only done for prescribing eyeglasses, it is not covered. If Medicare assumes the charge on the bill includes eye refraction, it will automatically deduct 20% from the amount of the bill before determining the reasonable charge. So if it wasn't done, the bill should say so; otherwise you are losing an automatic 20%. Ideally, eye refraction should be itemized on the bill as a sep-

arate charge; then Medicare will have a better idea as to how to process the bill.

2. "Office visit" is generally a poor description. If you went to the doctor for breathlessness and he took an EKG, the charge for the EKG would be covered because of your symptom (if the doctor puts down the symptom). If the bill just reads "office visit" and includes the charge for the EKG without specifying, the bill will seem too high and a larger proportion will be disallowed. For instance, an ordinary office visit might be billed at $15; an office visit that included an EKG and some X rays might be billed at $100. If Medicare gets a bill for $100 for an office visit that doesn't list other services, it will allow only what it would pay for a routine office visit. The more information the better, providing it is of the right kind.

You may not know what the bill should itemize, but if it doesn't seem to list services you know you got, you might ask the secretary; eventually you will learn and it could increase your benefits appreciably.

In some instances, the "reasonable" charge may seem very unreasonable indeed. For instance, I know of a case where an orthopedic surgeon billed $300 for setting a broken hand, putting it in a cast, removing the cast and providing follow-up care. It was a difficult procedure and it was very skillfully done by a surgeon with a first-class reputation. Medicare allowed only $125. I checked with other orthopedic surgeons in the area and found that $300 was the average charge for the services provided. So I called Medicare and asked why they had allowed so little.

The explanation was that the doctor had not performed that particular procedure within the past calendar year. If he had done it several times, and if it had been for Medicare beneficiaries, so that Medicare had a record of his bills, he would have been allowed a much larger amount, more in line with his actual charges. The surgeon was board-certified, taught at Yale Medical School and did not need to prove his qualifications to do what he did. Yet because of sheer happenstance—not having performed that particular type of operation within a certain time period— either he or the beneficiary was being penalized: he, if he accepted the assignment; the beneficiary, if he didn't.

In an emergency such as a broken hand, it is unlikely that you will be in any frame of mind to shop around. But with a different type of medical need, it might pay to check with Medicare and find out what they will allow for that particular service performed by that specific physician. If it is so low that he will be discouraged from accepting the assignment, try to find someone for whom Medicare will allow a higher reasonable charge.

As surgeons become more in favor of accepting the assignment, perhaps they will arrange among themselves to spread the various types of procedures so that each of them gets his quota and thus the highest possible reasonable charge.

Often, knowing how much Medicare will allow will get a reluctant doctor to accept the assignment. He may have good reason to think that he will be settling for a lot less than his usual charge if he accepts Medicare's reasonable charge, but he can be influenced in your favor if you can quote dollars and cents to show that this is not the case.

17

How to Read the Explanation
of Medicare Benefits (EOMB) Form

Next to your claim form, the Explanation of Medicare Benefits (EOMB) form is the most important form you have to deal with. It contains a great deal of information and it is the only official record you have of how your claims have been dealt with.

WHAT THE EOMB FORM IS

The EOMB form is Medicare's response to your claim for benefits (which you filed on 1490S). You will receive a copy for each Part B (SMI) claim form filed, regardless of whether you or the doctor or other provider had filed the claim, and regardless of whether the provider had accepted the assignment or not.

Let us look at an actual form, filled out for an imaginary claim, as a sample of the information it will contain (see page 172). Since each form is designed by the carrier, your form may look a little different from the one shown; forms vary from state to state and within the state from carrier to carrier. All forms, however, must contain the same information; you may find it in a slightly different place on the form, but it has to be there somewhere, and

CONNECTICUT GENERAL LIFE INSURANCE COMPANY
200 PRATT ST • MERIDEN, CONNECTICUT 06450

DATE OF NOTICE	HEALTH INSURANCE NUMBER	CONTROL NUMBER
04/01/79	000-11-2222A	9001-11111-00

BENEFICIARY

John Q. Public

FOR HEALTH INSURANCE
SOCIAL SECURITY ACT

John Q. Public
21 Main Street
Anytown, Connecticut 06492

NOTICE OF NON PAYMENT

- - - - - - - - - (If payment was made on this claim, your check would be attached here) - - - - - - - - -

EXPLANATION OF MEDICARE BENEFITS

THIS IS A STATEMENT OF ACTION TAKEN ON YOUR MEDICARE CLAIM. KEEP THIS NOTICE FOR YOUR RECORDS

1 SERVICES WERE PROVIDED BY	2 WHEN FROM MO DAY	TO MO DAY YR	3 AMOUNT BILLED	4 AMOUNT APPROVED	5 EXPLANATION OF ANY DIFFERENCE BETWEEN COLUMNS 3 & 4 MEDICARE DOES NOT PAY FOR	SERVICE CODES SEE BACK
John Fixum, M.D.	02 05	03 10 9	30.00	27.00	See Item 5 on back	1 A
John Fixum, M.D.		02 05 9	5.00	5.00		1 E
John Fixum, M.D.		03 10 9	3.00	3.00		1 E
John Fixum, M.D.		03 10 9	25.00	25.00		1 A

	TOTALS ▶	63.00	60.00

		MEDICARE PAID	
INPATIENT RADIOLOGY AND PATHOLOGY PHYSICIANS' SERVICES AND OR CERTAIN LABORATORIES PAID IN FULL	▶		THIS IS A STATEMENT OF THE ACTION TAKEN ON YOUR MEDICARE CLAIM. BE SURE TO READ THE IMPORTANT INFORMATION ON THE BACK OF THIS NOTICE
AMOUNT PAYABLE AT 80% AFTER THE ANNUAL DEDUCTIBLE	▶	60.00	
AMOUNT APPLIED TOWARD THE ANNUAL DEDUCTIBLE	▶	60.00	YOU HAVE MET 60.00 OF THE DEDUCTIBLE FOR 1979
BALANCE PAYABLE AT 80%	▶		IMPORTANT WHEN WRITING HI NUMBER 000-11-2222A
DATE 04/01/79	TOTAL MEDICARE PAYMENT ▶		PLEASE REFER TO BOTH CO NUMBER 9001-11111-00

BENEFICIARY OR REPRESENTATIVE

John Q. Public
21 Main Street
Anytown, Connecticut 06492

REMARKS:

Payment information has been forwarded to
Blue Cross/Blue Shield of Connecticut for
Supplemental Benefits.

(PLEASE SEE THE EXAMPLE OF THE REVERSE SIDE OF THE MEDICARE STATEMENT ON PAGE 15.)

13

KEEP THIS NOTICE FOR YOUR RECORDS.
USE THE ATTACHED REQUEST FOR MEDICARE PAYMENT FORM THE NEXT TIME YOU WISH TO CLAIM MEDICARE BENEFITS.

CAT #175497
MC 4 REV 6-77

This is an example of an EOMB form. In this case, there is no payment
due from Medicare so it is a "notice of non-payment." These forms
differ, depending on the carrier, and samples of some of these variations
are shown in the Appendix.

the forms will not differ so much that you will have trouble reading one that is a little different from the one shown here. Let us examine the form illustrated.

HEADING

The top part of the form gives the following information:

- the name of the carrier (the insurance company that administers Medicare Part B in your area);
- the date the claim was received from you;
- the control number (see explanation, page 180);
- the name and health-insurance claim number (from your Medicare card) of the beneficiary and the date the form is being sent to you.

THE MAIN BODY OF THE EOMB

This section gives the details of your claim, as Medicare has picked them up from the bills you attached, and tells you how the claim has been disposed of. It shows:

COLUMN 1:   the name of the doctor or other provider.

COLUMN 2:   the date the services were provided.

COLUMN 3:   the amount charged by the provider.

COLUMN 4:   the amount approved ("reasonable charge").

COLUMN 5:   an explanation of the difference between columns 3 and 4.

You should check to make sure the information taken from providers' bills agrees with the information in columns 1, 2 and 3. Every item on the bill will be given its own separate line on the EOMB. You can see how important it is that the doctor (for instance) carefully itemizes the services he has provided and does not lump them under a general category (such as "office visit"); Medicare may cover one service and not cover another.

You will not receive back the copy of the bills you sent to Medicare, so you should have a copy (or keep the original and send Medicare a copy) in your files.

EXPLANATION OF COLUMNS 4 AND 5

The information in these columns will vary, depending on a number of factors. The two most important are whether the service is covered at all, and if it is, how much of the actual bill is the reasonable charge or allowable amount that Medicare will pay.

Column 4, the "Amount Approved," tells what Medicare will pay. Column 5, "Explanation of Any Difference Between Columns 3 & 4 Medicare Does Not Pay For," explains if the amount in column 4 differs from column 3. It is important that you understand the reason given because this is where you would find your first clue that Medicare has made a mistake, or that the information given in the claim or on the doctor's bill was inadequate. The explanation may be written out in this space (column 5), in which case it might say, "More than the allowable amount." This means that the amount Medicare approves (column 4) is less than the amount of the actual bill (column 3). Instead of a written explanation, column 5 may simply say something like, "See Item 5 on back." This refers you to the paragraph on the back of the form that explains that the actual amount is more than the allowable amount.

If the amount in column 4 is zero, the explanation may read, "Services not covered." This would happen, for instance, if the doctor's bill listed a charge for a routine physical exam or some other noncovered service.

Somewhere on the form you may see a note, something like "benefits paid to the provider." This indicates that the doctor or other provider has accepted the assignment and that therefore the check is not enclosed but has been sent to the provider.

THE TOTALS—THE BOTTOM PART OF THE EOMB

In column 3, you will find the total amount of all *bills* attached to this claim. In column 4, the total will indicate all the *approved* amounts.

EXAMPLES OF BENEFITS

Example 1: The doctor has not accepted the assignment and you have not met any of your $75 deductible. (See page 176.)

In example 1, you had not met any of your deductible, so the entire $75 was deducted ("amount applied toward the annual deductible") from the $125 that Medicare approved. This completed your deductible payment for the year, and future claim forms this year will show you have met $75 of your deductible, so there will then be no "amount applied toward the annual deductible." In other words, the deductible will not be subtracted from column 4 in any bills you receive for the rest of the year.

"Amount payable at 80% after the annual deductible" shows the amount left for Medicare to partially pay after the deductible has been met. In this example, $125 minus $75 equals $50 for Medicare to partially pay. This figure is repeated on the line "balance payable at 80%," and in the next box ("Medicare Paid") is the amount Medicare actually pays. In this example that amount is 80% of $50,

EXPLANATION OF MEDICARE BENEFITS

1 SERVICES WERE PROVIDED BY	2 WHEN						3 AMOUNT BILLED	4 AMOUNT APPROVED	5 EXPLANATION OF ANY DIFFERENCE BETWEEN COLUMNS 3 & 4 MEDICARE DOES NOT PAY FOR	SERVICE CODES SEE BACK
	FROM			TO						
	MO	DAY	MO	DAY	YR					
E. Smith			12	23	2		220.00	125.00	MORE THAN ALLOWABLE AMOUNT	3
						TOTALS ▶	220.00	125.00		

	AMOUNT APPROVED	MEDICARE PAID	
INPATIENT RADIOLOGY AND PATHOLOGY PHYSICIANS' SERVICES AND OR CERTAIN LABORATORIES PAID IN FULL	▲	.00	.00
AMOUNT PAYABLE AT 80% AFTER THE ANNUAL DEDUCTIBLE	▲	50.00	
AMOUNT APPLIED TOWARD THE ANNUAL DEDUCTIBLE	▲	75.00	
BALANCE PAYABLE AT 80%	▲	50.00	40.00
	TOTAL MEDICARE PAYMENT ▶		40.00

THIS IS A STATEMENT OF THE ACTION TAKEN ON YOUR MEDICARE CLAIM. BE SURE TO READ THE IMPORTANT INFORMATION ON THE BACK OF THIS NOTICE.

YOU HAVE MET $75.00 OF THE DEDUCTIBLE FOR 1982

IMPORTANT WHEN WRITING PLEASE REFER TO BOTH

HI NUMBER 000–11–2222A

CO NUMBER 9001–11112–00

DATE 8/31/82

or $40. A check for this amount will be the top part of this
form, unless payment has been made directly to the doctor.

With the information on this form, you can figure out
how much of the charges shown on the claim form you will
have to pay. In this example, here is how it works out:

You pay:

Your deductible of $75:	$ 75
20% of Medicare-approved balance of $50:	10
The difference between the doctor's bill and	
Medicare's approved amount:	95
Total you pay:	$180

So, out of the doctor's bill of $220, Medicare pays $40
and you pay $180.

Example 2: The doctor has not accepted the assignment
but you have met all of your $75 deductible. (See page
178.)

Since, in example 2, you have already met all of your
deductible, nothing is subtracted from the Medicare-approved amount of $125. Medicare will therefore pay 80%
of that amount, or $100, and a check for that amount will
be sent to you or to the provider. (If to you, it will be
enclosed.)

You can now figure out that your share of the doctor's
bill of $220 will be $120. Here's how:

20% of Medicare-approved balance of $125:	$ 25
The difference between the doctor's bill and	
Medicare's approved amount:	95
Total you pay:	$120

Example 3: The doctor accepts the assignment and you
have met all of your deductible. (See page 179.)

You will note that the form looks exactly the same as

EXPLANATION OF MEDICARE BENEFITS

1 SERVICES WERE PROVIDED BY	2 WHEN FROM MO DAY	TO MO DAY YR	3 AMOUNT BILLED	4 AMOUNT APPROVED	5 EXPLANATION OF ANY DIFFERENCE BETWEEN COLUMNS 3 & 4 MEDICARE DOES NOT PAY FOR.	SERVICE CODES SEE BACK
E. Smith		12 23 2	220.00	125.00	MORE THAN ALLOWABLE AMOUNT	3
		TOTALS ▶	220.00	125.00		

INPATIENT RADIOLOGY AND PATHOLOGY PHYSICIANS' SERVICES AND OR CERTAIN LABORATORIES PAID IN FULL ▲ .00

AMOUNT PAYABLE AT 80% AFTER THE ANNUAL DEDUCTIBLE ▲ 125.00

AMOUNT APPLIED TOWARD THE ANNUAL DEDUCTIBLE ▲ .00

BALANCE PAYABLE AT 80% ▲ 125.00

MEDICARE PAID .00

THIS IS A STATEMENT OF THE ACTION TAKEN ON YOUR MEDICARE CLAIM. BE SURE TO READ THE IMPORTANT INFORMATION ON THE BACK OF THIS NOTICE.

YOU HAVE MET 75.00 OF THE DEDUCTIBLE FOR 1982

100.00

IMPORTANT WHEN WRITING PLEASE REFER TO BOTH

HI NUMBER 000-11-2222A

CO NUMBER 9001-11112-00

DATE 12/31/82   TOTAL MEDICARE PAYMENT ▶ 100.00

EXPLANATION OF MEDICARE BENEFITS

1 SERVICES WERE PROVIDED BY	2 WHEN FROM MO DAY YR	TO MO DAY YR	3 AMOUNT BILLED	4 AMOUNT APPROVED	5 EXPLANATION OF ANY DIFFERENCE BETWEEN COLUMNS 3 & 4 MEDICARE DOES NOT PAY FOR:	SERVICE CODES SEE BACK
E. Smith	12 23	2	220.00	125.00	MORE THAN ALLOWABLE AMOUNT	3
	TOTALS ▶		220.00	125.00		

		MEDICARE PAID	
INPATIENT RADIOLOGY AND PATHOLOGY PHYSICIANS' SERVICES AND OR CERTAIN LABORATORIES PAID IN FULL	▲	.00	THIS IS A STATEMENT OF THE ACTION TAKEN ON YOUR MEDICARE CLAIM. BE SURE TO READ THE IMPORTANT INFORMATION ON THE BACK OF THIS NOTICE.
AMOUNT PAYABLE AT 80% AFTER THE ANNUAL DEDUCTIBLE	▲	125.00	
AMOUNT APPLIED TOWARD THE ANNUAL DEDUCTIBLE	▲	.00	YOU HAVE MET 75.00 OF THE DEDUCTIBLE FOR 1982
BALANCE PAYABLE AT 80%	▲	125.00	IMPORTANT WHEN WRITING HI NUMBER 000-11-2222A
TOTAL MEDICARE PAYMENT ▶		100.00	PLEASE REFER TO BOTH CO NUMBER 9001-11112-00
DATE 12/31/82		100.00	

the form in example 2. The difference is that your share of the doctor's bill is only $25. Here's how:

20% of Medicare-approved balance of $125:	$25
Total you pay:	$25

You do not have to pay the difference between the doctor's bill and Medicare's approved amount, because in accepting the assignment the doctor has agreed to accept the Medicare-approved amount.

WHAT IS A CONTROL NUMBER?

The control number is a number assigned to each individual claim; it helps identify that claim among the millions of claims your Medicare office processes each year. It will appear on every check you receive from Medicare and also on the EOMB form. It may be called either "Control number" or "CO #."

Whenever you have a question about your claim, you should be prepared to give the control number for that claim, as well as your health insurance (Medicare) number, your name and address, and the date on the claim (which may be called the "date of notice"). Have this information handy before you place your call.

LOOK AT THE BACK OF THE EOMB FORM

The back of the form contains a great deal of useful information. For instance, item #5 is a brief explanation of "reasonable charge"—the most common reason for Medicare's charge being less than the doctor's bill. In addition, it will enable you to translate the codes (as in column headed "service codes") into understandable terms.

MEDIGAP INSURANCE AND THE EOMB

If you have an insurance policy that picks up some of the charges Medicare does not pay, that company may require this form before it will honor your claim. If possible, send them a copy. If they insist on receiving the original, be sure to make a copy for your own files. These forms should be part of your permanent medical record.

YOUR RIGHT TO REVIEW

The last paragraph on the back of your EOMB form is headed, "Your right to review of the case." It reads:

If you have a problem or question about the way your claim was handled or about the amount paid, please get in touch with the (name and address of carrier) within 6 months of the date of this notice. We will give your request full consideration.

Your nearest social security office will also be glad to help you with a request for a review of your claim if this is more convenient for you.

This means that you can appeal the decisions Medicare has made in paying your claim. For example, you may not think that you or the doctor or other provider has been paid enough, or you may think there is an error in the way Medicare has analyzed your claim. If coverage has been denied, you may wish to discuss the reason, or if you know the reason, you may disagree with the ruling. In the next chapter, you will learn how to disagree with a Medicare ruling—and win most of the time.

18

If You Disagree—How
to Appeal a Medicare Claim

**THE EOMB, THE UTILIZATION NOTICE AND YOUR RIGHT
TO APPEAL**

As we have seen in the previous chapter, the back of your
Explanation of Medical Benefits form has a paragraph
telling you of your right to appeal Medicare decisions. You
may, for instance, question Medicare's "reasonable
charge," if you feel it is too little. You may also question
denial of coverage. In the latter case, there is a specific
rule that may help you; it is called "Waiver of Beneficiary
Liability" and we will discuss it shortly.

**IF YOU APPEAL, YOU WILL PROBABLY WIN HIGHER
BENEFITS**

According to surveys conducted by HCFA and the AARP
(American Association of Retired Persons), only 2% to 3%
of Medicare beneficiaries who are dissatisfied because of
denials of claims or too low an allowable charge ever do
anything about it. Most of them feel, "Oh, what's the use.
Nobody's going to pay any attention to me." Don't be like
that. You can increase your benefits appreciably by speaking up. And the chances of getting satisfaction are excellent. Medicare estimates that *over 50%* of the Medicare

payments that are questioned are settled in *favor of the beneficiary*—claims that have been denied are paid, and low allowed charges are increased. That's money in your pocket that you don't have to pay taxes on; don't lose benefits through inertia or timidity.

WHAT IS A "WAIVER OF BENEFICIARY LIABILITY"?

It sometimes happens that you receive services that are not covered, but that, at the time you received them, you thought were covered. Under certain circumstances, even though they were not covered and Medicare has denied coverage, Medicare will change its mind and agree to pay for them.

The Waiver of Beneficiary Liability rule may apply when coverage has been denied for the following reasons:

1. When services were custodial.
2. When covered services were received after your coverage ceased.
3. When the services were deemed not "reasonable or necessary."

If your claim was denied for any of the above reasons, and—for Part B services—if the doctor or the provider has agreed to accept the assignment, it may be that you can still get payment under the Waiver rule. Note that it is necessary with Part B services that the assignment be accepted; most providers will gladly accept the assignment in this instance if it means the difference between Medicare covering or not covering the service.

There are two ways the Waiver rule can be applied. The first may find that the provider has exercised due care under the Medicare policy and has given the services in good faith that they were covered. In this instance, the government waives payment of Medicare's share.

The second way may find that the provider should have

known better but that the beneficiary had no way of knowing noncovered services were being provided. An example of this might be when a beneficiary loses his Medicare hospital coverage but is not notified by the hospital that this has happened. Under certain circumstances, if the beneficiary has not been notified that coverage has ended, Medicare will rule that the hospital must pay Medicare's share and that the patient is covered for those services.

Ignorance, however, is no excuse. If, for example, Medicare has denied coverage because you have put in a claim for items that are never covered, such as eyeglasses or hearing aids, you cannot invoke this rule.

Once you have invoked the Waiver of Beneficiary Liability rule, you cannot use it again for the same kind of services. The second time around it is assumed that you have learned the rules and can no longer plead that you didn't know them. If you think Medicare's denial of claim could be reversed under this rule, it is a simple matter to phone the Medicare office and ask them. If the rule does not apply, they will explain why not. If you still dispute the way they have handled the claim, you can then appeal.

HOW TO APPEAL A PART A CLAIM

If, upon receiving Medicare's explanation of the reason for denial (for Part A, this will be a "disallowance letter"), you disagree with the decision, you have a right to question this decision. There is a specific process to follow and it is different from the process for appealing Part B claims, so you should know how.

Step One: Request an Explanation

This sounds more formal than it is. Simply phone the Medicare office and tell them why you think their denial of the claim is incorrect. Have all your information handy—the services you received, when you received them, whatever you can tell about them, and all your personal identification, such as name, address, Medicare number, as well as a copy of the utilization form or disallowance letter. If the explanation you get at this time is not satisfactory, you can take Step Two.

Why You Shouldn't Both Phone and Write

Your first step in questioning a claim is, as we have said, to phone the Medicare office. Some people prefer to write so that they have a record of their complaint.

Medicare asks that you do one or the other but *not both.* If you phone and write at the same time, you will involve more than one Medicare department, and will create extra work for them as well as slowing up the processing of your complaint.

If you wish to phone and then follow up with a confirming letter, be sure to refer in your letter to the fact that you have previously discussed this matter by phone, and give the date of your call and the name of the person you spoke to. Ideally, do not phone and write about the same problem.

At some point after the initial phone call, you may wish to start putting everything in writing. If so, be sure you refer to previous phone calls (by date and Medicare person) and document carefully.

If you write first and then get impatient and phone to find out what has happened, have a copy of the letter handy, as well as all the information listed at the beginning of Step One.

Step Two: Request a Reconsideration

The important thing here is timing; you can lose the right to a reconsideration if you do not act promptly.

If all of your claim is denied, you must request a reconsideration within 60 days from the date you are notified of the denial (the "notice of denial" from Medicare).

If only part of your claim is denied, you can request a reconsideration immediately, or you can wait until you receive the second notice, which will give you more details (the benefits that were paid as well as the benefits that were denied). You must, however, request reconsideration no later than 60 days after you receive the second notice.

Requests for a reconsideration must be made in writing on a specific form; it may be easier to get it from your local social security office than from Medicare, but try both places. At the social security office someone will help you fill it out.

The information needed for the form is simply your name, address, health-insurance claim number, where and when you received the services and the name of the Medicare intermediary (usually Blue Cross) that made the initial decision, as well as why you are dissatisfied with the denial and any additional information you think may be helpful. Sometimes a written statement from your physician will help support your position.

If you have been denied payment because Medicare thinks you are not eligible for the program, it will be comparatively easy to establish that you are: simply give your Medicare claim number from your red, white and blue Medicare card.

Medicare will turn your request over to entirely different persons from the one's who processed your original claim and you will get a completely new decision. You will then receive a notice of the new (reconsideration) decision.

If the coverage is denied because the services are not covered services, but you had no way of knowing they were not covered, you may still get benefits under the Waiver of Beneficiary Liability rule. This does not apply very often and it is best to make every effort to determine that the services you are receiving are covered services.

Step Three: Request for a Hearing

In the event that you still do not agree with Medicare's decision and if the amount in question is $100 or more, you may request a hearing. You have 60 days from the date you receive the reconsideration denial to make this request. It must be in writing and you can get the forms the same place you got the reconsideration forms.

If your request is granted (and it usually is), you will get at least ten days' notice of the date you are scheduled to appear and where the hearing will be held. The hearing is conducted by the Office of Hearings Appeals of the Social Security Administration. It is informal but you may have someone represent you—in fact, you don't have to be present at all—and you can even have witnesses to testify on your behalf. If you have additional evidence on your side, you may present it at this time, and you should bring copies of all correspondence and forms to date. You will be asked to testify under oath and the hearing will be presided over by an administrative law judge.

You will very seldom have to go this far to resolve a disagreement with Medicare Part A, but it is comforting to know that you have the right to do so if you wish.

You will be notified in writing as to the decision, with an explanation of it.

Step Four: Request for Review by Appeals Council

If you are still not satisfied, you may request a further review, this time by the Appeals Council of the Office of Hearings and Appeals, within 60 days of the date you receive the decision of the hearing.

Step Five: Court Action

Your next recourse is to bring suit in a Federal district court; you may do so if the amount in dispute is $1,000 or more. Presumably, if you have taken the matter this far, you are fairly sophisticated or have the advice of someone who knows these procedures, so I will not attempt to explain them further.

HOW TO APPEAL A PART B CLAIM

One of the important differences in the way Part A and Part B claims and disputes of claims is handled is the intermediary. The intermediary is the insurance company that locally administers the Medicare program; there is always more than one intermediary within a state. The intermediary for Part B is always referred to as the "carrier." In Connecticut, for example, Blue Cross is one of the three private insurance companies that are the intermediaries for Part A (HI), and Connecticut General is the carrier for Part B (SMI). Since you do not file Part A claims, you will not have any contact with the Part A intermediary unless part of the claim is denied. The Part B claims you file will go to the Medicare office in your state and you will not be aware of who the carrier is unless you notice the name on your EOMB form (it is always given).

If the provider of Part B services, such as your doctor, accepts the assignment, he will send in the claim form to the same carrier.

The steps in appealing a Medicare Part B payment or denial of payment are similar to those of Part A, but have slightly different names in some instances.

DEPARTMENT OF HEALTH, EDUCATION, AND WELFARE
HEALTH CARE FINANCING ADMINISTRATION

Form Approved
OMB No. 066R0043

REQUEST FOR REVIEW OF PART B MEDICARE CLAIM
Medical Insurance Benefits - Social Security Act

NOTICE Anyone who misrepresents or falsifies essential information requested by this form may upon conviction be subject to fine and imprisonment under Federal Law.

Carrier's Name and Address

1 Name of Patient

2 Health Insurance Claim Number

3 I do not agree with the determination you made on my claim as described on my Explanation of Medicare

Benefits dated:

4 MY REASONS ARE *(Attach a copy of the Explanation of Medicare Benefits, or describe the service, date of service, and physician's name—NOTE.—If the date on the Notice of Benefits mentioned in item 3 is more than six months ago, include your reason for not making this request earlier.)*

5 ☐ I have additional evidence to submit. *(Attach such evidence to this form)*

☐ I do not have additional evidence.

COMPLETE ALL OF THE INFORMATION REQUESTED SIGN AND RETURN THE FIRST COPY AND ANY ATTACHMENTS TO THE CARRIER NAMED ABOVE. IF YOU NEED HELP, TAKE THIS AND YOUR NOTICE FROM THE CARRIER TO A SOCIAL SECURITY OFFICE, OR TO THE CARRIER. KEEP THE DUPLICATE COPY OF THIS FORM FOR YOUR RECORDS.

6 SIGNATURE OF **EITHER** THE CLAIMANT **OR** HIS REPRESENTATIVE

Representative ➡

Claimant ➡

Address

Address

City, State, and ZIP Code

City, State, and ZIP Code

Telephone Number | Date

Telephone Number | Date

Form HCFA-1964 (1-78) (Formerly SSA-1964)

CLAIMANT'S COPY

(over)

This is the first form you would file if you disagreed with Medicare's settlement of your claim. It is very easy to fill out and uncomplicated. It even tells you right on the form where to get help in filling it out if you feel you cannot do it yourself.

Step One.

Same as for Part A.

Step Two: Request for Review

This is similar to Part A Request for Reconsideration, except you use form HCFA-1964. You have six months from the date of the EOMB you are disputing in which to file this form with Medicare.

Step Three: Request for a Hearing

This is similar to Part A Request for a Hearing; the amount in question must also be $100 or more; the form is HCFA-1965.

Step Four: No Recourse

Under Part B, the decision of the hearing is final. You may not ask for judicial review, appeal to the Social Security Administration or go to court on any basis. Unless you can persuade the carrier or the hearing officer to reopen the case or to reconsider the decision, you have gone as far as you can go.

FREQUENCY OF APPEALS

Medicare feels that not nearly as many beneficiaries question Medicare claims as should. Asking for at least an explanation is a good way to discover errors, and Medicare will cheerfully correct them once they are discovered. With such an enormous volume of claims to process, mistakes are bound to be made and it is up to each beneficiary to examine his or her payments and complain if something seems to be wrong.

On the other hand, what you may turn up can be somewhat upsetting. Take the case of the beneficiary in a nearby town who had an operation for cataracts in her right eye. The hospital required her to have preadmission tests before she could check in to the hospital. These tests were routinely required and were not related to her cataract operation. She sent in the bills for them along with the rest of the bills for the operation and the doctor's services, and Medicare paid them all in the usual fashion (80% of the allowed charge).

Two years later, she had to have the same operation on the left eye. Afterward she sent in all the bills—the same as for the previous operation—and Medicare denied payment for the preadmission tests. She protested that Medicare had paid these bills before but Medicare simply said that had been a mistake. She went to the Legal Aid Society and finally to her senator, but no one was able to help her. I suggested she apply the Waiver of Beneficiary Liability Rule, since Medicare itself had misled her into thinking those tests were a covered service. Medicare thought about it a bit, then ruled that she *was* covered under the Waiver, but that if she insisted on getting paid for the second set of tests under the Waiver, Medicare would then bill her for the first set of tests that she had mistakenly been paid for. (Medicare has a procedure for recovering what it deems "overpayments.") Since this was obviously a no-win situation, she gave up. In a way, she was lucky to have gotten one set of the tests paid for, but in another way, I feel Medicare should have paid for both sets since it misled her by its first payment. In any case, I do not think the medical consumer should be put in the middle, between the hospital's requirements and Medicare's refusal to pay for them; some more equitable way should be found than to dump the problem on the patient.

19

The "Reasonable Charge"
—How Reasonable Is It?

The basis of all Medicare and Medigap insurance benefit payments is the so-called reasonable or allowable charge. When Medicare says it will pay 80% of a bill, it means 80% of the amount it has determined is reasonable and allowable. This is often considerably less than the actual bill and is the reason most doctors and other providers hesitate to accept the assignment. Since there is no way you can influence the determination of the reasonable charge (although, as we have seen, there are ways to increase the amount of your benefits), you may not care to concern yourself with the details. However, in case you are interested, this chapter will present a brief discussion of the nature of the reasonable charge.

WHAT IS IT?

The reasonable or allowable charge is the amount Medicare establishes annually (July 1) for each provider of certain specific services. There is no set fee schedule for a service—such as an appendectomy or an X ray—that all providers are allowed. For this reason it is impossible to know, unless you ask Medicare, what the allowable charge will be for any given service.

HOW IS IT DETERMINED?

The reasonable or allowable charge is determined by compilation of three sets of figures:

1. the actual charge;
2. the customary charge;
3. the prevailing charge.

The Actual Charge

The actual charge, or the amount shown on the doctor's actual bill, is in some ways the least important. Its primary function is to help establish the customary charge. The only time it plays an active role is in a negative sense; if the actual charge is *less* than what Medicare determines as the reasonable charge, Medicare will pay the actual bill rather than the reasonable charge. This rarely happens; usually the actual bill is higher than the reasonable charge.

The Customary Charge

Customary charges are theoretically what the doctor or other provider bills as his median charge—the lowest point below which at least 50% of the actual charges fall.

For example, let's look at actual bills from Doctor A and Doctor B:

DOCTOR A	DOCTOR B
$6	$145
6	146
7 median	148
8	155
	160 median
	170
	180
	200
	210

In this example, the median or customary charge for Doctor A would be $7; for Doctor B, it would be $160. Obviously both doctors charge different patients different amounts; Doctor B may charge one patient $145 and another $210 for the exact same service. This is normal billing procedure and Medicare takes it into account by arriving at the customary charge in this fashion.

It should be noted that these actual charges are compiled from the claims that are filed with Medicare; non-Medicare bills are not included in the equation. And obviously, when a doctor raises his fees this raises his customary charge (although there are restrictions as to how much of a raise Medicare will accept in a given period). A doctor moving into a new area does not have a record with Medicare and is, so to speak, starting with a clean slate. He may easily establish a higher customary charge than can a doctor who has been in the area for some ten or twenty years; this is a source of irritation to established doctors.

The Prevailing Charge

In order to arrive at the prevailing charge, Medicare gathers together all the customary charges in a given geographical area; each state is divided into many such areas. The prevailing charge is the lowest charge, on an array of customary charges, that is high enough to include 75% of all the customary charges.

This is not a simple process; it involves three basic steps:

1. weighting the customary charges;
2. arraying the weighted customary charges;
3. finding the 75th percentile of the array.

How the Customary Charges Are Weighted

Medicare records the number of times a particular service (such as an X ray) was performed by a particular doctor; it also adds this figure to a cumulative total for all doctors in the locality.

The result could look like this:

NUMBER OF TIMES THE SERVICE WAS PERFORMED	DOCTOR	CUSTOMARY CHARGE	CUMULATIVE TOTAL SERVICES
25	Smith	$6	25
50	Brown	6	75
40	Richards	7	115
35	Bean	8	150
25	Elroy	9	175

The weighting is arrived at by the indication that the service was performed 25, 50, 40, 35 or 25 times.

How the Customary Charges Are Arrayed

The charges in the table are already arrayed: they have been put in order according to the amount of the charge, from the lowest to the highest charge.

How the 75th Percentile Is Arrived At

The 75th percentile is found by examining the arrayed charges to find the lowest figure in the list of cumulative totals that includes at least 75% of all the charges. In this example, if you multiply 175 (the cumulative total) by 75%, you get 131. The lowest figure in the cumulative total that includes the 75th percentile (131) is 150. The pre-

1980 PREVAILING CHARGE SUMMARY DATA   B/S OF FLORIDA

FLORIDA
COMBINED LOCALITY DESIGNATION

	PROCEDURE DESCRIPTION	AREA A	AREA B	AREA C
1	INITIAL BRIEF OFFICE VISIT	17.00	20.00	25.00
2	INITIAL LIMITED OFFICE VISIT	18.00	25.00	25.00
3	INIT INTERMED OFFICE VISIT	20.00	25.00	30.00
4	INIT COMP OFFICE VISIT	40.00	46.00*	45.00
5	MINIMAL F/U OFFICE VISIT	6.00	8.60*	7.50
6	BRIEF F/U OFFICE VISIT	12.00	15.00	15.30*
7	LIMITED F/U OFFICE VISIT	15.00	15.00	15.60*
8	EXTENDED F/U OFFICE VISIT	15.00	17.00	20.00
9	COMPLETE F/U OFFICE VISIT	25.00	20.00	25.00
10	BRIEF F/U HOME VISIT	30.00*	20.00	40.00
11	LIMITED F/U HOME VISIT	15.00	20.00	30.00
12	INTERMDIATE F/U HOME VISIT	23.00*	20.00	25.00
13	EXTENDED CARE FACILITY VISIT	17.00	20.00	35.00
14	BRIEF F/U NURSING HOME VISIT	15.00	20.00	20.00
15	INITIAL BRIEF HOSPITAL VISIT	13.30*	15.00	18.40*
16	INIT INTERMED HOSPITAL VISIT	40.00	45.00	50.00
17	INITIAL COMP HOSPITAL VISIT	40.00	50.00	55.00
18	BRIEF F/U HOSPITAL VISIT	46.00*	53.70*	70.00
19	LIMITED F/U HOSPITAL VISIT	15.00	18.00	20.00
20	INTERMED F/U HOSPITAL VISIT	16.90*	18.40*	25.00
21	EXTENDED F/U HOSPITAL VISIT	20.00	20.00	25.00
22	BRIEF EMERGENCY ROOM VISIT	20.00	25.00	25.00
23	INTERMED EMERGENCY ROOM VISIT	16.00	18.00	20.00
24	LIMITED EMERGENCY ROOM VISIT	22.00	25.00	30.00
25	INTERMED EMERGENCY ROOM VISIT	22.90*	25.00	30.00
26	LIMITED CONSULTATION	46.75*	35.25*	41.40*
27	EXTENSIVE CONSULTATION	50.00	50.00	50.00
28	COMPREHENSIVE CONSULTATION	60.00	60.00	75.00
29	PSYCHOTH000930 E HOUR	50.00	53.70*	61.30*
30	PSYCHOTHERAPY-HALF HOUR	25.00	30.00	40.60*
31	CHIROPRACTIC OFFICE VISIT			
32	INITIAL PHYSIOTHERAPY	12.00	12.30*	15.00
33	F/U PODIATRIC OFFICE VISIT	15.00	15.00	15.60*
34	ELECTROCARDIOGRAM (EKG)			
35	EKG-INTERPRET.REPORT ONLY			
36	SPIROMETRY			
37	ELECTROENCEPHALOGRAM (EEG)	35.00	45.00	50.00
38	CHEMOTHERAPY			
39	COLLECTION OF SPECIMENS			
40	SEBRIDEMENT OF NAILS	15.00	15.00	16.70*
41	SKIN BIOPSY			
42	CHEMOCAUTERY	3.00	5.00*	5.90*
43	RADICAL MASTECTOMY	905.80*	937.10*	1004.10*
44	OPEN REDUCTION OF FRACTURE	1005.00*	1093.30*	1171.40*
45	ARTHROCENTESIS-MAJOR JOINT	20.00	20.00	20.00
46	ARTHROTOMY	15.30*	18.00	20.00
47	ARTHROPLASTY-REPAIR OF HIP	1500.00*	1500.00*	1500.00*
48	NEEDLE PUNCTURE OF BURSA	18.90*	19.50	20.00
49	BRONCHOSCOPY	200.00	191.60*	191.60*
50	THORACENTESIS	35.00*	37.10*	41.30*
51	CATHERIZATION OF HEART	500.00	500.00	500.00
52	INSERTION OF PACEMAKER	1149.75*	1080.00	1000.00
53	PARTIAL COLECTOMY	766.50*	843.20*	1004.10*

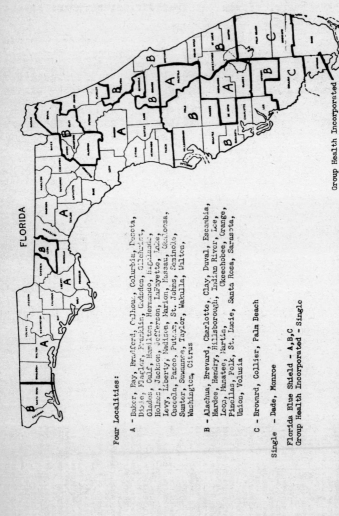

FLORIDA

Group Health Incorporated

Four Localities:

A – Baker, Bay, Bradford, Calhoun, Columbia, Desoto, Dixie, Flagler, Franklin, Gadsden, Gilchrist, Glades, Gulf, Hamilton, Hernando, Highlands, Holmes, Jackson, Jefferson, Lafayette, Lake, Levy, Liberty, Madison, Marion, Nassau, Okaloosa, Osceola, Pasco, Putnam, St. Johns, Seminole, Sumter, Suwannee, Taylor, Wakulla, Walton, Washington, Citrus

B – Alachua, Brevard, Charlotte, Clay, Duval, Escambia, Hardee, Hendry, Hillsborough, Indian River, Lee, Leon, Manatee, Martin, Okeechobee, Orange, Pinellas, Polk, St. Lucie, Santa Rosa, Sarasota, Union, Volusia

C – Broward, Collier, Palm Beach

Single – Dade, Monroe

Florida Blue Shield – A, B, C
Group Health Incorporated – Single

Two pages from the *Medicare Directory of Prevailing Charges 1980* showing how Florida is divided into localities for the purpose of determining "prevailing charges."

vailing charge in this example is, therefore, $8. (The 50th, rather than the 75th percentile, is used for services a physician has not performed often enough to have established an up-to-date customary charge.)

We have now determined the customary charge for a particular service performed by a particular doctor as well as the prevailing charge in his locality. Now we have to apply a further rule.

Lowest Charge Levels

In arriving at the reasonable charge, Medicare chooses the *lowest* figure among the actual charge, the customary charge and the prevailing charge. In addition, however, Medicare states that payment for items and services that do not generally vary significantly from one supplier to another cannot exceed the *lowest charge levels* at which they are widely and consistently available in the locality. The lowest charge level is set at the 25th percentile of actual charges and is revised twice a year. This limit, however, applies only to certain laboratory tests and two items of durable medical equipment (the standard wheelchair and hospital bed); it does not, at present, apply to doctor bills.

HOW UP-TO-DATE ARE REASONABLE CHARGES?

They aren't up-to-date at all; at worst they can be as much as two and a half years out-of-date. Considering that they are compiled by an industry that manages to update automobile insurance figures every six months, it seems extremely puzzling that this is the best they can do with health-care costs. Here is why they are so inaccurate.

Reasonable charges are adjusted each July 1 based on actual charges from bills submitted to Medicare for the previous calendar year (January through December). The previous year's charges may have been billed anywhere from January to December. Under this system, if a July 1 reasonable charge has been based on actual charges of the previous December, the July 1 reasonable charge is already six months out of date the day it goes into effect. December, however, is the latest charge, so *even the most current reasonable charge is six months out-of-date.*

Since the reasonable charge is updated only on July 1, and since it is based on the previous year's charges (January through December), a reasonable charge determined on July 1, 1982, and based on charges of December 1981 would be 6 months out-of-date, but if it were based on charges of July 1, 1981, it would be 12 months out-of-date. And if it were based on charges of January 1, 1981, it would be 18 months out-of-date.

If we then consider that the reasonable charge that is determined on July 1, 1982, is in effect until June 30, 1983, we see that a June 1983 reasonable charge could be based on an actual charge of January 1981.

In other words, it works this way:

Date of Actual Bill	Bill on Which Reasonable Charge Is Based	Reasonable Charge Out-of-Date by
July 1, 1981	December 30, 1980	6 months
July 1, 1981	July 1, 1980	1 year
July 1, 1981	January 1, 1980	1½ years
December 30, 1981	January 1, 1980	2 years
June 30, 1982	January 1, 1980	2½ years

Of course, the customary charge for a doctor is not usually based on a single bill, but it could be, and it has been necessary to simplify the example to show the nature of the reasonable-charge procedure.

WHY DON'T DOCTORS JUST RAISE THEIR FEES?

To some extent they do. A September 21, 1981, issue of the *Washington Report* said that the overall Consumer Price Index had gone up 9.4% but hospital room charges had risen 13.6% and doctors' fees 12.8% in the same period. There is, however, a law limiting how much Medicare can increase prevailing fees in a given year; it is called the "Economic Index Limitation."

THE ECONOMIC INDEX LIMITATION

Generally an economic index is a measure of the price changes for a specified item or service in the economy from one time period to another. Medicare's Economic Index is based on increases since the year 1971 in the costs of doctors' office practices and in the earnings levels of workers in general. Since fiscal-year 1973 prevailing charges are based on calendar-year 1971 charge dates, doctors' charges that are higher than those of fiscal-year 1973 are permitted only if they can be justified on the basis of actual economic changes. For example, using 1980 as the fee screen year (and remember, that began July 1, 1979), Medicare's Economic Index allowed prevailing charges for 1980 to increase no more than 53.3% over fiscal-year 1973 prevailing charges. In other words, the 1980 doctor bill could be 53.3% higher than the 1973 bill. As a result of this limitation, many doctors don't attempt to raise their fees themselves; they consult with Medicare to find out how much of an increase the formula will allow.

At this point you may well wonder what is done in countries with a national health plan. It's really much simpler: the government usually establishes a fee schedule for each service; all doctors and providers participating in the plan agree to it; and everyone knows exactly where he or she stands. It works in other industrialized countries in the world, and if it's not perfect, neither is the system we have here—and it takes care of a lot more people than Medicare does.

20

The Professional Standards
Review Organizations and You

Every day we are subject to decisions that influence our lives, but most of the time we are unaware of them and do not know the decisions that have been made, let alone by whom. In the case of the Professional Standards Review Organizations, always referred to as PSROs, we cannot help but be aware of the decisions made, but we may not know how these decisions have been arrived at. Since the decisions can have a seriously detrimental effect on our lives, we ought to have some idea of the organization that makes them and how it works.

DECISIONS THE PSRO MAKES THAT AFFECT YOU

All Medicare coverage is based on the determination that the covered service is "medically necessary." Since Medicare will not accept the judgment of even the most prestigious physician or surgeon as to what is "medically necessary," the question naturally arises, "If my doctor doesn't know, who does?" The answer is the PSRO or the utilization review committee. One of these two committees examines each and every Medicare claim and rules on whether or not it is "medically necessary." If the determination is yes, Medicare will approve the claim. If the determination is no, the claim will be disallowed as "not medically necessary."

HOW WILL A NEGATIVE DECISION AFFECT YOU?

Every time a PSRO or utilization committee decides a service is not medically necessary, you will be notified that Medicare will not cover that service. If you are in a hospital or nursing home, you will quickly have to decide whether to leave or to stay on at your own expense.

A PSRO may determine that you no longer require hospitalization, but that you do require nursing home (SNF) care. If there is no opening in nearby nursing homes (SNFs), the PSRO may approve your continued stay in the hospital until a bed becomes available in a nursing home.

If you enter the hospital for elective surgery, the PSRO will decide whether or not the operation was medically necessary. If you want to know the decision before you incur the expense of proposed elective surgery, you can get a ruling before you schedule the operation.

A PSRO will determine whether you need to be in a nursing home (SNF) and for how long. If it determines that your stay is no longer medically necessary, you will have to go home or stay at your own expense.

Much is made of the fact that you are not "thrown out" of the hospital if the PSRO decides your stay is not medically necessary, but for the majority of Medicare beneficiaries who cannot afford to pay for hospitalization out of their own pockets, that is what really happens. Unless, of course, you choose to use up all your financial resources in paying your hospital bills until you become eligible for Medicaid.

Any treatment you receive from your doctor, therapist or home health-care agency is similarly subject to review by the PSRO. In fact, any time Medicare is expected to cover a service, it will do so only if it is deemed medically necessary.

The two points to remember in connection with "medically necessary" are that coverage will be denied even for covered items if they do not meet this requirement, and that your doctor is not the judge of what is medically necessary. He may strongly disagree with the decision but his opinion, while it will be taken under consideration, is not what counts in the end.

WHAT CAN YOUR DOCTOR DO ABOUT A NEGATIVE DECISION?

Before the PSRO disapproves of services, it is mandated by law to give your doctor a chance to explain why he feels the service is medically necessary. If his reasons are persuasive or add information that had not been available to the organization, the decision to disapprove may be reversed and you will never know how close you came to a denial. Doctors tend to fight for their patients because they know the personal hardship and anguish a denial may inflict, but unless they clearly understand the factors that influence the PSRO, they will strike out more often than not.

You may think a good way to get more favorable treatment might be to choose as your personal physician a doctor who is on a PSRO. Theoretically this will not help, because he is precluded by law from ruling on decisions involving his own patients.

WHAT CAN YOU DO ABOUT A NEGATIVE DECISION?

You will not be in direct contact with the PSRO. The first you will know of its decision will be a denial of your claim by Medicare. Chapter 18 tells you how to appeal a Medicare claim with which you do not agree.

HOW CAN A PSRO POSSIBLY REVIEW SO MANY SERVICES?

It would be difficult for the organization to personally evaluate all the covered services under its bailiwick, so certain procedures have to be set up to make this easier.

Among the procedures are written norms, criteria, and standards of care, diagnosis and treatment. These are arrived at by observation and compilation of statistics, and establish typical patterns in the area for such services as length of hospital or nursing-home stay, adjusted for age and diagnosis. Presumably the information provided by your doctor will establish the reason, if you need more care or a more extended hospital or nursing-home stay than the average patient in your situation. Any deviation from the average established by these standards would probably have to be justified. For instance, if half of the patients with the same medical problems you have are being discharged from the hospital after one week, it will be up to your doctor to show why you need to be hospitalized for two weeks.

Doctors and institutions are made understandably nervous by the existence of a review organization, and the more timid doctors will tend to lean over backward to avoid denial of treatment they have recommended. There is, however, a sound reason for the existence of this type of organization, even if its decisions are sometimes somewhat arbitrary.

WHY SHOULD THERE BE A PSRO?

As we have seen in the section on unnecessary surgery, health-care providers are no different from any other group in needing some supervision and some check on their operation. The PSRO performs three functions: (1) it determines whether the covered services were actually needed; (2) it examines whether the services provided met standards of professional quality; and (3) it determines whether the service is being provided appropriately.

Services Actually Needed

Unnecessary surgery is an example of a service that might be provided when it was not actually needed. While denial of coverage may work against a beneficiary in that it may deny services that the doctor may honestly think are needed, it also works for the beneficiary in that it tends to discourage a proliferation of services that put the patient under mental, physical and financial strain and are not needed at all. We all know instances where doctors have called for numerous office visits and where the patient learned subsequently that these were not necessary, the suspicion arising that the doctor was using this comparatively painless way of augmenting his income. Similarly, a hospital with a large number of empty beds may be reluctant to lose its patients to a nursing home, even though they no longer require hospital-level care. Outside review acts as a check on rising health-care costs and can benefit the consumer of health-care services. The fact that there are also disadvantages is unavoidable and simply must be recognized and dealt with through the appeals process.

Professional Quality

Quality control is even more essential in the delivery of health care than it is, for example, in the production of safe automobiles. Any effort in this direction should be encouraged.

Appropriate Service

In any area where specialized knowledge is needed, it is difficult for the consumer of the service to evaluate the need for it. An example of this is the ability of automobile mechanics to talk you into unnecessary work on your car: you have no way of knowing whether a certain gizmo is shot and really needs replacing, and you must depend on the honesty of the mechanic. Or it may be that you do need the gizmo, but you do not need to have the oil changed and liquid added to your window-washer reservoir at the same time. Tacked-on health-care services are difficult for the consumer to recognize, but the PSRO keeps a sharp eye out for them and will question any that come to its attention.

WHO SERVES ON THE PSRO?

The PSRO is made up entirely of physcians and any physician may serve on a voluntary basis.

WHAT IS THE DIFFERENCE BETWEEN THE PSRO AND A UTILIZATION COMMITTEE?

There is no difference in function. Sometimes it is the PSRO, sometimes a utilization committee, that makes the determination of "medical necessity." Changes are constantly being made; for instance, in my area the PSRO has just been replaced by the utilization committee.

IF INSTITUTIONALIZATION IS DENIED, HOW MUCH NOTICE IS GIVEN?

If the PSRO determines that your hospital stay or extended stay in a nursing home (SNF) is no longer medically necessary, it will notify you that Medicare coverage is about to end.

The question that naturally arises is how much notice are you given—in other words, how much time do you have to make arrangements to leave or to decide to stay on at your own expense?

Generally speaking, you are given 24 hours' notice. Since in some cases, such as leaving the hospital for an SNF, it may take longer than that to complete the arrangements, you may be granted an additional three days. This extension may also be granted if you are going home but need time to arrange for someone to be there to take care of you. This extension is not automatic; it is granted on a case-by-case basis and you must explain why an extension is needed.

Sometimes the hospital is informed of denial of further Medicare coverage but neglects to tell you about it right away. If you do not leave in time because of this, the Waiver of Beneficiary Liability comes into play and you will be covered under those terms; however, you must still leave within the usual period after the hospital has notified you.

One to four days is not much notice, so it is well to be aware, when you are in the hospital or nursing home (SNF), that this can happen. Your doctor can often warn you ahead of time that your condition is such that this may happen, and you should talk over with him what plans you should make in that eventuality.

V
BEYOND MEDICARE—MEDIGAP INSURANCE

21

What Is Medigap Insurance and Why Do You Need It?

Medigap insurance is insurance that pays some of the health-care costs that Medicare does not; for instance, the deductible and coinsurance of Medicare Part A (HI) are often paid by Medigap insurance. Since the majority of Medicare recipients own Medigap policies, any thorough discussion of Medicare should include a look at Medigap.

The reason so many Medicare recipients own Medigap policies is because they realize the inadequacy of Medicare coverage. It is estimated that Medicare pays less than 40% of total health-care costs of the elderly. You must pay for the majority of health-care costs out of your own pocket, and each year the percentage you must pay grows larger. A beneficiary pays far more for health care today, with Medicare coverage, than he would have had to pay 60 years ago (adjusted for inflation) before Medicare.

People who depend solely on Medicare to cover their health-care costs are like a sleeper trying to keep warm in a double bed under a stadium throw: most of the area will be out in the cold.

Most people realize that they cannot hope to have enough income or assets to meet health-care costs for any serious illness. As we have seen, an extended hospital stay with full Medicare coverage can cost over $10,000 out-of-pocket, not including the bills from physicians, surgeons and all the other health-care services for which the hospital patient is billed. It is obviously essential, if you can possibly afford it, to supplement Medicare coverage with private health-insurance coverage. The decision is easy to make; it is not, unfortunately, so easy to implement.

IS THERE ANYONE WHO DOESN'T NEED MEDIGAP INSURANCE?

If you were very rich and didn't have to worry no matter how high your health-care bills ran, I guess you wouldn't absolutely need extra insurance. But in that case, you would probably be smart enough to buy it anyway.

About the only other time you don't need it is if your income and assets are low enough to qualify you for Medicaid. Your income must be very low, and you can own practically nothing, before you can qualify; if you think you may be in this category, get in touch with your local social security office.

Don't hesitate to apply for Medicaid if you think you can get it; Medicaid coverage beats Medicare all hollow. It covers many more services and comes much closer to the national health plans of other industrialized nations.

If you don't qualify now, keep it in mind. Many seniors who thought they had enough to manage on for the rest of their lives find their assets quickly depleted once they run out of Medicare coverage and are paying all their health-care costs themselves. In a situation like that, Medicaid may be a true safety net.

WHAT MEDIGAP WILL NOT DO

If you are contemplating buying a Medigap policy, it is important that you do not do so with unreal expectations.

Medigap policies are misleadingly named, because they do not cover all the gaps by any means.

Here are some examples of gaps in Medigap policies:

- Medicare covers only those nursing homes classified as SNFs; Medigap policies do too. What most people think of as nursing homes are not covered by Medicare and usually are not covered by private insurance either.

- Medicare pays only 80% of covered charges; Medigap policies pay only 20% of covered charges. In other words, unless your doctor or other provider accepts the assignment, chances are you will have to pick up the amount over and above the covered charge, even with Medigap insurance.

- In Medicare, hospital coverage ceases after 90 days' hospitalization in a single benefit period (unless you use your Lifetime Reserve days). Most Medigap policies stop paying hospital costs when Medicare does. If possible, look for a policy that pays when Medicare doesn't.

A Federal Trade Commission report on Medigap insurance concluded: "Although the definition of inadequate coverage is open to debate, it is indisputable that Medicare supplement policies often fail to cover important gaps in Medicare."

The Federal Trade Commission also took a dim view of the benefits to be gotten from a Medigap policy compared to its costs: "Medicare supplement policies pay back in benefits only a relatively low percentage of dollars paid in premiums. Loss ratios for hospital indemnity, nursing home and low-value Medicare supplement policies run around 40 percent. Expense factors of 50 to 60 percent are not uncommon."*

* Federal Trade Commission *Report on Medigap,* 1978.

As Medicare beneficiaries look into Medigap insurance, they become aware of its deficiencies and, in an effort to gain security, often end up buying several policies and duplicating coverage.

In 1978, the Federal Trade Commission issued a two-volume report which opened with the following paragraph:

Health care costs are a major expense and source of concern for the elderly. Medicare covers only 38% of their health care costs [1976 figures]. People over 65 must pay for many kinds of care which Medicare will never cover, including drugs, dental care, eyeglasses, hearing aides, routine examinations and most nursing home care. Even after Medicare and private insurance, the average per capita health care expenditure for the over-65 age group was $403—much more than they paid out-of-pocket before Medicare.

Since that study, out-of-pocket costs have doubled.

In its study, the FTC found that not only do over 50% of seniors have at least one policy but that 23%—almost half—have two or more policies with "unnecessary duplication in coverage." The Commission also found that most of these unnecessary policies were sold door-to-door or through mail-order advertisements. Most of these policies are sold by playing on the individual's fear that he or she would not be covered in the case of a serious illness. The fear is real but the solution offered by policies of this sort is not; even a good Medigap policy does not provide complete health-insurance coverage. Because of the situation uncovered by this study, the government has recently passed certain laws regulating Medigap policies, and many states, such as Connecticut and Wisconsin, have tightened up their insurance regulations. The consumer is better protected today than at any time in history but he or she must still beware.

It is not easy to find a good Medigap policy and you

cannot depend on the salesman to have your best interests at heart—he may, but you cannot depend on it. Since this is such an important purchase, let us see what we can learn about buying a good policy.

22

How to Buy a Medigap Policy

One of the things that make it so difficult to compare policies is the lack of standardization. The best way to deal with that is to learn the different categories into which Medigap policies fall. There are four basic types.

MEDICARE SUPPLEMENT POLICY

This type of policy will pay some or all of the deductibles and coinsurance you would otherwise have to pay out-of-pocket. It follows Medicare's guidelines as to covered services and reasonable charges. There are many variations in this type of policy. Some will pay for only Medicare Part A deductibles and coinsurance; some will pay for only Medicare Part B; some will cover both. You must read the policies and compare what they offer with the cost of the premium.

The best Medicare supplement policy covers both Medicare A and B. The best policy also goes beyond Medicare coverage and covers hospital or nursing-home expenses even when Medicare coverage has ended. It also covers some prescription drugs and other medicines that Medicare does not cover.

It may be, however, that this type of policy will be too expensive for you or may not be worth the amount of the premium. If you cannot find a policy that gives you all these features at a price you can afford, look around until you find one you can afford and see what you have had to give up. You may be able to find a policy at a lower premium that gives you a pretty good deal; you will have to shop around and compare policies to see which is best. If you have to choose, it is generally considered more important to have good Part B coverage, but this is not necessarily true.

CONTINUATION OR CONVERSION OF PRE-65 INSURANCE

If you have had a policy prior to becoming eligible for Medicare, you may be able to convert it to Medigap coverage. Most Blue Cross/Blue Shield policies are convertible; so are many of the policies you will have through your job. You should examine the policy to see what you get for your money, but there is a good chance that this type of policy will be satisfactory. If it is, there are certain advantages. First of all, the insurance company already knows your physical condition, so it will not require a physical or medical record or information from your doctor. Second, and most important, it will not exclude any health problem you may have as a "pre-existing condition." You will get continuous coverage without a waiting period. If you have this type of insurance through your job, your employer may continue to pick up all or part of the premium (the premium will be much smaller because of your Medicare coverage).

In the event you decide on this type of policy, be sure your husband or wife is covered; you may have to buy a separate policy for him or her.

INDEMNITY POLICY

There are three kinds of indemnity policies: hospital indemnity, nursing-home indemnity and medical indemnity (based on Medicare Part B services, such as doctor bills). Sometimes a policy will overlap categories and cover parts of each one of the three, but all come under the heading of "limited coverage policies."

The feature all indemnity policies have in common is that they do not pay specific bills but pay you specific cash amounts. You are free to use this cash any way you want to and these policies seem to be very attractive to a large number of people. Since these policies pay in addition to any other insurance you have, it often appears that this type of insurance will allow you to plug any leaks in your other health policies.

Many insurance experts feel that indemnity policies are not as good an insurance investment as more comprehensive policies would be. One way you may be able to decide is to compare the amount paid with the amount of the premium; often the premium is so high that the amount you are likely to collect doesn't even cover the premium.

Amounts paid vary considerably from one policy to another. One policy, for instance, may pay you a dollar amount for each day you are in the hospital, starting with the day of admission; the amount may vary from $7 a day to $20 or more a day. Since Medicare pays 100% of hospital charges from the 1st to the 60th day, this is really money you can spend on other costs. Other policies may not start payments until you have been in the hospital a week (which is still within the 100% coverage period). Since the average hospital stay is about a week, you may never collect anything on this part of the policy.

The inadequacies of the policy become more evident

when you begin to pay hospital coinsurance. For instance, when Medicare required a coinsurance of $51 a day for the 61st to the 90th day, Colonial Penn paid only $10 a day. So even with the policy, you would have had to pay $41 out of your own pocket. If you bought a more expensive policy that covered you for 371 days, it paid $9.50 at a time when Medicare paid nothing; $9.50 a day wouldn't go very far toward paying a hospital bill.

The Federal Trade Commission, after studying indemnity polices, concluded, "Although owners of indemnity policies could use the dollars they receive to pay Medicare deductibles and coinsurance, the rate of return on these policies is so low that they would be better to place their money in another form of investment."

DREAD-DISEASE POLICIES

Policies of this type offer very limited coverage, usually only for a specific disease. The insurance salesman for this type of policy usually tries to play on your fear about cancer, for instance, and paints a grim picture of the costs you can incur if you get it. This type of policy is so poorly thought of that some states won't even allow it to be sold. Generally speaking, any good health policy will give you the same coverage, plus much, much more, at a comparatively reasonable premium.

In addition to the fact that the basic premise of the policy is not sound, many of these dread-disease policies have a maximum amount they will pay that is far below what you can reasonably expect treatment to cost. They also have restrictions as to the type of treatment they will cover and the type of facilities where you can receive covered treatment.

Consumers Union warns that the dread-disease policies it has examined "offer only fragmentary protection against the cost of treatment . . . [and] offer no coverage at all for your numerous other disease that can also be expensive to treat."

Most policies you will be offered will contain elements of one or more of the above types. The many variations each company offers means that inevitably there will be an overlapping; a policy may be both supplementary medical *and* indemnity. Since one company offers 77 different types of policies, you can see that shopping for a good one is not an easy task.

THE IMPOSSIBLE DREAM

Once you know what Medicare doesn't cover, it would seem to be easy to look for a policy that covers all other health-care costs. The reason it isn't is because no such animal exists. The State of California, in a study of health insurance, noted there is "a great demand for a supplemental policy which would provide complete coverage, but [we have] rejected the idea as unworkable because premiums would be too high." The FTC study reached the same conclusion: "The cost of a policy that really filled the gaps would be prohibitive." You won't find the perfect Medigap policy—one that pays all your health-care expenses not covered by Medicare.

In its 1978 report on Medigap insurance, the FTC found that no existing policy covered physicians' charges above the level Medicare determined to be reasonable. Since the spread between Medicare's so-called reasonable charge and the actual fees physicians are charging is widening every year, and since fewer and fewer physicians in the most high-priced areas are accepting the assignment, the over-65 patient is paying more and more of his own doctor bills and other health-care costs every year.

No Medigap policy, the FTC says, will pay for items and services Medicare does not cover. Since these include such absolute necessities as hearing aids and eyeglasses, many seniors are making do with old appliances and devices that are no longer appropriate for their condition. When the cost of a new pair of eyeglasses can easily run over $100—especially for bifocals—many social security recipients must make do with old and inadequate ones.

There are a few policies, carry-overs from group insurance, that cover part of prescription drugs or dental care. The sparseness with which these policies exist or are available to the elderly is shown by the extent of coverage: in 1975 only 16.9% had coverage for prescription drugs and only 1.9% had coverage for dental care.

No Medigap policy covers custodial care in a nursing home or in one's own home. Since Medicare coverage for most nursing-home care is nonexistent, this is one of the most serious of all gaps.

In the area of the SNF—the only kind of nursing home covered even partially by Medicare—Medigap policies cover, at most, the Medicare deductibles. Since these benefits cease after 100 days in an SNF, you aren't buying as much as you might think with a Medigap policy that covers only the deductible for the first 100 days.

If the Medigap policy you are considering includes "nursing-home coverage," be sure you understand exactly what kind of nursing home is meant and the extent of the coverage. If it is limited to the kind of coverage provided by Medicare, there is no coinsurance for it to pay on the average stay because Medicare pays 100% of the first 20 days of an approved stay in an approved nursing home. Unless the policy picks up the cost from the 20th day on, or unless it pays for custodial care or care in a nursing home that is not an SNF, it must offer a sizable benefit of some other sort to be worth the premium.

Many policyholders expect Medigap to cover the amount of the provider's bill that is over and above what Medicare approves as the reasonable charge. Most policies will pay the 20% coinsurance of the reasonable charge but no more than that. Keep in mind that most policies use Medicare guidelines in deciding what to cover. Even with Medigap, you will usually have heavy out-of-pocket expenses if the provider refuses to accept the assignment.

Once you know that you cannot find the perfect policy, you will realize that you will have to make a decision as to which benefits are most important to you and how much you can afford to pay for them. You can lower your premiums by accepting a higher deductible and by eliminating those provisions for which you may have least need.

Many experts, for example, feel that you shouldn't buy a policy that pays the deductibles and coinsurance; they think coverage should begin beyond those costs. There are many reasons for this viewpoint but these are still the features that most beneficiaries find attractive. Compare the cost and coverage of policies that do not cover these items and see whether you do not benefit greatly by paying those costs yourself.

CATASTROPHIC OR MAJOR-MEDICAL POLICIES

Although you want to beware of duplication of policies, this type of policy is important to have, either in addition to, or instead of, a regular health-care policy. Its function is to protect you against major health-care costs, and because of this, it usually has a high deductible—$1,000 or more. Unfortunately, this type of policy is usually not available except as a group policy and, as far as I know, does not exist for the over-65 person. If you are under 65 and have a good health policy, you may be able to get this kind of coverage after 65 by conversion. If you can possibly afford it, it is desirable—if you can get it.

THINGS TO CONSIDER WHEN LOOKING AT A POLICY

1. Buy from a Reputable Company

You still have to be a careful consumer and not be lulled into a false sense of security by a well-advertised name, but an insurance company with a good reputation is a better bet than some fly-by-night outfit you have never heard of. A good company is not necessarily the one with the most television advertising. It is a company your insurance friends speak of with respect and one that projects a certain amount of dignity and concern in its advertising and promotion. Its salesmen will not use disreputable tactics (which we will go into later), nor will they be reluctant to explain the benefits and show you where in the policy these benefits are guaranteed. On the other hand, they are in business to sell policies, and it wouldn't make sense for them to lose the sale by telling you about a better policy sold by a competitor. What you have to remember about an insurance salesman is that no matter how friendly he is, he is not your friend.

2. Look for Easy-to-Understand Language

Policies are now supposed to be written so that the average person can understand them; if yours is not, be suspicious.

3. Look for Easy-to-Read Printing

Companies that put provisions in small print or on shaded or colored backgrounds are hoping you won't be able to read them, or that it will be so much trouble that you will skip that part. Small print or hard-to-read areas are not a good sign, and you should make an effort to read those areas extra carefully even if you have to use a magnifying glass to do so.

4. Look for the Delivery Provision

A policy should state how soon it will be delivered after you sign it. No insurance company should take more than thirty days to send you the policy. If it does, ask the company for a written explanation of the delay. If sixty days go by, get in touch with your State Insurance Department.

5. Check the Loss Ratio

Loss ratio is a way of measuring the percentage of premium dollars that the company returns in benefit payments. It shows very clearly whether the company is weighting the odds too heavily in its own favor. The lower the ratio, the less chance you will get your money's worth out of that policy. It's a little bit like house odds on a roulette wheel; the worse the odds for the individual gambler, the poorer chance he has of winning.

You can't figure out the odds on your getting a particular illness or of needing certain coverage, but the insurance company can, and that is how they set their rates. If they don't pay out a reasonably high percentage of their premium money in benefits, they have given themselves too much margin. Loss ratios for hospital indemnity, nursing-home and poor Medigap policies run about 40%. The Blues are highly regarded for their Medigap policies partly because their loss ratios are 85–90%; in other words, you get more for your premium dollar with the Blues than with many other companies. In an example cited in the FTC report, they found that a Wisconsin Blues policy with fairly comprehensive Medigap coverage cost $95.40 a year while a rival insurance company's policy, offering much poorer coverage, cost $200 a year.

6. Study the Pre-existing Condition Clause

From the standpoint of the purchaser of health insurance, this is one of the most dangerous clauses in the policy; from the standpoint of the insurance company, it is often one of the most lucrative.

A company that makes a practice of not paying claims can do wonders with its interpretation of this clause. Not only can they deny coverage for pre-existing conditions for a considerable length of time, they can decide that *new illnesses are the result of old ones.* For example, if you have a disease that includes dizziness among its symptoms, and you subsequently fall and break your hip, the insurance company may refuse to pay the claim for the hip on the grounds that the fall was caused by the pre-existing condition (dizziness). It is amazing how ingenious the companies can be, and the policyholder, unless he or she is willing and able to go to court, has no recourse.

It is a clause that puts a special burden on the elderly because by the age of 65, most people have a health record that includes at least a few chronic conditions. The more obvious ones like diabetes or arthritis are clearly excluded from coverage by this clause, but—by the very nature of these diseases—it is entirely possible to argue that most of your other troubles stem from these diseases. What this means is that the illnesses for which you are most liable to need coverage are the very ones that may not be covered. A health-insurance policy that will pay for practically no diseases that you can acquire, except bubonic plague or an ectopic pregnancy, isn't much good to you.

One of the advantages of a health maintenance organization is that there is no pre-existing limitation on HMO coverage (see Chapter 24). However, if that option is not available to you, get the policy with the shortest waiting time on exclusions, and do not buy any policy that will *never* cover pre-existing conditions.

This pre-existing condition clause is one of the devices that unscrupulous agents—the kind that tell you to cancel your old policy because they will write you a better one—use to keep from ever having to pay any of your claims. Each time you take out a new policy, you enter a new waiting period; these agents often time their visits to coincide with premium payments. They tell you not to send in the premium but to give them the check instead; then they use it to write you a new policy, canceling your old one. Or they sell you a new and "better" policy, without pointing out that your old policy has now become effective for pre-existing conditions and that buying a new policy will lose you that advantage and will put you in a new waiting period.

Not all insurance salesmen are dishonest by any means, but even the honest ones are not always selling the best policy you could buy because their company—possibly a very reputable company—may not be writing the best policy of that particular sort.

If you have a good reason for taking out a new policy and canceling your old one, do not cancel the old one as soon as you take out the new. Keep the old policy in effect—even if it means paying one additional premium—until the waiting period for the exclusion for pre-existing conditions is over and the new policy is completely in effect. HCFA suggest this as a way of protecting yourself in the event a pre-existing condition should worsen before your new insurance covers it.

7. Don't Buy Too Many Policies

As we have seen, no one policy will cover everything. Any salesman can show you where his policy will cover something your present policy will not, but he will not point out all the areas where you are paying for duplicate coverage. You cannot collect from more than one policy for the same coverage no matter how many premiums you pay. So any duplication of coverage is a waste of your money. The only way to compare policies is to make two columns and list in one all the coverage from one policy, and in the other all the coverage from the other policy. This is the only way you can compare benefits without becoming totally confused. The salesman may try to discourage you from doing this because it may make the areas of duplication of coverage very clear.

8. Look for the Maximum Benefit

Even when a policy covers a certain area, they probably have a limit as to the total amount of money they will pay you in your lifetime. The limit may be dollars per disease; it may also be expressed as number of days or visits or something similar. If you cannot find this information in the policy, ask to be shown where it is. If the salesman can't find it but promises you his company is good for such-and-such coverage, insist on having it in writing from the company. If it isn't in writing, you won't be able to collect a penny.

9. Check the Conditions for Renewal

A policy that is "renewable at company option" is like a rug that can be pulled out from under you at any time.

The company may decide not to renew because you have become ill and, after years of paying premiums, are now in a position to collect. It should not be possible for a company to make any changes in your policy unless it is, at the same time, making those changes for all its policyholders.

10. Ask About a "Free Look"

You can't compare policies if you can't get hold of the policies. Even if you have already paid the first premium, you should have ten days in which to change your mind. Do your homework by comparing the promotional material each reputable company puts out—with lists of benefits clearly stated—so that you have a fairly good idea how one stacks up against the other. Make your columns for comparison. Then go through the actual policy or policies to see if there are any booby traps—clauses the salesman forgot to mention and the company forgot to put in its promotion. Here is where the nine points we have just discussed can act as a checklist.

TWO HEADS ARE BETTER THAN ONE

When you are considering buying health insurance, talk it over with as many friends and acquaintances as possible. You may uncover stories of experiences they have had that will be helpful to you. You might even consider having insurance salesmen come to speak to your senior center—a different one each luncheon. The salesmen will have to adjust their sales pitch when they find themselves confronted with a roomful of prospects rather than one, but that could be a good thing. Then your group could make a project of comparing policies, and what could otherwise be a somewhat tedious project could become a very interesting one. You should all feel free to ask questions at this time. Be prepared to sit on the member who wants to buy a policy "because he was such a nice young man."

Include in your consideration policies from such organizations as the AARP (American Association of Retired Persons), who do not send salesmen but who will send you complete information so that you may compare their policies with the others.

23

The Hard Sell—When Not to Buy Medigap Insurance

While most insurance salesmen and most insurance companies are reputable, there are some that are not a credit to the industry. Since this type of insurance is most often sold to the elderly, it is well for you to be aware of what goes on and to learn to recognize the signs that the pleasant young man at your door is no better than a con man.

Here are some signs that should warn you to be extra careful of any policy the salesman tries to sell you.

A Salesman Who Claims He Is Selling a Government Policy

The government is not in the insurance business (unless you count Medicare), and it certainly does not send salesmen around door to door to sell health-insurance policies. Fly-by-night companies sometimes give themselves vague names that make them sound as if they are part of the government. They even print up their literature to look as if it came from Washington, D.C., complete with official-looking seals, promotional material with a government "look," envelopes just the size of social security envelopes, and direct-mail letters that start out, "Dear Medicare Member..."

Their job is made easier by the confusing names that the government gives some programs. For example, Medicare Part B is called Supplementary Medical Insurance and Medicare literature refers to Medigap as "Medicare Supplemental Policies." That is a little too close for comfort and can easily be confusing to a Medicare beneficiary.

A Salesman Who Is Vague About His Company or Himself

The first thing you ask any insurance salesman, even if he has called and made an appointment to see you, is for his business card. If the card has only his name on it, if it lacks a phone number or a business name and address, ask him for that information and write it down. If he refuses to give you that information (and he may not refuse outright but may try to distract you), insist, and do not continue the conversation until you have it. If he gives you that information, phone the number as soon as he leaves and see if the information checks out and if it really seems to be a business office.

A Salesman Who Cannot Produce Proof of Licensing

Insurance companies must meet certain requirements in order to do business within the state. Proof that they have met these requirements is a license. Agents, also, must be licensed by the state and must carry the proof of licensing on them at all times. This license must show the name of the agent and the name of the company. If the salesman cannot produce this proof, do not talk to him further.

A Salesman Who Offers You a Break If You Pay Your First Premium in Cash

Never, *under any circumstances,* pay cash at any time. If you do not have a checking account, you can get a money order or a bank draft. Make sure the payment is made in the name of the company. Never make out a check, money order or bank draft in the name of the salesman; no proper salesman would even suggest it.

A Salesman Who Asks You to Sign a Blank Application Form and Says He Will Fill It Out for You

This practice is called "clean-sheeting." You and only you should fill out the application form. Get a friend to help you if you find forms a little confusing. Do not sign a blank form. Your policy will be granted on the basis of the information in the form. If it is inaccurate in any way, the insurance company may grant the policy but refuse to pay when you make a claim, on the grounds that the information was incomplete or incorrect. Remember, insurance companies exchange information, check with doctors and hospitals and have many sources of information about the state of your health. You fool only yourself when you give inaccurate or untruthful information. The salesman may try to talk you into omitting or minimizing certain health problems in order to get the policy through the company, but you will be paying premiums for nothing because you will not be able to collect when the time comes.

A Salesman Who Suggests He See You Alone

Any salesman who suggests he see you alone should not be seen at all. If he has an honest presentation to make, why should he object to your having a friend present? (Don't ask him; he'll have a glib answer.) Even if you don't know someone smart about insurance, have someone there anyhow. For all the salesman knows, your friend is an expert, so he will automatically be more careful in his sales pitch if a third person is present. Also, a salesman will be more likely to be intimidated if your friend is a man.

A Salesman Who Tries to Switch Your Policies

A salesman makes money only on the policies he sells and the largest commissions are earned in the first year a policy is in effect; sometimes the entire first year's commission goes to the salesman.

With this kind of an incentive, it is no wonder a salesman may try to sell you a new policy when the one you have is all you need. Instead of suggesting you need another policy, he may suggest that you can improve your coverage by canceling your old policy and taking out his new one. This practice is called "twisting" or "rolling over" a policy. Compare his policy with your present one and you will soon see whether what he says is true. Remember to take into account the "pre-existing conditions" clause and any other exclusions or waiting periods.

A Salesman Who Tells You the Policy Has a Number of Benefits That Aren't Listed in the Sales Brochure

The company won't pay on his say-so; if he can't show you the benefits in writing in the sales literature, and later in the actual policy, assume he is exaggerating and that those benefits are not really part of the policy.

A Salesman Who Tries to Sell You More Insurance Than You Can Afford

No reputable salesman will try to sell you insurance that is so far beyond your means that you have to borrow money to pay the premiums. Yet unscrupulous salesmen have done just that. Before you talk to an insurance person, you should go over your finances and have an idea of how much you can afford to spend per year for premiums. If you can't afford it, don't buy it—you'll just lose whatever money you do put into it.

UNSAVORY PRACTICES

In case you think I am exaggerating the problems you may run into when trying to buy health insurance to supplement Medicare, let me tell you about some of the information gathered by congressional hearings on Medigap insurance.

In 1978, Senator Lawton Chiles conducted a hearing before the Special Committee on Aging to look into the problems and abuses of Medigap policies. Speaking at that time he said, "I was distressed to hear from consumers and state insurance commissioners that many older Americans were clearly being taken advantage of by unscrupulous insurance agents eager to make high commissions.

"We were also distressed to hear that in some cases insurance company policies encourage oversale and misrepresentation of health insurance policies to the elderly— while the insurance company at the same time does not take the responsibility for its own agents. . . .

"We have heard of insurance salesmen offering door prizes at senior centers and other programs for older

Americans to obtain membership lists—lists which are then routinely used to sell insurance policies.

"Sales agents have described company directives requiring them to sell new policies on every service visit, to write new policies rather than to renew current ones, and to delete medical histories on new policy forms.

"We have also had reports of companies routinely denying claims when they first come in—taking the better-than-average chance that the elderly policyholder will not challenge their judgment and re-submit a claim.

"Relatives have written who were outraged when they discovered an elderly parent with many insurance policies and large accumulations of canceled checks to insurance companies. One from Marathon, Florida, said:

'Last spring I learned that my 88-year-old aunt . . . whose income is less than $5,000 a year . . . had been sold more than $10,000 of health insurance in approximately a one-year period.'

"Age, rather than income, targets the group at which these salesmen aim. Wiley L. Cheatham, District Attorney from Cuero, Texas, testifying at the hearing, described examples from his area: 'Both the rich and poor alike are victims of these schemes. We had an ex-Governor's close relative who was victimized regularly. . . . We have a district judge's elderly mother and aunt who were regularly taken each year for considerable sums of money, unbeknownst to the judge. This is one area that the younger relatives might want to take note, because these elderly people like to feel that they are handling their own business; that they are getting insurance and won't have to fall back on their children; so very often they don't tell their closest relatives of the business transactions they have had. . . . We had several wealthy widows, one of them who has a ranch in excess of 10,000 acres in Texas, and much more land in New Mexico. She was one of the regular customers. They would more or less vie for who would go in there and write a big policy.

"'Then, of course, [Cheatham continues] you have many of the poorer senior citizens living in low-cost housing units. We have found quite often that the agents would have to time their visits so that they would get there after the social security checks came in so they could take advantage of the social security checks.'

"If the typical victim can be either rich or poor, are there any common characteristics and how do so many salesmen discover these vulnerable persons?

"The typical victim is over 65 and usually living alone. It may be a man or a woman, but is more likely to be a widow. The victims are not, as one might expect, senile but they are lonely and tend to judge the salesman by external appearance. A good-looking, friendly, well-dressed salesman who is sympathetic and appears helpful can soon win the trust of many of the people he talks to; that is his main skill. The elderly person comes to look forward to his visits and to trust in his advice. Since health insurance is complicated—and made to appear even more so by the language and format (small print, gray color blocs) of the policies—the prospective purchaser tends to take the salesman's word for what the policy covers and whether or not it is needed.

"In this area the victim tends not to consult with children or relatives. In an effort to maintain independence and to retain a feeling of control over her affairs, she will try to handle purchases of health insurance on her own.

"As soon as a salesman discovers a 'hot' prospect, he passes the word around. The victim list that is thus compiled is known as a 'Goose List' and is something like the mark tramps used to put on house fences and back doors to tell other tramps it was a good spot for a hand-out. Here is a sample of listings from an actual goose list [addresses and telephone numbers deleted]:

MAGGIE.   This is a *cinch* sale, easy to talk to.

MYRTLE.   This one is a good deal but she likes Reserve Life, so handle with ease—sell on idea of lowering rates she now pays.

WILMA.   This one is tough but has always been sold heavy, but you have to stroke it on her—

EULA.   This lady is as goosy as two skinks. Cinch sales, $200–$250.

EVA.   This is a jamp-up good one for anyone.

LOTTIE.   E.J. has sold this deal four or five times. He can't write nothing but goosies. Try her.

WILLYNE.   These are two sisters here and another one that lives somewhere else; they buy for her too—good for $2,000 or $3,000. Cinch.

ADDIE.   This is a small deal, but is a sale.

ZELA.   This lady is a goose. Talk to her about her quilts that she makes. Buy one from her—pay her half and stroke it on her—

PAULINE.   This is a goose but watch out for her daughter.

REMA.   This one is just a plain old goose; not too big but sale inevitable.

RUTH.   This is a good one; handle easy, nice to talk to.

ZORA.   This one is goosy for a policy that pays everything for home and office calls.

ULYSSES.   This is an old man and is a good deal. Go in and talk about playing guitar; he likes that kind of ———. Has daughter but she don't mess with his business.

LAURA.   This is a sale, but don't have very much money (sorry about that).

MOLLIE.   This lady has always bought good. She wants a policy that pays for rest home. She won't have anything else. Go to back door.

RUBY.   This one is hot as a three-dollar bill, so send someone on this.

MYRTLE.   This one is a cinch. Make like you are lowering her principle."

Senator Chiles has this to say about this type of insurance salesman: "I think the information that is on this goose list gives you an idea of the type of people who are preying on the elderly, and their total and complete lack of any kind of feeling whatsoever. I can't think of anything much more heinous than people who would run this kind of scheme."

Are you on the insurance salesmen's goose list? Do not let that friendly, pleasant young man distract you from reading the policy, and, best of all, always have a friend sit in on any sales pitch.

DOES ALL THIS MEAN I SHOULDN'T BUY MEDIGAP INSURANCE?

Not at all. As long as you realize that no policy is going to pay all of your health-care costs and as long as you politely usher to the door any salesman who says, "I have a policy that will cover everything that Medicare doesn't cover," there is no reason why you shouldn't buy some peace of mind with a carefully chosen policy.

If you use the loss-ratio method of rating policies, you can be sure of at least getting your premium dollar's worth. Do not be carried away by the emotional appeal of certain benefits—such as the thought of all the cash an indemnity policy will put in your hands in case of illness. The California Department of Insurance estimates that it cost, on the average, $30 a year to buy insurance for the $60 annual Part B deductible (now $75). The loss-ratio method would have kept you from buying that policy.

Do not hesitate to ask the salesman what the loss ratio is on the policy he is trying to sell you. If it is good, he will be delighted to tell you so. If it isn't and he hedges, look at some other policies.

24

HMO—More Than
Alternative Health Insurance

The typical health-insurance policy has been described as "a hunting license . . . a permit to go look for care." At best it pays after the fact; getting the people to provide the health care you need is your problem. In contrast, an HMO—health maintenance organization—guarantees *delivery* of the very services for which you are buying insurance coverage. Primary-care physicians, specialists, therapists, nursing staff and the necessary equipment and laboratory technicians are immediately available when you need them. It is not necessary to search out personnel or a facility each time; no need to trot around from office to office; and you are freed from the awkwardness of asking the doctor and supplier to accept the assignment—as well as the distinct possibility that your request may be refused.

Clearly, in considering a health-insurance policy to supplement Medicare, the senior citizen should consider prepaid health-care plans such as the health maintainance organizations or HMOs. Not only will an HMO provide everything in the usual Medigap policy, it will include much preventive medicine and the convenience and accessibility of a complete health-care service. The basic premise of an HMO is that prepaying health-care costs reduces them. It has been clearly established that HMO members have a lower rate of hospitalization than non-HMO members—partly due to the beneficial effects of preventive medicine, partly to a reduction in nonessential surgery and partly due to discharge planning that works with the patient to arrange for post-hospital care.

John Nelson, president of the Greater Delaware Valley Health Care, Inc., an HMO in Radnor, Pennsylvania, describes the decline in hospitalization in the HMO that services the UAW (among others) in Detroit: "When Medicare was introduced in 1965, the opportunity was provided for auto workers to continue during retirement as members of the HMO. Today, the members have aged in the plan—about 7,000 older citizens, people over 65, are Medicare beneficiaries. They are using approximately 2,300 inpatient days of hospital care per 1,000 enrollees per year. Now that rate is considerably less than the going rate nationally which I believe . . . is close to 3,500 to 4,000 days per 1,000. Kaiser reports in a recent issue of Group Health News that their over-65 population is using something on the order of 1,950 days per 1,000 members per year. The savings on inpatient days are used to provide more comprehensive benefits beyond the Medicare benefits to their senior population which they have enrolled."

In other words, not only has HMO membership lowered the cost of health care, it has enabled the over-65 members to avoid the illnesses that require hospitalization and has reinvested the savings in such a way as to broaden the benefits covered.

A PROVEN RECORD

You may never have heard of an HMO but it is far from a new idea. The first one was formed in 1927 and the one that is presently the largest in the country, the Kaiser Permanente Plan, was started in 1938. Since its small beginnings, the HMO movement has grown until it has received the federal government's stamp of approval—so much so that every employer with a health-care plan must offer HMO membership as an alternative, if there is an HMO available. As a result, unions—such as the United Automobile Workers—are large participants in these plans, and membership is growing by leaps and bounds every year.

In 1979, Senator John Heinz sponsored two bills (S. 1485 and S. 1530) "to address some of the inherent flaws in our current reimbursement system for health care services and to open greater options in the delivery of health care services for older Americans . . . [and to] encourage greater participation by older persons in health organizations by offering incentives to HMOs to serve this population group."

The government's opinion of HMOs is demonstrated by the fact that Medicare beneficiaries are now encouraged to join an HMO and HMOs are allowed to participate in the Medicare program.

In speaking on the need for supplemental programs, Senator Heinz said, "The Medicare program, with all of its good intentions for meeting the health needs of older Americans, is falling farther and farther from its goal. Unable to keep pace with the soaring cost of health care services, Medicare leaves older persons with ever-increasing out-of-pocket costs. . . . There is ample evidence that most HMOs deliver high quality care at lower cost than the fee-for-service sector. . . ."

In speaking before the Senate Special Committee on Aging in 1979, George Hauck, of the Pennsylvania Department of Aging, had this to say: "Medicare does not pay for many of the most expensive, yet necessary, health care needs—prescription drugs, dental care, to name a few—of the elderly. The famous gaps in Medicare, coupled with the increasing health care expenditures of Medicare beneficiaries for noncovered, out-of-pocket, necessary health care services, and life on fixed incomes in an inflationary economy, create a real hardship of uncertainty and fear for senior citizens.

"Integration of health maintenance organizations on a risk basis into the Medicare system offers great hope for helping Medicare beneficiaries who freely elect to enroll in this very attractive alternative. HMOs, representing prepaid health care delivery systems offering comprehensive service benefits to a voluntarily enrolled population, when opened to the Medicare population . . . show great promise for coming closer to the ideal of health care services to the elderly. . . ."

Among the specific benefits Mr. Hauck sees HMOs offering are: "HMOs don't just pay for care, they organize a delivery system and assume responsibility for the delivery of services to their subscribers. HMOs offer comprehensive benefit packages with an emphasis upon preventive health care services, ambulatory care, and cost-effective usage of inpatient hospitalization. HMOs emphasize quality health care services through formal quality assurance systems, organized grievance resolution systems, periodic choice of the consumer to transfer without penalty into alternative health insurance mechanisms, and freedom to choose a personal family physician among those primary care physicians participating in the HMO. . . . And finally, HMOs offer Medicare beneficiaries, through prepayment, freedom from many of the burdens associated with deductibles, coinsurance, paperwork, finding physicians who will accept assignment under Part B, and so forth."

Again, the bottom line is that HMOs are good for Medicare beneficiaries.

Further proof that HMOs must be doing something right is the fact that private insurance companies are now getting into the act. At the same Senate hearing the Insurance Company of America reported: "Our health care operations make us one of the largest hospital management organizations in the world. We also operate two health maintenance organizations serving 170,000 members. It is the intention of the INA Health Care Group to continue our pace of expansion in the HMO field." So it would seem that the HMOs are not only good for the consumer, they are also good for business.

HOW AN HMO WORKS

Each HMO is a complete entity (except for the very large plans, such as Kaiser-Permanente, which has a number of branches in various areas) and, to some extent, makes its own rules. Because of this, the services provided and the premiums and out-of-pocket costs will vary from one to another. Upon enrollment you agree to pay a fixed premium, monthly or quarterly (depending upon the HMO). The amount of this premium is not affected by how much use you make out of the services because it is, in effect, a group plan and the charges are based on averages.

Since service is provided by a specific group of health-care personnel who work in teams or in cooperation with one another, it is available only to a limited area. There are now a great many more HMOs than there were ten years ago, but it is still possible that you will not have one near you. Check with your senior center, public-health nurse or social worker to find out. Some states, such as California, have fairly good coverage; others have none. As HMOs become increasingly accepted, it is hoped they will proliferate; until recently generous funds have been available from the federal government to help new HMOs over the initial difficulties of the first few years.

HOW DOES AN HMO PRACTICE PREVENTIVE MEDICINE?

Neither Medicare nor private health insurance pays for preventive medicine. The HMO, on the other hand, makes preventive medicine available to the elderly in several ways. First of all, it actually covers the cost of routine physicals, immunization shots and other practices associated with preventing illness rather than treating it only when it has already happened. Not all HMO plans cover these services (as you can see if you compare the High and Low option plans offered by our sample HMO on page 259), so be sure to look for the one that does; all HMOs do have such a plan available. Preventive medicine saves not only money but lives, not to mention minimizing the discomfort and risks of a serious illness. Catching an illness or disease in its early stages means treatment can be much less drastic and have a much higher rate of success and cure.

In addition, belonging to an HMO acts as preventive medicine because you know that your monthly premium will be your only expense no matter how often you see the doctor or need other services. You do not have to hesitate to check out a symptom because your budget is tight that month and you cannot afford any extra, unplanned-for bills; with membership in an HMO, you will be able to budget your health-care costs, with a few exceptions. The lower hospitalization rate of HMO members is thought to be largely due to the greater availability of health services and the greater freedom with which members use them. If, by the way, you wonder whether HMO members do not abuse these services just because they can be used without charge, you will be interested to know that studies have shown this is not the case. Knowing they can call on a doctor without getting a bill each time does not result in unnecessary visits, and, of course, catching an illness early cuts down on the number of necessary visits.

TYPES OF HMOs

PPGP—Prepaid Group Plans

This is the type of HMO which we will deal with in further discussions. In my opinion it offers the most advantages and is the kind I would choose if I had an option.

The management of all federally qualified HMOs is by a board of directors, one third of which must be representative of the people enrolled in it. This means, of course, that the members have an opportunity to participate in decisions that affect them and to help determine policy. Further, government requirements assure that the HMO will be run for the benefit of its members and that increased profits will result in increased benefits and expanded services. Unlike a private physician whose profits do not directly benefit his patients, the profits from the health-care services provided by an HMO are supposed to be shared with its members in this way.

Also known as a staff HMO, this type is housed in a central facility that contains all the health-care personnel and equipment except for that normally furnished by hospitals or skilled nursing facilities. They are outpatient facilities with X ray and other equipment, specialists, therapists, skilled nurses and emergency-room services all under one roof. The emergency-room services are on all 24 hours a day. Your medical records are kept in a central office and are quickly available to anyone on the staff. General practitioners are generally internists and act as your personal physician, together with a team that is assigned to you when you join.

For an elderly person especially, it is very convenient to have all these services right at hand. For instance, if you go to your doctor with a general complaint and if, after examining you, he thinks it advisable for you to be seen by a specialist, he simply makes an in-house phone call. The specialist, who may be as far away as the floor above, may be able to see you quickly and you will be saved the need to make another trip to another location. In addition, your records will be sent right up to the specialist's office, and if he wishes any X rays or tests, they can usually all be performed right in the same building. This eliminates much traveling and wear and tear on the patient, and because of the nature of an HMO, there is no worry about how much it will all cost.

A large HMO will have a number of teams and you are encouraged to change if you do not like the team to which you have been assigned. You will generally find everyone very pleasant and helpful because they are not in competition for patients and will tend not to feel personally offended if you ask for a change.

Once you have become familiar with the members of the team, you will feel very comfortable about calling for advice on the phone and you will often find one member available and helpful if another is busy. Since your team will be familiar with your health record, you will not be totally dependent on a single person. Many people I know who belong to HMOs are particularly pleased with the relationships they develop with the nurses; they feel less timid about "bothering" a nurse with a question than they would calling the doctor, and the nurses will quickly refer the matter to the doctor if necessary.

This type of HMO will probably be the best buy for your money, if it is a good one.

MCF—Medical Care Foundation Plan

This type of plan is organized along the lines of group-practice plans, with which most of us are familiar. It is a group of physicians who organize to provide prepaid health-care services, rather than the fee-for-service system where you pay for each visit and each service provided.

Physicians who belong to an MCF do not give up their private practice; patients in that category are billed in the usual way. But in addition to their private practice, the group has patients from whom the plan collects fixed-rate premiums that deliver all the usual services without any additional charge.

The individual physicians have, therefore, two kinds of patients—private and HMO. Services rendered to HMO patients are monitored by the group to make sure that they are kept to a certain limit; physicians will not be reimbursed for services that are judged unnecessary or excessive, and the individual physician might find himself out-of-pocket since he cannot, under the contract, collect from the patient. While this will tend to reduce unnecessary visits, it may also reduce services that the physician believes are truly necessary but for which he may not be reimbursed. There is also a question as to whether a physician would tend, in these circumstances, to favor his private patients.

IPA—Individual Practice Association

This kind of HMO is by far the most loosely organized since it is formed by individual physicians in their own offices who merely join together into a group that provides services as an HMO, at the same time retaining their private practice. Its chief advantage is that it allows those who enroll to go to the physician of choice, rather than having to choose among a group of physicians who may not include the family doctor.

It is the kind of HMO generally suggested to medical students with an interest in that kind of thing.

QUALITY CONTROL

HMOs are closely watched and regulated by the federal government, which generally approves of them in theory. All HMOs, regardless of what kind they are, must meet certain government standards and provide certain minimum services in order to call themselves an HMO. Because of their track record in delivering cost-effective and good-quality health care, they have been certified to handle Medicare recipients, and that should give you some confidence in the system. The fact that they have come so far in the face of a distinct lack of enthusiasm on the part of the American Medical Association and of many individual doctors is also in their favor.

WHAT ARE THE DISADVANTAGES OF AN HMO?

There are a few so-called disadvantages of an HMO; let us examine them to see if they are real.

1. You Cannot Choose Your Own Doctor

If by that you mean that you cannot pick a name out of the phone book, or that you cannot continue with your present doctor if you join an HMO to which he does not belong, that is quite true. Chances are, however, choosing a doctor from the HMO staff will be at least as good as picking one at random out of the phone book. As to having to leave your own primary-care physician, this could be a problem. If you have a very good relationship with him and he has been your family doctor for many years, if he is still taking just as good care of you today as he did when you were younger (and perhaps better able to pay his bills), if he isn't getting ready to retire himself, and if he agrees to accept the assignment, you will want to think twice about making a change. But that is a lot of ifs.

There's a good chance that you already belong to an HMO through your job, so you can continue that membership and the same doctor. Or there's a good chance you may want to relocate, in which case you'll have to get a new doctor wherever you move to. Or you may find that your doctor is not up on, or interested in, geriatric medicine, and that he tends to fall back on the clichés of doctors who stereotype the elderly: "You'll just have to live with it," or "You aren't getting any younger, you know." If his approach to your symptoms is becoming increasingly jocular and offhand, you ought to think about making a change—just as you shouldn't put your six-year-old car in the hands of a young mechanic who says, "Are they still making parts for this?" in a tone of considerable skepticism.

While you may not be able to go to the primary-care physician you are now using (although you may be surprised to find he is associated with an HMO), you will still be able to choose your physician. The larger the HMO, the greater the number of physicians on its staff and the wider your choice. And you are not stuck with your first choice; you can ask to change to another doctor if you wish.

2. The Facility May Be in the Next Town and, Therefore, Inconvenient

If you have been going to a doctor who is practically around the corner, this might be an inconvenience for the visits you make for minor symptoms or to get flu shots. But it is more than offset by the tremendous convenience of having all the services under one roof when your primary physician wants to refer you to a specialist or send you to a lab for tests or have more complicated X rays taken than the ones usually done in a doctor's office. (And the HMO won't charge you for the flu shots.)

3. You Have to Wait a Lot

I have talked to a number of people around the country who belong to HMOs and I find this varies considerably. Sometimes there is a delay in getting an appointment, and sometimes there is a long wait in the doctor's office. But I found the same sort of complaint from people who go to doctors in private practice. One of the leading doctors in my area, a specialist, is known for the long time he keeps patients waiting; it is not unusual to cool your heels for an hour in his waiting room. On the other hand, some doctors—and some HMOs—won't keep you waiting more than five or six minutes. And an HMO usually treats any emergency situation with considerable dispatch; if your own doctor isn't available, someone else just as qualified takes over and has all your records handy to help in making any decisions that may be necessary.

The HMO May Go Out of Business

Private physicians tend to think of HMOs as very unstable and continually on the verge of bankruptcy. The fact is that many have been in continuous operation for decades and the number of successful HMOs is growing every year.

There is no doubt, however, that starting an HMO is a difficult procedure, and running it in the black is not easy and not likely to occur during the first few years of operation. If it were truly part of a national health plan this would not be the case, but because it is not, and because membership is voluntary, it takes time to educate people in the area to the point where they join in enough numbers to make the plan work. If there are unions and large companies in the area, membership usually increases rapidly, which explains why you do not yet find HMOs in small towns.

Until recently the federal government has provided financial aid to HMOs when they need it, because they are recognized as a good health-care buy for the consumer; today much of that aid has been cut out of the federal budget and some of the HMOs may not be able to continue operating. If you are thinking of joining an HMO, you might want to ask about its situation. You certainly should take a tour of the facility and see for yourself whether it seems to be functioning properly. Look for cleanliness, equipment in good repair, a staff that seems reasonably happy. Ask how long the HMO has been in business and what its plans are for future expansion of services or facilities. Do remember, though, you aren't *buying* the HMO, you are only committing yourself to a monthly premium and you can always change your mind if it doesn't work for you—for whatever reason.

25

A Look at an HMO

We have seen how HMOs work; now let us look at a specific example. Keep in mind that this is how one particular HMO works; the ones in your area may not have exactly the same setup or coverage.

Community Health Care Center Plan, Inc. (CHCP), in New Haven, Connecticut, is a model HMO. It has been in existence approximately ten years, so it has weathered the financial difficulties that beset many prepaid medical plans when they first start up. It has connections with the prestigious Yale–New Haven medical facilities, including the teaching hospital, and access to what is considered some of the finest medical personnel in the country. Admittedly, it is a better facility than many HMOs—possibly better than the one that may be available to you—but at least it shows the potential in this kind of care. Let us see how you would fare as a Medicare beneficiary using the CHCP for your Medigap insurance.

ELIGIBILITY

Anyone of any age and any physical condition may join. The only limitation is that you must live within a 20-town area, including New Haven. For practical purposes, this is hardly a limitation since it wouldn't make much sense to belong to a medical facility that was too far from your home.

PRE-EXISTING HEALTH CONDITIONS

Most Medigap insurance policies have a pre-existing, or "pre-X," clause that requires a waiting period before the policy will cover illnesses or other health problems you may have had at the time you took out the policy. Since this waiting period is usually from six months to a year, you may find yourself with fairly heavy health-care bills that you must pay out-of-pocket during that period, even though you have an active Medigap policy. Some companies disallow any condition for which you are taking medication, which could effectively deny you coverage for high blood pressure, diabetes or any other chronic illness for which you must take regular medication.

CHCP does not have any pre-X clause: you are covered for all your illnesses, new or old or chronic, from the moment you join.

You may find that your family physician is not well informed about this aspect of HMOs. I had a surprising number of physicians tell me quite positively that HMOs would take only healthy people and that you could not join if you were not well. To make sure I was getting correct information on this, I checked with CHCP. They assured me the state of a person's health was not a factor in qualifying for membership. To be absolutely sure I then asked, "You mean even if I came crawling in over the threshold on all fours with a terminal disease, I could still join?" The answer was "Yes."

MEDICARE INSURANCE REQUIREMENT

The only requirement for a Medicare beneficiary is that he or she must *be* a Medicare beneficiary. In other words, you must be receiving Medicare in order to qualify for membership under the Medigap part of the HMO plan. Ideally, CHCP works best when you are receiving both Part A Hospital (HI) and Part B Medical (SMI) benefits, but you may enroll if you have only Part B coverage. In that case, however, you will be covered only for those services covered by Medicare Part B, which means you will have no CHCP coverage for hospital charges and other items covered by Medicare Part A.

ENROLLMENT PERIODS

If your application is received by the first of the month, your enrollment will be effective the first of the following month.

FILING MEDICARE CLAIMS

With CHCP, as with all HMOs, there are no claim forms for you to file. All that is taken care of for you by CHCP and you will have no obligation in connection with services covered, except for payment of your monthly premium. This does not apply, of course, to charges for uncovered services. Occasionally you may receive a bill for a covered service that you have been authorized to incur outside of CHCP; CHCP will process these bills for you.

EMERGENCIES AWAY FROM HOME

Since you are required to use CHCP personnel in most instances, you may wonder what would happen if you were to become ill when traveling. If you are temporarily away from home and beyond the service area, and if it is an emergency, CHCP will approve payment of your medical care, including hospitalization.

THE MONTHLY PREMIUM

Since you must be a Medicare beneficiary, you must pay your Medicare Part B premium just as you always do. In addition, you must pay a monthly premium to belong to CHCP.

The amount of the premium depends on which plan you choose; you have two choices, CHCP-M (Low) and CHCP-M (High).

THE DIFFERENCES IN THE OPTIONS

CHCP-M (Low) is similar to the usual Medigap policy that pays the deductibles and coinsurance you would otherwise have to pay out-of-pocket. It does not cover any services Medicare doesn't cover, does not provide a discount on prescription drugs and does not include preventive medicine. In deciding whether this is good value, you should compare the annual cost of the premiums with the cost of other Medigap policies with similar coverage. You should also keep in mind that the Senate Committee on Aging and the Federal Trade Commission in their report on Medigap insurance felt this kind of insurance was not as desirable as catastrophe insurance.

CHCP-M (High) offers much more than the Low Option. In addition to all the coverage of the Low, it provides many services not covered by Medicare, such as more in-hospital days, immunizations (such as flu shots), tests for hearing aids (though not the cost of the hearing aids) and routine eye and physical examinations. In addition, while it does not offer 100% coverage of prescription drugs, it sells them in the CHCP pharmacy at cost plus 40%, a considerable savings over the usual markup.

WEAKNESSES IN HMO COVERAGE

As with all health insurance, there are weaknesses even in CHCP coverage. For instance, it is still greatly influenced by Medicare's exclusions, and, though it fills some of the gaps, does not fill them all by any means. Even with Medicare Part A and Part B and the High Option CHCP membership, you will still find yourself paying some of your bills out-of-pocket. For instance, you will still have to pay extra for a private room in the hospital and for private-duty nursing. Dental care, except for the very limited coverage offered under Medicare, is excluded. No cosmetic surgery is covered, nor are the costs of eyeglasses, hearing aids or routine foot care. (Some HMOs do cover these services.) Custodial care, the big gap in Medicare, does not even receive token coverage. If there is more than one HMO in your area, you might find some of these services offered by one and not by another; it always pays to shop around. I do not, however, know of any HMO that covers all health-care services.

CHCP SERVICES: At the Facility

SERVICE	CHCP HIGH OPTION COVERAGE	CHCP LOW OPTION COVERAGE
Physicians	Fully covered for office visits and surgery. For psychiatrists, covered for up to $500 a year.	Same coverage
Laboratory tests	Fully covered	Same coverage

X rays	Fully covered	Same coverage
Physicals, hearing tests and other preventive services	Fully covered	No coverage
Immunization (flu shots, etc.)	Fully covered	No coverage
Prescription drugs: Administered in facility	Fully covered	Covered to extent of Medicare allowance.
Bought in CHCP pharmacy	You pay CHCP's cost plus 40%.	You pay the full price.
Physical therapy	If provided in the facility, covered to extent of Medicare allowance.	Same coverage
Speech therapy	If provided in the facility and approved by CHCP, covered to extent of Medicare allowance.	Same coverage
Prosthetic devices and appliances	Covered to extent of Medicare allowance.	Same coverage

CHCP SERVICES: In the Hospital

Service	CHCP High Option Coverage	CHCP Low Option Coverage
Days covered	Fully covered for 485 days in each benefit period when arranged by CHCP physician. Does	90-day coverage plus one-time 60 reserve days.

	not cover services not covered by Medicare.	
Psychiatric hospital	Lifetime limit of 190-day coverage.	Same coverage
Physician's services	Fully covered when provided or arranged by CHCP physician.	Same coverage
Blood	Fully covered	Same coverage

CHCP SERVICES: *Emergency*

SERVICE	CHCP HIGH OPTION COVERAGE	CHCP LOW OPTION COVERAGE
Within CHCP area:		
24-hour-a-day service—physician always on call at facility	Fully covered	Same coverage
Ambulance	Fully covered when authorized by CHCP.	Fully covered if authorized by CHCP and approved by Medicare.
Outside CHCP area:		
Hospitalization	Fully covered for up to 120 days, including care outside U.S.	Same coverage
Physician	Fully covered in U.S. Outside U.S. covered for up to $500.	Fully covered in U.S. Outside U.S., no coverage.

| Ambulance | Fully covered in U.S. if medically necessary. Outside U.S., no coverage. | In U.S., fully covered if approved by Medicare. Outside U.S., no coverage. |

CHCP SERVICES: In Skilled Nursing Facility

SERVICE	CHCP HIGH OPTION COVERAGE	CHCP LOW OPTION COVERAGE
SNF	Covered to extent approved by Medicare and if arranged and authorized by a CHCP physician. Custodial care not covered.	Same coverage

CHCP SERVICES: For Home Health Care

SERVICE	CHCP HIGH OPTION COVERAGE	CHCP LOW OPTION COVERAGE
Home health-care services allowed by Medicare	Covered to extent approved by Medicare and if arranged and authorized by a CHCP physician.	Same coverage

WHAT DO THE TABLES TELL YOU?

Generally speaking, the Low Option picks up the deductibles and coinsurance but little else. Services covered follow Medicare guidelines closely, except in a few minor instances, such as the cost for blood (Medicare charges for the first three pints; CHCP pays for these). This is comparatively limited coverage and leaves a large gray area for you to pay out of your own pocket. If you go with this kind of plan, you will probably want to compare the premiums with those charged by other insurance companies. The only apparent advantages the HMO would seem to have over any other similar policy would be the convenience of having all the services you require right at hand in one facility, having all your medical records immediately available to all the health-care personnel you will be using and having all the forms filled out and sent in for you.

The biggest advantage of all is not so obvious. You don't have to ask the doctor or other provider to accept the assignment, because you will never be charged more than Medicare's allowable charge, and between Medicare coverage and CHCP coverage, all your health-care costs that are approved by Medicare will be *fully covered.* With the large percentage of physicians in certain areas refusing to accept the assignment, this could be a big savings in your out-of-pocket health-care expenditures.

The High Option plan has all the advantages of the Low Option plan plus some benefits that go considerably beyond Medicare. The most obvious improved coverage is in the length of a covered hospital stay. Where Medicare and the Low Option plan provide only 90-day coverage, this plan provides full coverage for 485 days. It is important, however, to understand that this coverage applies only when hospitalization with skilled nursing care is required and not when it is used for custodial care.

In addition to improved hospital coverage, the High Option plan provides some preventive-care coverage for services that are the hallmark of an HMO: routine physicals, immunizations, hearing tests (though not hearing aids) and a break on prescription drugs.

Additional coverage that is useful to travelers is coverage for emergency care when out of the United States. Although limited, it is still better than Medicare or the Low Option plan, which provide no coverage (with certain exceptions).

VI
QUESTIONS AND ANSWERS

26

The 100 Most-Asked Questions

Here are the 100 most-asked questions gathered from senior centers, social workers and Medicare offices around the country. Many of the questions have been rewritten to be composites but all deal with the basic information that was requested. If you do not wish to read the text, you may find your question and the answer to it among those in this chapter. For convenience, the questions have been grouped as much as possible by subject matter.

All of the information in the answers can be found elsewhere in the book, in much more detail. If you wish a fuller explanation, look in the index for the appropriate section or sections.

If you count, you will find that there are more than 100 questions in this chapter; it really should have been entitled "One hundred most-asked questions—and some others people seem to be confused about." The additional questions arose out of seminars and meetings with social workers, volunteers and all who deal with Medicare beneficiaries, and represent questions they would like the answers to. Medicare recipients seem to find some areas more confusing than others and it was felt that in some instances the question-and-answer format was the clearest way to get the answer across. If you prefer just to read the text, you need not read this chapter; on the other hand, even after reading the text, you may find these questions helpful.

MEDICARE ELIGIBILITY

Who is eligible for Medicare?
- Everyone over 65 who is eligible for social security benefits is eligible for Medicare. Also those eligible for survivor benefits or railroad retirement pensions.
- If you are under 65 and have been receiving disability payments for at least 24 months.
- Certain individuals requiring kidney dialysis. See "How can I tell if I can qualify for Medicare if I have kidney disease?" on page 271.
- Certain individuals who can qualify under a provision called "transitional entitlement." See how you can get Medicare under transitional entitlement, on pages 272–273.

When will I be eligible for Medicare?
You will be eligible for Medicare the first day of the month you become 65 years of age. It is important to apply three months before that, or your application will not have had time to be processed and you may find yourself *without health-care coverage* for three months because your regular health insurance may expire on your 65th birthday.

You may also be eligible at an earlier age if you are disabled. See below.

I am a widow and I have never worked so I am not eligible for social security. However, I intend to apply for my share

of my husband's social security benefits next year when I reach 65. Will I be able to get Medicare then?

Yes. Be sure to apply three months before you reach age 65.

Is it possible to be eligible for Medicare before reaching age 65?

You may be eligible anytime you have been receiving disability benefits for at least 24 months, regardless of the age-65 limitation. If you become well, you will lose coverage unless you have reached the age of 65 in the meantime. It is possible, however, to qualify again if you subsequently become disabled again.

Why do foreigners, who are not American citizens, get Medicare coverage?

Medicare is based on work record, not on citizenship. If you have worked long enough to be entitled to social security benefits, you are automatically entitled to Medicare.

I am on disability and getting disability benefits. As soon as I have been getting them for 24 months, I plan to apply for Medicare. Will my wife get Medicare coverage when I do?

No. You will be automatically enrolled in Medicare A and B if you are still receiving disability benefits after 24 months, but your wife cannot get Medicare until she reaches the age of 65. Disability benefits are not the same as social security benefits, even though the amount of the benefits coincide.

I began receiving social security payments last year because I was disabled. I was 60 years old. Now I am 61 and wonder if I am eligible for Medicare yet, or do I have to wait until I am 65?

You don't have to wait until you are 65 if you are receiving disability benefits. You become eligible for Medi-

care at any age after you have been receiving disability
benefits for 24 consecutive months.

Are kidney disease disability benefits the same as total disability benefits?

In a number of ways the rules are easier.

1. The waiting period is shorter. Instead of the usual
   24-month waiting period, a dialysis patient is eligible
   for Medicare after three months on dialysis.

   Even this three-month waiting period is waived for
   those who enter a training program for self-dialysis
   before the beginning of the third month after the one
   in which dialysis begins.

   The waiting period is waived, also, if you have discontinued dialysis but then have to resume it.

2. If you are a candidate for a transplant operation,
   your coverage begins the month you are hospitalized,
   providing the transplant operation takes place within
   three months of your entering the hospital.

3. To encourage self-dialysis at home, Medicare covers
   all health-care costs for supplies and professional or
   provider help and supervision that is needed for home
   self-dialysis.

4. You need not be totally disabled—that is, unable to
   do any gainful work—in order to qualify for this kind
   of disability. As long as you are on a regular dialysis
   program, you may work as much as you are able
   without your earnings affecting your disability status.

I am receiving Medicare because I have kidney disease. How long will my coverage last?

If you are covered by Medicare because you are on dialysis, you will be covered for 12 months after the month
in which you discontinue dialysis.

If you have had a kidney transplant, you will be covered

for three years after the month in which you have had the operation.

If your transplant is not successful and you then have to go back on dialysis, you do not have the usual three-month waiting period but are entitled to Medicare from the first day of dialysis.

How can I tell if I can qualify for Medicare because of kidney disease?

Anyone who is in "that stage of kidney impairment that appears irreversible and permanent and requires a regular course of dialysis or kidney transplantation to maintain life" is eligible for Medicare, regardless of age, after three months on dialysis.

It is not necessary to be totally disabled in this instance. Sometimes people on dialysis are able to continue working; this does not affect their eligibility for Medicare.

Dependents, however, do not become eligible under these circumstances.

Incidentally, Medicare coverage includes the entire insurance program, not just those expenses connected with renal disease.

If I take early retirement at age 62, will I be eligible for Medicare?

No. You are not eligible for Medicare until age 65 or over, unless you are disabled or require kidney dialysis.

If I decide not to apply for social security benefits when I reach 65 years of age, can I still get Medicare?

Yes, if you qualify for social security benefits, you are entitled to Medicare coverage from the day of your 65th birthday. It is important to enroll for this coverage three months before your 65th birthday, because many health-insurance policies will no longer cover you after the age of 65 for any benefits that you could be receiving from Medicare.

If I am not eligible for Medicare Part A, is there any way I can still get it?

Yes. The following persons 65 years of age or older may voluntarily enroll in Medicare Part A, even if they are not eligible, by paying a special monthly premium:

1. A citizen of the United States.
2. A resident of the United States or an alien admitted for permanent residence with at least five years' continuous residence prior to the month in which he or she applies.

IMPORTANT: In addition, you must also enroll in Medicare Part B. You must continue to pay Medicare Part B premiums as long as you live or you will lose your Part A Medicare coverage.

If I am not eligible for Medicare Part A but can qualify for voluntary enrollment in this program, what will it cost me?

Since the monthly premiums tend to be increased each July, check with your local social security office to get the latest information.

For the period July 1981 through July 1982, the monthly premium is $89; it is scheduled to go up to $113 July 1, 1982.

In addition, you must be enrolled in Medicare Part B. The monthly premium for the period July 1981 through June 1982 is $11. (As of July 1, 1982, the premium will be $12.20.)

Therefore, your total monthly premium for Medicare coverage from July 1981 through June 1982 is $100—$1,200 a year.

I have heard that even if my work record does not entitle me to Medicare, I still may qualify under something called "transitional entitlement." How can I find out if it applies to me?

If you are a resident of the United States, or a citizen of the United States, or an alien with permanent resident status who has lived in the United States continuously for at least five years immediately before the month in which you file your application for Medicare, and if you reached age 65 before 1968, you may qualify for Medicare coverage under the "transitional entitlement" provision.

If you reached 65 between the years 1968 to 1974, you might qualify if you have three covered quarters for each year from 1968 to the year in which you reached 65. For instance, if you became 65 in 1970, you would need nine quarters—three for 1968, three for 1969 and three for 1970—to qualify.

There are certain restrictions to qualifying for this coverage, but you should apply immediately to your local social security office if you think you qualify. You may be pleasantly surprised because, if you qualify, you may receive retroactive payments for the 12 previous months.

I am thinking of moving to Italy. I am receiving social security benefits and Medicare. Will I still be covered by Medicare?

No. Medicare coverage extends only when a beneficiary is in the United States, with a few exceptions.

I am divorced and took early retirement under which I receive social security payments based on my ex-husband's earnings record. Will I be eligible for Medicare when I am 65 and if so, how do I apply for it?

You will be eligible for Medicare when you reach 65. You don't have to apply for it because you already get social security payments, so you will automatically be enrolled in Medicare Part A and Part B when you become eligible.

However, mistakes happen, so look for your Medicare identification card around your 65th birthday and contact

Medicare immediately if you don't receive it.

I took early retirement when I reached 62, but now I will be 65 this year and eligible for Medicare. Where and when do I apply?

You don't have to apply. Since you are getting social security benefits, your enrollment in Medicare will be taken care of for you automatically.

Of course, if you do not receive your Medicare card by your 65th birthday, you might want to inquire at your local social security office to make sure the computer hasn't made a mistake.

If I am eligible for Medicare, will I be automatically enrolled in the program when I reach 65?

Not unless you are already receiving social security benefits. If you are not receiving social security benefits, you should call your local social security office three months before your 65th birthday. Be sure to say you want to be enrolled in Medicare Part B as well as Medicare Part A, although it should be automatic.

You do not have to actually start receiving social security benefits, if you don't want to, to receive Medicare coverage; you just have to be eligible.

I'm 65 and retired and I like to travel. Will I be covered by Medicare if I become ill in a foreign country?

With a few exceptions, you will not be covered by Medicare outside of territory that Medicare calls "United States" (see "What territory is included in the term 'United States' as used by Medicare?" on page 308).

If you receive medical treatment in Canada or Mexico, check to see if you are covered under one of the exceptions. If you are in the United States but a hospital in Canada or Mexico is the nearest one, you should also check your coverage.

It is possible, however, that you may become ill in a

country with a national health plan that covers travelers within that country.

Once I qualify for Medicare because of reaching age 65, can I count on its coverage for the rest of my life?

Not necessarily. For instance, if you are hospitalized, you are entitled to all or partial coverage of most costs for the first 90 days. If your illness requires continuous hospitalization for more than 90 days, you may use up a once-in-a-lifetime reserve of 60 days. If you are in the hospital after 150 days, you will no longer be covered by Medicare for any part of your hospital costs.

It is possible, therefore, to use up all your Medicare Part A hospital coverage within 150 days after your 65th birthday. If your illness continues, without a break, to require hospitalization, it is possible that you may never again have any Medicare coverage for that part of your hospital-care costs.

Who pays the expenses for someone who is not eligible for Medicare but who is willing to donate a kidney?

Medicare pays 100% of all the health-care costs incurred by kidney donors in the course of the donation. Donors do not have to pay any deductible or coinsurance premiums for this coverage. Donor Medicare coverage lasts until the donor has recovered from the transplant operation.

Medicare Part A
Hospital Insurance (HI)

Will my Hospital Part A Medicare pay my entire hospital bill?

No. Your expenses for the hospital stay (as of January 1, 1982) will be as follows:

$260	For the 1st to the 60th day
$ 65 a day	For the 61st to the 90th day
$130 a day	For the 91st to the 150th day (these 60 "reserve" days may be used only once in a lifetime)

In other words, a 60-day stay will cost you $260.

A 90-day stay will cost you $2,210.

A 150-day stay will cost you $10,010.

From the 151st day of a hospital stay in any one benefit period, *you* must pay the entire hospital bill.

At any time that you leave the hospital or skilled nursing facility and are out of it for 60 consecutive days, you start a new benefit period.

What does "Part A Deductible" mean?

Part A or "hospital" Medicare coverage does not require a monthly premium, but it does require that you pay a deductible amount the first time you enter a hospital during a spell of illness (benefit period).

The amount of the deductible is determined each January 1. It has gone up steadily from $40 in 1966 to $260 in 1982.

If you are hospitalized more than once in a single benefit period, you are required to pay the deductible only the first time and not on subsequent admissions. The deductible is all you must pay for all hospital covered services for the first 60 days of hospitalization.

What is a "benefit period"?

A benefit period—also called "a spell of illness"—begins the first day you enter a hospital and ends when you have been home from the hospital or skilled nursing facility for at least 60 consecutive days.

The term applies only to coverage under Medicare Part A (HI); there are no benefit periods for Medicare Part B.

How many benefit periods am I allowed under Medicare Part A?

There is no limit to the number of benefit periods you are entitled to.

What are "Lifetime Reserve days"?

Under Medicare, you are covered all or partially for the first 90 days you are in the hospital in any single benefit period. If you have to stay in the hospital more than 90 days, you may still be partially covered by Medicare for another 60 days, if you choose. These 60 days are known as "Lifetime Reserve days" because they can be used only once in a lifetime. Once you have used them up, Medicare will pay for only 90 days of hospitalization in any benefit period.

If you wish, you can use part of this reserve and save the rest. For example, you could use 10 of your 60 days and save 50 for another time.

You need not use your reserve days just because you are in the hospital more than 90 days. If you wish to save them, you can do so by paying the hospital yourself for the in-hospital stay after the 90th day.

You have 90 days after your discharge from the hospital to decide whether to use your reserve days, or to change your mind if you had decided to use them, provided you agree to pay the charges for those days and the hospital agrees to accept your payment. To avoid hassles, let the hospital know as soon as possible.

If I am covered by Medicare, may I go to any hospital I want?

No. the hospital must be what Medicare defines as "a qualified provider." A qualified provider, in this instance, is a hospital that has been certified as meeting all the requirements of the definition of such an institution.

Most hospitals have been so certified, but you may occasionally find a hospital—especially a private one—that is not. Generally speaking, if you show your Medicare card upon admission, when asked what insurance you carry, the hospital will tell you if it is not covered. If in doubt, ask.

I am a Christian Scientist. Are Christian Science sanatoriums covered by Medicare under my hospital coverage?

Sanatoriums operated or listed and certified by the the Church of Christ Scientist in Boston, Massachusetts, are included in Medicare's definition of covered hospitals.

Remember, however, that the services you receive may not be covered even though you receive them in a certified facility. I would suggest you check with your Medicare office to make sure what you are entering the sanatorium for is one of the covered services.

I am planning to enter the hospital and my doctor has chosen one covered by Medicare but with only private rooms. I understand that Medicare pays for semiprivate rooms and wonder how much more my room will cost me?

If there are no semiprivate accommodations in the hospital, you will be completely covered by Medicare in a private room and should not receive a bill from the hospital for your room in the first 60 days of your stay.

If the hospital has both semiprivate and private rooms but the semiprivate rooms are all filled up, Medicare will pay for your stay in a private room until a semiprivate becomes available.

Will Medicare pay for a private room if I need one?

Usually Medicare will pay only for a semiprivate room (which may include two, three or four beds). However, there are circumstances under which Medicare will pay for a private room:

1. When necessary for the health of the patient or of others. If, for instance, you have a very contagious disease.
2. When the hospital or skilled nursing facility has no semiprivate accommodations.
3. When all the semiprivate accommodations are taken and the patient requires immediate hospitalization.

The private room must be ordered by the physician on the grounds that it is necessary under one of these three circumstances. Under no circumstances will Medicare pay the extra cost of a private room ordered by the patient or the patient's family.

If I request a private room in the hospital, must I pay the entire cost or will Medicare pay part of it?

If you request a private room or other expensive accommodations, you are liable only for the difference between the customary charge for such a room and for the semiprivate room. Medicare will pay the hospital the same amount it would if you were in a semiprivate room.

I understand the hospital will send a bill to Medicare for my hospitalization, but I would like to see an itemized bill so that I can check the charges. How can I do this?

You are entitled to see an itemized bill even though it will be paid for, mostly, by Medicare or an insurance company. You may have to insist on receiving it, however. Some hospitals have taken to just sending a total and indicating what portion of it you must pay. This is usually a negligible amount—$15 or $20 or less—but that is no excuse for not sending you an itemized statement. Hospitals are notorious for inaccuracies in their billing and you should demand an itemized statement and check it over carefully when you get it. If you do not understand a charge, call up the business office and ask about it. If the person who answers the phone is not forthcoming with answers, ask to speak to the next in charge. The higher up you go, the nicer the person will be.

Remember, health-care costs are increasing partly because of billing inaccuracies; do your part in making sure Medicare is not charged for a service the hospital did not deliver.

Incidentally, if the hospital posts *The Patient's Bill of Rights,* you will usually find that it lists the right to see an itemized bill for your charges, regardless of who pays it.

I have received a bill from the hospital for a recent illness. I do not understand why I got a bill since I think that between Medicare and my Medigap insurance I don't owe the hospital anything. What should I do?

Wait. Hospitals often mistakenly bill for charges covered by insurance. It is usually straightened up later, but you may have a problem getting your money back if you have paid a bill you didn't really owe. If the hospital begins to send you dunning letters, call the business office and ask for an explanation of charges and ask why they are not covered by your insurance. If you don't think the answers are correct, check further—with Medicare, your insurance company and so on.

If you have Medigap insurance, the insurance company will pay after Medicare has paid (otherwise it doesn't know how much is due) and it is very likely that you may be billed for the amount Medigap will pick up. Do not be intimidated by the business office and do not pay a bill unless you are sure you owe it.

If I am hospitalized for a very short stay and the covered charges I incur are not as much as the deductible amount I paid upon admission, can I get my money back from the hospital?

It's very unlikely you will incur charges less than the amount of the deductible no matter how short your stay. However, if that should occur, you may be entitled to a refund.

You may find, however, that the hospital bill is different from the amount they credit toward your deductible. This can happen because Medicare allows the hospital to use either the actual charges or its "customary" charges—whichever is higher. For instance, your actual charges may have been $100 but the customary charges may be $150. In that case, the hospital will use $150 in figuring your deductible credit.

My mother required an emergency admission to a hospital and the hospital insisted they had to have a check for the deductible amount before they would admit her. Is this proper procedure?

Medicare tells me they consider this improper procedure inasmuch as they guarantee the hospital that Medicare will pay the deductible when the hospital is unable to collect it from the Medicare beneficiary. So it is not only unconscionable, it is also unnecessary for the hospital to have such a rule, since they are not taking any risk either way.

Can the hospital charge me, instead of Medicare, if I leave later than discharge time?

It depends on why you have overstayed. If the delay was due to medical reasons—for example, if you are bedridden and have to wait for transportation—Medicare will pay and the hospital should not bill you.

If the delay is due to personal reasons and merely a matter of convenience, the hospital may charge you. However, the hospital is obligated to give you reasonable notice of date of discharge, and reasonable notice is usually construed as not less than 24 hours prior to time of discharge.

Does Medicare cover blood for blood transfusions?

The first three pints of blood used by an inpatient are not covered by Medicare. You may avoid the charge if you agree to replace the blood you use.

I said I would replace some blood I needed for a transfusion so the hospital did not bill me for it. The hospital did, however, bill me for administering the transfusion. Will Medicare cover the bill?

Medicare will not cover the bill because there shouldn't be any bill. The hospital is not allowed to charge you for administering the transfusion; Medicare reimburses the hospital directly.

My doctor has prescribed certain medication for me to take while I am in the hospital but I do not have any at home. He says he will give me a prescription, but I am being discharged by the hospital on a Sunday and will not be able to get it filled until the next day. Does Medicare allow me to take medicine out of the hospital?

There is special provision made for the hospital to give you a limited supply of medication to take with you when you leave the hospital.

If your doctor says it is medically necessary in order to permit or make easier your discharge from the hospital, Medicare will pay for enough of this take-home medication to last until you can get some from your usual pharmacy.

My doctor says I have to go to a nursing home. As long as I choose a skilled nursing facility, will I be sure of Medicare coverage?

Not necessarily. Your condition must *require* the services provided by a skilled nursing facility. Medicare will review your case upon admission, and periodically thereafter, to determine whether you really need those services.

If Medicare determines you do not, you will not be covered even though you are actually staying in the facility.

My mother is very feeble and cannot feed or dress herself but she doesn't have any specific illness. She would like to go to a nursing home where someone could take care of her daily needs. Will her Medicare insurance cover this?

No. Not even partially. Medicare specifically excludes care that it defines as "custodial." Custodial care is that which is primarily "for the purpose of meeting personal needs and could be provided by persons without professional skills or training." Even if your mother would die without someone to feed her, Medicare does not consider this medically necessary.

What are examples of custodial care?

Custodial care includes: help in walking, in getting in and out of bed, in bathing or getting dressed, in eating and taking medicine, in going to the bathroom, preparing food for oneself—in other words, all the essential needs of daily existence not related to or caused by an illness.

Custodial care is not covered by Medicare, and a hospital or nursing-home stay that is required primarily for custodial care is not covered.

During my hospital stay, my doctor wanted me to take a medication that was not carried by the hospital pharmacy. He had me order it from my pharmacy. Did I do the right thing?

Drugs and medications supplied by and used in the hospital are covered by Medicare. Drugs ordered from outside the hospital and paid for by the patient are not. You should have asked your doctor to order it through the hospital—they could have obtained it from wherever it was available—and then Medicare would have paid for it. It does not have to be available in the hospital pharmacy to be covered by Medicare; it only has to be ordered and paid for by the hospital—even if it was supplied to the hospital by your local pharmacy.

If I need a private-duty nurse in the hospital, will Medicare pay for any part of her services?

No. Even if the hospital engages the private-duty nurse for the patient, and even if the hospital makes payment initially for the nurse's services, the patient is still liable and must reimburse the hospital for the full amount. Some hospitals exercise a great deal of control over private-duty nurses and supply them to patients from a pool. However, unless the nurses are actually on the hospital staff, they must be paid for by the patient and will receive no reimbursement from Medicare. Be sure you *mean* to order private nurses, and do not be confused into thinking they are part of your hospital service merely because the hospital takes care of it for you.

My mother was in the hospital and is now in a skilled nursing facility. She has used up her Medicare coverage and must pay all her health-care expenses herself. Can I count the day she began paying her own expenses as the beginning of the 60 days toward a new benefit period?

No. Whether or not Medicare coverage still exists, you cannot begin a benefit period so long as the patient is still in the hospital or nursing home. If your mother continues to be in the nursing home for the rest of her life, she will never again be eligible for that Medicare coverage.

My doctor says I need the care of a skilled nursing facility, but Medicare says I do not and will not pay its share. Doesn't my doctor know best?

Medicare has the final word. Even if your doctor says your life will be endangered if you are not in a skilled nursing facility, Medicare may determine that this is not the case. You can, of course, appeal Medicare's decision if you and your doctor do not agree with it.

I am a Christian Scientist. I need to go to a nursing home and want to know whether I will get Medicare coverage in a Christian Science sanatorium.

Sanatoriums operated, listed, and certified by the First Church of Christ Scientist, Boston, Massachusetts, can come under Medicare as a "skilled nursing facility," but they do not have the same coverage as other skilled nursing facilities. Differences in coverage are as follows:

1. Extended-care services are covered, partially, for only 30—instead of the usual 100—days.
2. You must pay the coinsurance daily rate from the day of admission, instead of after 20 days. After 20 days, you are no longer covered by Medicare for the skilled nursing facility and must pay all of such bills yourself.

If I am covered by Medicare, may I go to any nursing home I want?

No. The nursing home must be a "skilled nursing facility," or SNF (see Chapter 6), and must be what Medicare defines as a "qualified provider." The great majority of nursing homes do *not* qualify as skilled nursing facilities, and a number of those that do are not certified as a qualified provider. Always ask about Medicare coverage before entering a nursing home.

If Medicare approves coverage for my care in a skilled nursing facility (the only kind of nursing home that is covered), will I be covered for as long as I need to stay there?

No. You will be partially covered (see page 52 for specific amounts payable by you) for 100 days, at the most. If you require further SNF care, you will have to pay for all of it yourself. Medicare will not pay any part of your nursing-home costs after the first 100 days.

My neighbor went to the hospital for dental surgery in connection with a broken jaw. I thought dental services weren't covered, so why did Medicare pay for it?

Most dental services aren't covered, but hospitalization and surgery in connection with a broken jaw and with certain other procedures are covered. The law has recently been amended to make coverage slightly more liberal, so check with your dentist if you are considering dental work and want to know if it is now covered.

If I am in the hospital and run out of Medicare Part A coverage but decide to stay in the hospital at my own expense, can I receive coverage for laboratory tests and similar services on an outpatient basis?

I had to go to Medicare to get the answer to this one, but the answer is yes.

My wife recently had a hip operation and the doctor said she would need 48 hours of round-the-clock care by registered nurses. I ordered them because he said it was necessary but now Medicare refuses to pay the cost. Is this correct?

Yes. Medicare never covers private nursing care, even though the doctor says it is necessary. Sometimes even the hospital says it is necessary, but Medicare will not cover it under any circumstances.

I have been told I need surgery and I want to get a second opinion. I know Medicare covers a second opinion but I want to be sure I understand just how. Will the bill for the second opinion be covered even if I decide not to have the operation?

Yes, the bill will be covered regardless of what you decide.

My mother is confined to home and receiving home health

care that is covered by Medicare. She cannot prepare her own meals, but there is a local catering service that will bring in meals each day for a very reasonable charge. She cannot afford it unless Medicare can help pay for it but Medicare says it cannot pay for it. Is it possible that Medicare would pay for physical therapy and doctor visits and all, but not for food, when otherwise she will go hungry?

Food is considered custodial care and Medicare does not pay for custodial care even if it is required to sustain life. The only way to change this situation is to change the Medicare law; your congressman can help you do this.

I am getting home health care and a nurse comes fairly often to supervise my treatments. Since my daughter is a registered nurse, I would like her to take care of me and earn the money but the home health-care agency says Medicare will not pay a relative. Is this true?

Yes. Medicare will not cover "services performed by immediate relatives or members of your household."

MEDICARE PART B SUPPLEMENTARY MEDICAL INSURANCE (SMI)

Why do I have to pay a monthly premium for Part B (SMI) coverage and not for Part A?

Part B works entirely differently. Both A and B have deductibles but A goes by benefit periods (spells of illness) and B by the calendar year. Also, A has 100% coverage for early benefits; B (with very few exceptions) never covers more than 80% of the reasonable charge. And, Part A claims are filed for you; Part B claims are not (unless the provider accepts the assignment or does you a favor).

I went to the doctor because I was having chest pains and he took an X ray. His bill was $100 but Medicare only

allowed the same amount they had allowed previously for an ordinary visit. Doesn't Medicare cover the cost of X rays?

It sounds as if your doctor's bill was not itemized sufficiently. Take a look at it. If the bill just says "office visit" or something similar, without mentioning the X ray, Medicare will have processed it as a regular office visit. If this is the case, call Medicare and explain about the X ray (and any other services you may have received during the visit), and explain that the reason you went to the doctor was because you were having chest pains. Your doctor may have to submit a new bill, correctly itemized, but Medicare does cover the X ray under these circumstances and you are entitled to partial payment.

My doctor agreed to accept the assignment but he still sent me a bill. How can he do this?

There are a number of reasons why he may still send you a bill. For instance:

1. You will still owe him the 20% coinsurance Medicare doesn't pay.
2. You will owe him the full charge for any noncovered service, such as a flu shot.
3. He may not have received payment from Medicare yet, so the bill will not show a credit for the Medicare payment.

If you do not understand the bill, call the doctor's office and ask to speak to the secretary; she will be glad to explain it to you.

I will be 65 next year and will be applying for social security benefits. I understand that I will then be enrolled in Medicare Part A automatically, but that I need to make a special point of it if I wish to be enrolled in Medicare Part B. How do I apply for Medicare Part B?

You used to have to sign up for Medicare Part B (SMI) separately, but that is no longer the case. When you enroll in Part A automatically, you are also automatically enrolled in Part B. Your monthly premium will be deducted from your social security checks.

I am going to be 65 shortly and will automatically get Medicare Part A, but I am pretty healthy and thought maybe I would put off getting Part B since that would cost me over $100 a year. What do you think I should do?

If you possibly can, sign up for Medicare Part B as soon as you are eligible. If you don't, you will be penalized and end up paying more than you need to. If you do not sign up in the year in which you become eligible, you will be penalized by a 10% increase in your premium for every year in which you could have signed up but didn't—and you will pay this increased premium for the rest of your life.

In addition, you can never be that sure you won't need it. Even if you are healthy, you might have an accident that would require the use of a wheelchair or something similar. Medicare Part B would help cover the cost of this necessary equipment. And the premium is comparatively small.

If you find the premium beyond your means, it is possible that you might qualify for Medicaid.

I understand I must pay a deductible each time I enter the hospital in a new benefit period. How are benefit periods for the Part B deductibles measured?

The Part B deductibles must be paid only once in a calendar year. As soon as you have medical bills totaling the amount of the deductible, you will be covered for 80% of the reasonable charges for Part B bills for the rest of that year.

I just had my annual physical examination. My doctor says Medicare won't pay for it. Is this right?

Unfortunately, yes. Medicare does not pay for preventive medicine or for well-patient care. You have a physical checkup to try to keep yourself healthy and to catch any disease in its early states. This is sensible and means an illness will probably cost less because you are catching it while it is still easy to treat, but Medicare isn't that logical. Unless you go to the doctor for treatment for illness, you are not covered for Medicare.

A person on limited funds will tend to wait until illness manifests itself before he or she goes for diagnosis and treatment. This means, for instance, that a person may risk blindness because of inability to pay for a routine eye examination that would have detected eye disease in its early—and treatable—stages.

When does Medicare cover the cost of an ambulance?

Medicare Part B covers the cost of an ambulance under the following conditions:

1. when the ambulance equipment and personnel meet Medicare requirements;
2. when the ambulance is medically required; that is, when transportation in any other vehicle could endanger your health;
3. when transportation is from the scene of an accident to a hospital, or from your home to a hospital or SNF, or between hospitals (if medically necessary) and SNF, or a hospital or SNF to your home.

Any time the ambulance takes you to a place that is not the nearest facility, you may find you are covered only for the cost that would have been incurred if you had gone to the nearest facility.

When might ambulance charges be denied by Medicare?

Medicare covers charges for use of an ambulance if it is ordered by your doctor and if it is deemed medically necessary—which could happen in an emergency when no doctor is present. Be aware, however, that your doctor may order an ambulance under circumstances that Medicare would rule not medically necessary. If, for instance, your doctor transfers you from a large hospital to his small, private hospital, Medicare may rule that change was not medically necessary. In this event you would have to pay the entire cost of the ambulance yourself.

I understand why Medicare did not pay my entire doctor bill because I know it will pay only what is a "reasonable charge," but I do not understand why they did not credit the entire bill toward my deductible. After all, I had to pay the whole bill. Was this a mistake on Medicare's part?

Unfortunately no. Medicare is allowed to credit only the amount it allows as a "reasonable charge" toward deductibles. You are thus penalized twice—you have to pay the amount over the "reasonable charge" and you don't even get credit for it—but that is the way the law is set up. This is another reason why it is important for you to find doctors who will accept the assignment.

Last year I paid a doctor bill that I had filed a Medicare claim form for because the doctor was dunning me for the money. Now I am filling out my income-tax form for that year. Can I deduct what I paid the doctor as a medical expense even though I will be reimbursed for at least part of it sometime this year?

Yes, because medical expenses are deductible in the year they are paid. However, when you receive your check from Medicare, you will have to report as income the amount that the deduction for the bill you paid reduced your taxable income for the year in which you paid it. This may mean that only part of the reimbursement is taxable. Check with your local IRS office if you do not understand how to figure this.

How can I use the fact that Medicare updates its "reasonable charges" each July 1 to lower my medical costs?

When Medicare updates its reasonable charges, it usually raises the amounts of the doctors' bills it will pay. Waiting until after July 1 to incur medical charges means that a doctor who doesn't accept the assignment will be allowed a higher reasonable charge, so there will be less difference between what Medicare pays and what is left for you to pay. This will reduce the amount you have to pay.

My doctor refuses to accept the assignment. Does that mean I must pay his entire bill or will Medicare still pay part?

Medicare will still pay 80% of the amount it determines is a "reasonable charge." You will have to pay whatever Medicare does not pay—it may amount to more than the part Medicare pays.

What does "accepting the assignment" mean?

Medicare rarely pays as much as a doctor or a supplier bills for a service or a product. The doctor or supplier who accepts the assignment agrees that whatever Medicare allows (the "reasonable charge") will be the amount of his bill. In this event, Medicare will pay 80% and you will have to pay 20%.

My doctor accepted the assignment and Medicare paid him, but he still sent me a bill. Why do I owe him money if he accepted the assignment?

Even if he accepts the assignment, Medicare will pay only 80% of the "reasonable charge." You must still pay the remaining 20%.

In the case of hardship, many doctors will waive the 20% and accept what Medicare pays as full payment of their bill. It doesn't hurt to ask.

How do I ask a doctor or supplier if he will accept the assignment?

Look him straight in the eye and speak clearly and matter-of-factly, as if you expect the answer to be yes.

If you look down in your lap, twist your fingers and speak in a very low voice, he is much more liable to refuse.

Don't take no for an answer the first time, especially if he fails to look at you when refusing. Argue a little in a nice way, pointing out that you cannot afford his bills otherwise and will need time to pay them.

How can I find a doctor who will accept the assignment?

Medicare may have a list. If not, you will just have to phone doctors' offices and ask. It is sometimes difficult to determine until the doctor has met you, because many doctors will not accept the assignment if they think you are affluent.

I have very bad arthritis and nothing has helped, so my doctor has suggested a treatment that he says is still experimental but that he thinks might help. Now, however, Medicare will not pay for any of it. How come?

Medicare makes many decisions as to the necessity or appropriateness of health care. In your case, it is possible that there is no proof or record that the treatment really works or has any beneficial effects. In that case, Medicare will not pay for it.

Ask your Medicare office why the claim was denied. Since their office made the decision, they should be able to tell you the basis for it.

In the future, if a doctor proposes unusual treatment, get the details and check with Medicare to be sure you are covered for that specific health-care service. If you are not, you may be able to talk your doctor into charging you very little, since you are taking part in an experiment from which he may benefit professionally.

I use oxygen regularly and have for the past several years. Medicare has always paid for it but now they have suddenly stopped. What has happened?

Medicare sometimes decides that a covered service is being "overutilized." In your case, it would mean that you are using more oxygen than Medicare considers necessary for your illness. Speak to your doctor; if he says you need the amount of oxygen you are using, ask Medicare to review the claim. Often a mistake is made in this area and payments will be reinstated.

If coverage is resumed, you will be reimbursed for any bills that were not paid (up to 80%).

I go to an acupuncturist who is a regular doctor. Will Medicare pay his bills?

Medicare doesn't pay for acupuncture, no matter who does it.

Will Medicare pay for me to get insulin injections for my diabetes?

No. Medicare considers insulin injections as something the beneficiary can do for himself or herself.

I understand that Medicare pays for detoxification facilities, but when I sent in the bill, the EOMB came back with the notation that this was a noncovered service. How come?

There has been a change in the law; Medicare no longer covers detoxification facilities.

I have cataracts. My doctor says they are not operable yet, but asks me to come in twice a year to see if they have reached that point. Will Medicare reimburse me for these visits?

Yes. Medicare covers eye-doctor visits for cataracts; it does not cover routine eye examinations.

I had to go to three different doctors. The first charged me $20 and Medicare allowed $15. The second charged me $25 and Medicare allowed $15. The third charged $45 and Medicare allowed $30. Why did Medicare allow different amounts?

Medicare's reasonable charges may vary from doctor to doctor because of the way the reasonable charge is arrived at. If you really want to know how this is done, read Chapter 19.

I was in an automobile accident recently and need plastic surgery, but my friends say Medicare won't pay for it. Is this true?

Check with your surgeon and with Medicare. In the case of an injury or an accident, Medicare will often cover the cost of plastic or rehabilitative surgery.

My ophthalmologist has recommended that I have laser surgery for an eye condition, but he says Medicare won't pay for it. How can that be?

Although laser surgery has been widely accepted by ophthalmologists, Medicare disallows coverage for it as "not an accepted procedure." However, this can change at any time since all new procedures undergo review regularly and may be included at any time. Check just before you set up arrangements and you may find the rules have been changed in your favor.

When I first retired in 1979 at age 65, I went to live in England because my mother was still alive there. When she died earlier this year, I came back to the United States. I hadn't enrolled in Medicare Part B (SMI) when I was in England because I wouldn't have received any benefit from it, since Medicare coverage doesn't apply when you are in England. Now Medicare is asking me to pay a much higher premium for Part B coverage than anyone else I know pays. I didn't get it at age 65 because I wouldn't have had any use of it; why should I be penalized for using common sense?

Medicare penalizes late enrollment, regardless of the reason. However, you may still have gained because you saved all the money you would have spent on premiums for the years in which you didn't enroll. If you figure out how much your increased amount is (10% for each year you didn't enroll), and divide it into the amount of the premiums you would have paid, you may find that it will be ten or more years before you are actually paying out any more in actual cash than if you had enrolled at age 65 and paid monthly premiums since then at the regular rate.

In any case, the penalty is imposed on all late enrollees and cannot be appealed.

My claim for a doctor bill was processed without any allowed amount; the reason given was "charges previously submitted." I never sent in this bill before—what does Medicare mean?

This is a mistake commonly made in processing doctor bills. Part of the reason is that doctor bills tend to be cumulative; they often list charges that have already been submitted and paid by Medicare, along with new and recent charges. To avoid confusion, it would help if you put a line through those charges for which you have already submitted claims.

You will also find this won't happen as often with the new super bills that many doctors are now using.

My eyelids were all wrinkled and crepey and made me look even older than I am, so I had them fixed. Medicare wouldn't pay for the surgery but it paid for it when a friend of mine had it done. Shouldn't Medicare be consistent?

It does sometimes happen that Medicare isn't consistent, but it also happens that the two claims may seem the same and really be quite different. For instance, your operation was clearly cosmetic surgery and would never be covered by Medicare. The same operation, however, might be medically necessary if the condition of the upper eyelids were such that they were actually interfering with vision. In that case, the operation to correct the condition of the upper lids would be covered. If the lower lids were also operated on at the same time, that would not be covered unless it could be shown that in some way the condition of the lower lids was also interfering with vision.

My teeth are very bad and my dentist says they must all be pulled. It will be very expensive so I asked him to accept the assignment, but he said this service is not covered by Medicare. Is he right?

Yes. Very few dental services are covered by Medicare. Filling teeth, pulling teeth, root-canal work and the cost of dentures are all necessary services that are not covered.

What is a prosthetic device?

Generally speaking, it is a device needed to replace an internal body organ. Examples of prosthetic devices are: pacemakers; corrective lenses needed after a cataract operation; colostomy bags; breast prostheses and artificial limbs and eyes. Dentures, however, are not included.

I have had a mastectomy. Will Medicare pay for a surgical brassiere?

Surgical brassieres are covered items, but I would suggest you check with Medicare as to what kind is approved. If there is a very fancy one on the market, Medicare will approve only the basic kind.

Does Medicare cover treatment for allergies?

Allergies are treated just like any other illness.

My father is mentally ill and I have been sending the doctor's bills to Medicare. They paid some but now the claims are coming back (on the EOMB form) with the notation that they are noncovered services. Isn't this a mistake?

Probably not. You are thinking of the coverage for doctor bills as being 80% of the allowable charge. But coverage for outpatient treatment of mental illness is limited to

$250 in a calendar year. And it would be even less than that if your father had not met any of his Part B deductible of $75. In that case, the effective coverage maximum would be only $175.

I have very flat feet and lately they have gotten worse. My doctor has written a prescription for adapting regular shoes so that they give me more support, but Medicare says it will not pay for the cost of these changes. Is that right?

Medicare does not pay for any special shoes unless they are part of a leg brace.

I haven't paid my doctor bill because I haven't gotten the money yet from Medicare. He is getting very cross and writes unpleasant notes on the bills. Why doesn't he understand my predicament?

Medicare payments aren't usually so slow that the doctor should become that impatient. In Connecticut, for instance, payment is usually made within two weeks—sooner if the doctor accepts the assignment. If it has been much longer than that, maybe something has happened on Medicare's end; you should call the Medicare office and ask about the claim.

I have had a cataract operation in both eyes and Medicare has covered my eyeglasses. A friend of mine is wearing contact lenses for the same reason and Medicare has covered that. But now I find that my eyes have become very sensitive to bright sunlight and I would like to get sunglasses with the same prescription. Medicare says it will not cover sunglasses. It seems to me that they are just as medically necessary as eyeglasses and contact lenses; have the Medicare people made a mistake?

No. Sunglasses are never covered, even if they are prescription sunglasses. What you could do instead, maybe, the next time you get a pair of cataract lenses, is to get the kind that are tinted. This will provide some protection from the sun and Medicare will pay for regular tinted lenses for cataract glasses.

My husband has had a stroke and cannot feed himself, get out of bed to go to the bathroom, take a bath and so on. He is too heavy for me to lift and some days my arthritis is so bad that I cannot make meals or take care of him properly. The social workers say there is no Medicare coverage to help me out, but I don't understand—doesn't home health care provide for this kind of situation?

No, not if your husband's condition has stabilized and cannot be improved through therapy and doesn't require skilled nursing care. Everything you have described is called "custodial care," and coverage for custodial care is specifically excluded from coverage under the Medicare law.

FILING A CLAIM

My father has just gone on Medicare and he has some doctor bills. How does he get Medicare to pay them?

Call the doctor's office and ask whether the assignment has been accepted. If it has, the doctor will file the claim. If not, ask if they have copies of claim form HCFA-1490S. If you cannot get the form from them, you can get it from the social security office or from Medicare. (See Chapter 16.)

I've tried to get some claims paid, but Medicare says they are too old and that they won't pay them. Is there a time limit on claims?

Yes, there is. You have at least 15 months in which to submit a claim. The rule is: for services rendered from January through September of a year, claims must be filed by December 31 of the following year. For services rendered from October to December of a year, the time limit is extended by one year. In other words, a claim for services rendered in October 1982 must be filed by December 31, 1984.

Is it okay to send in more than one bill attached to the claim form?

Medicare says to send in as many as you wish. Do not, however, send in claims for different years. Send in claims for services rendered in one year, and another form for claims for the next year. Claims are processed by year and it's easier for you to sort them out than for Medicare to do so.

I know I can attach more than one bill to my Medicare claim form, but can I attach bills from different doctors and suppliers or do they all have to be from the same place?

You may attach as many bills as you wish from as many suppliers as you wish.

When I file a Medicare claim, why can't I just send in the doctor's bills? I hate filling out forms.

The doctor's bill would not contain all the information Medicare needs. The form you have to fill out has been greatly simplified, and you won't believe how easy it is until you make an effort to fill it out—it's much easier than following a recipe in your favorite cookbook. All it asks for is your name, address, Medicare card number (look at it even if you think you know it by heart) and the letter after the number. Sign and send it in. There are step-by-step instructions in this book, but after filling out the form once, you will never even need to refer to them again.

I travel around a lot visiting my family and sometimes have to go to a doctor in another state from the one in which I live. How will Medicare keep track of whether or not I have filled my deductible?

Don't worry. All Medicare claims are sent from the

state in which they are filed to a central computer. The computer keeps track and lets the states know when you have filled your deductible requirements. Of course, even computers—or the people who use them—sometimes make mistakes, so you should always keep track too.

I was visiting my daughter in Virginia and became ill. I phoned my doctor and he asked me to have certain tests taken. When I returned home, I sent the bill for the tests to my Medicare carrier but I was subsequently told I should have sent the bill to the Medicare office in Virginia. What is the rule about where to send bills?

You should send your Medicare claims to the Medicare office in the state where the charges were incurred.

Does Medicare pay for diagnostic tests performed out-of-hospital at a laboratory?

Medicare will pay part of the charges for your tests providing you use a laboratory that has been certified by Medicare to provide the services you require. Not all laboratories are certified for any tests, and of the ones that are certified, some may not be certified for the particular tests you require. Your doctor should know whether you are covered by Medicare for those tests performed at that laboratory. Be sure to ask him.

I have received my Explanation of Medicare Benefits form, together with a check reimbursing me for some of my medical expenses, but I do not think the reimbursement is correct. Whom should I call to ask?

Phone or write the Medicare office explaining why you think the reimbursement is incorrect. Be prepared to give all the information on the EOMB form. If you write, enclose a copy. The more information you give, the easier it will be for Medicare to determine whether an error has been made. Errors are made frequently, so do not hesitate to question a payment you feel is incorrect.

When is the worst time to send in Medical claim forms?
In December. Many people accumulate their bills and send them in all at once at the end of the year. This means a mountain of claims need to be processed all at once and results in a delay in sending out checks.

When should I send in my claim forms to Medicare?
As soon as you get them. You will get your money faster.

My grandfather died recently and he was a Medicare beneficiary. My neighbor tells me I have to pay all his bills before I can file a claim for them with Medicare. This would be very hard for me to do. Is there any other way?
The law has been changed so that you no longer have to pay bills for deceased beneficiaries in order for them to be covered by Medicare. You can file them before paying them, providing you accept liability for them.

How do I bill Medicare for my hospital bill?
You don't have to do anything; the hospital will bill Medicare direct without bothering you; you will be sent a utilization notice that Medicare has paid the bill.

After my recent operation I received a bill from two surgeons; Medicare has covered only one. Shouldn't both be covered?
Look at your Explanation of Medicare Benefits (EOMB) form. If it says "charges previously submitted" or "charges previously considered," or something like that, Medicare may be confused and may think one surgeon has submitted two bills. The only way you can be sure what has happened is to call Medicare and ask. Usually both bills would be covered if two surgeons were deemed medically necessary.

I understand Medicare encourages us to question claims we

think are incorrect. They say over 50% of the claims questioned are corrected and receive a higher allowed charge. How can Medicare be such a mess?

Medicare does fairly well considering the enormous number of claims it must process. In 1981 in Connecticut alone, Medicare processed over two million claims. In the same year Medicare personnel was cut drastically, just at a time when the over-65 population is growing. You can expect more errors when there is a smaller staff to process more claims.

Remember, also, that an incorrect determination is not always Medicare's fault. Medicare must work with the information provided on the claim. If the doctor's bill is inaccurate, incomplete or incorrect, your claim will reflect this. Medicare has no way of knowing if this is the case; you must be alert and try to clean up providers' bills so that you get proper coverage.

I have had two hip operations and each time the amount of the surgeon's bill Medicare allowed was so low that I questioned it; in each case Medicare increased the amount of its payment. How can Medicare keep making the same mistake?

The amount of the payment depends on the way the service is coded. If the wrong code number is put down, the claim will be incorrectly processed from then on, because Medicare personnel will no longer look at the original bill. This is what is called a "computer error," but it is the result of someone punching in the wrong code information to the computer. Fortunately, it is easy for Medicare to check when you question the amount of payment and to correct the allowed amount.

I have just moved into the area so I had to change doctors. The doctor I chose came very highly recommended but when I filed his bills for Medicare payment, Medicare de-

nied them because he has no Medicare number. How can this be?

Your doctor should have known better. All doctors who are willing to participate in Medicare obtain an identification number. It simply establishes that they are physicians, within Medicare's definition of the term, and meet the necessary requirements. Ask your doctor to do this, and meanwhile, try not to incur any further charges. Incidentally, all providers—doctors, suppliers of medical equipment, hospitals and so on—must conform to this rule. Simply ask if they are participating in Medicare and whether they have filed any Medicare claims and received any Medicare payments or approvals.

Medigap Insurance

What is Medigap insurance?

A name for insurance that pays some of the health-care costs Medicare doesn't; in other words, it fills the gaps.

The name is somewhat misleading because you will still have to pay some health-care costs out of your own pocket, even with Medicare *and* Medigap coverage.

Why do I need Medigap insurance?

Because Medicare does not cover—nor is it meant to cover—total health-care expenses.

I want to buy Medigap insurance. Does the federal government have a Medigap insurance policy I can buy?

There is no federal government Medigap insurance policy. Beware of any private company or agent that claims to be connected with the federal government.

Can I trust an insurance agent to look over my present medical insurance and tell me honestly whether I need any more policies?

Definitely not. You should carefully examine your present policies yourself and see where they are lacking coverage. Any new policies you are considering should be compared to what you already have to see whether they duplicate your present coverage. Most agents are not knowledgeable about other policies and may not know that what they want to sell you duplicates coverage you are already paying for. And some unscrupulous agents couldn't care less, and will try to scare you into buying policies you don't need and that will never be any good to you.

If you have trouble understanding insurance policies, ask a friend, a social worker or someone at your senior center to help you look over the actual policy.

You might also want to send for the free information pamphlet from the Health Care Financing Administration called "Guide to Health Insurance For People With Medicare," HCFA No. 02100.

If I have regular Blue Cross/Blue Shield insurance, should I notify them when I become eligible for Medicare?

Yes. But don't just let it lapse. This is the time to examine your health-insurance policies. Take into consideration your whole family's coverage (see question below).

If you decide to buy Blue Cross/Blue Shield as Medigap insurance, call the Blues office you deal with as soon as you receive your Medicare identification card. The Blues will convert your contract to one that supplements Medicare coverage—in other words, to a Medigap policy.

Your new premium will be lower than your old premium, but your new coverage will be different also. Be sure to read your contract when you get it so you know what you are getting under the new policy.

When I convert to Blue Cross/Blue Shield Medigap insurance, how will this affect my family?

If your present Blues contract includes coverage for members of your family, check with your Blues office to find out how much of this protection will be included when you switch to a Medigap policy. You will probably have to take out additional insurance for the other family members. Since Blues contracts vary from state to state, be sure to check with the one issuing your contract.

What is a prepayment plan?

A prepayment plan is a health-care delivery system where you pay a monthly premium, regardless of the care you have had, and that covers health care when you need it. An HMO, or health maintenance organization, is an example of a prepaid health-care plan. You never receive a bill from an HMO and the monthly premium covers almost all of your health-care needs.

Can I belong to an HMO when I have Medicare coverage?

Yes. There seems to be some confusion about this, and even some doctors do not know that your Medicare coverage will work with the HMO.

Since there are many different arrangements, ask the HMO you belong to or are thinking of joining if they take Medicare beneficiaries, how it works and what services, if any, are not covered when you join the HMO.

How can I find out if there is an HMO in my locality?

Call any social security office. It will give you the names of the ones that cover your area.

Medicare in General

What exactly is Medicare?

Medicare is health insurance paid for by the federal government and administered state-by-state by Blue Cross or private insurance companies. You earn the right to it the same way you earn the right to social security benefits, but there are ways you can get it even if you are not eligible for social security. It is not a national health plan because it doesn't cover everyone; many people over 65 are not eligible and some under 65 are.

Will Medicare cover all my health-care costs?

By no means. Presently it covers about a third. Medicare was never meant to cover all costs but only to help pay some of the costs of short-term care. It has been described as a "grossly inadequate, inflation-producing, fee-for-service health-care delivery system . . . without protection against catastrophic illness" or long-term care. It pays nothing for preventive medicine, most nursing homes or custodial care.

Where should I apply for Medicare?

At your local social security office.

It isn't necessary to go to the office in person. The person at the social security office will take the information for the application over the phone and fill out the form for you.

What is the difference between Medicare Part A and Medicare Part B?

Generally speaking, Medicare Part A covers part of the expense incurred while you are in the hospital, with the exception of bills from doctors who are not on the hospital staff, such as your personal physician, surgeon, usually the anesthetist, and so on. It also covers some home health-care costs. The longer the hospital stay, the less Medicare covers; after 90 continuous days of hospitalization you pay the total cost.

Medicare Part A is officially called "Hospital and Insurance Benefits for the Aged and Disabled." It is commonly referred to as Medicare hospital insurance, or HI.

Medicare Part B, officially called "Supplementary

Medical Insurance Benefits for the Aged and Disabled," or SMI, covers private doctor bills, surgeons' fees, and a number of health-care costs such as diagnostic tests, wheelchairs, oxygen used at home and other home health-care costs.

Participation in Medicare Part B requires payment of a monthly premium, which can be deducted automatically from your social security check once you have enrolled. If you elect not to take social security benefits when you reach 65 years of age, you will have to make direct payments of this premium. See page 000.

When should I apply for Medicare?

You should apply for Medicare *three months before* your 65th birthday.

I lost or mislaid my Medicare card. How do I get a new one?

Ask the people in the social security office to please get you a new one.

What territory is included in the term "United States" as used by Medicare?

All the 50 states, as well as Puerto Rico, the American Virgin Islands, Guam, American Samoa and the Northern Mariana Islands.

How can I find the telephone number of my social security office?

Look in your local telephone book under the heading "United States Government." Then look for the subheading, "Health and Human Services Dept." Under that it will say "Social Security Administration," and that is the number of your local social security office.

You can often save yourself a trip to the social security office by getting the information you need over the phone.

How can I find out about amendments to the Medicare program?

It's not easy, because often a change will be reported in the newspapers but your state carrier will not have guidelines from the federal government and will not, therefore, be putting the changes into effect. If you are fairly sure there has been a change that would favorably affect you, call your congressman or senator and ask if it has really been made into a law. Then call your local state carrier and tell them. If they still say they cannot implement the law just yet, get the name and title of the person you have spoken with and get back to your congressman and senator with this information.

If you have not heard anything within 14 days, call your senator and congressman again and politely inquire what is happening.

Medispeak Glossary:
Learning to Speak "Medicare"

Medicare is a special language in which common English words sometimes take on different or redefined meanings. You cannot understand what you are and are not entitled to under Medicare unless you know what Medicare means when it uses certain words. In this glossary we will try to explain the words you will encounter most frequently in Medicare. Use it for reference; reading it from start to finish would only depress you.

Accepting the assignment. This term applies to your relationship with your physician and other providers under Part B (SMI). If they agree to accept the assignment, they agree to accept as the total amount of their bill whatever Medicare determines is the "reasonable" and allowable charge. If they agree to this, Medicare will pay 80% of their bill and you will be liable for the remaining 20%. You should ask any doctor or any medical supply store whether they will accept the assignment each time you plan to incur a bill with them.

Beneficiary. Anyone entitled to Medicare benefits. You, for instance, if you are 65 or older.

Benefit period. A segment of time during which certain Medicare Part A (HI) benefits apply. A benefit period begins with the first day of hospitalization and continues until you have been out of the hospital or skilled nursing facility for 60 consecutive days. There are no benefit periods for Medicare Part B.

Calendar year. January 1 to December 31.

Carrier. The private insurance company selected by the Social Security Administration to administer the Part B (SMI) section of Medicare. The carrier is appointed state-by-state. The Medicare beneficiary sends claim forms to the carrier within the state in which the charge was incurred. (Part A claims are also administered by private insurance companies, called intermediaries.) Obviously, the Medicare law will be interpreted by the carrier; the beneficiary should always feel free to question the interpretation if he or she feels the amount that has been paid on the claim is too low.

Claim forms. The Medicare Part B forms you fill out and send to Medicare in order to get the partial payment you are entitled to for covered services.

Coinsurance. The amount of your health-care expenses that you share with Medicare. In Part A Medicare, you pay part of your daily hospital bill after the 60th day of admission; that is coinsurance. In Part B, you pay 20% of the "reasonable charge" made to you by your doctor or provider of services. Do not take this to mean that you pay only 20% of your health-care bills; on the average you pay over 60% even with full Medicare coverage because so many costs are not covered.

Covered services. Health-care services for which you are insured under Medicare and for which Medicare will partially pay. However, even covered services must be furnished by a participating hospital, or by a supplier approved by Medicare, or they will not be covered.

Custodial care. The kind of health care that does not require the services of a physician or a registered nurse. Lack of custodial care may be life-threatening but it is never covered by Medicare.

Deductible. The amount you must pay for health-care services before Medicare coverage becomes operable. For instance, you are liable to a deductible upon being admitted to a hospital for the first time in each benefit period. As of January 1, 1982, the Part A (HI) deductible is $260; it usually is increased every January 1. As of January 1, 1982, the Part B (SMI) deductible is $75; this deductible does not tend to increase as regularly as the Part A deductible, but it may be increased each January 1. Medicare does not pay any part of your Part B claims until this deductible has been met by you. That does not mean you have to have paid out that amount; it does mean you have to have incurred bills for that amount for services that are covered by Medicare. Since not all health-care services are covered, it does not mean that the first of your bills will be automatically credited toward the deductible. You could, for example, have a bill for $500 in prescription drugs, but not one penny of that would apply to your deductible because Medicare does not pay for out-of-hospital medicines.

Durable medical equipment. Durable medical equipment is defined by Medicare as equipment that can withstand repeated use, is primarily and customarily used to serve a medical purpose, is generally not useful to a person in the absence of an illness or injury, and is appropriate for use in the home. It includes: wheelchairs, crutches, commodes, walkers, oxygen therapy equipment and hospital beds. Medicare allows the recipient to either buy or rent this equipment depending on the circumstances.

End-stage renal disease (ESRD). Kidney disease that is covered by Medicare: "that stage of kidney impairment that appears irreversible and permanent and requires a regular course of dialysis or kidney transplantation to maintain life."

Extended care. As opposed to acute care, which requires hospitalization, extended care may not require hospitalization but may still require full-time professional nursing care and other health services. If these cannot be provided at home, Medicare will pay partially for your stay in a skilled nursing home for up to 100 days.

Inpatient. What you are when you are in the hospital overnight or longer.

Intermediary. What the Medicare Part A carrier is usually called. You will seldom have any contact with the intermediary.

Intermediate-care facility. Usually referred to as ICFs. Most nursing homes fall into this category. They are used by patients who do not require the services of a skilled nursing facility but still cannot take care of themselves. If you do not require skilled nursing on a daily basis, or if you do not require skilled rehabilitation services provided only at an SNF, or if in any way the care you require can be defined as custodial care, you will probably go to an ICF. Medicare coverage does not apply to ICFs if they cannot qualify under the requirements for SNFs, even though they may provide extensive nursing and rehabilitation facilities. If you are in doubt as to whether or not you will be covered by Medicare, ask before you go into the nursing home.

Level of care. Defines which services can be offered by a provider in order for that provider to qualify for Medicare coverage. For instance, a nursing home is not automatically covered by Medicare; it must be a "skilled nursing facility." The level of care in a skilled nursing facility is much higher than in any other type of nursing home.

Medicare. A two-part (A and B) health insurance program that partially pays for some health-care expenses for most people living in the United States who are 65 years of age or older.

Medicare Part A. Also known as hospital insurance (HI) because it partially pays primarily for in-hospital expenses.

Medicare Part B. Also known as supplementary medical insurance (SMI) because it partially pays primarily for doctor and health-supplies bills.

Medigap insurance. Private insurance that is purchased by Medicare recipients in an effort to cover health-care costs not covered by Medicare. Many companies offer Medigap policies and policies should be carefully compared to see which one is best. None completely cover all health-care costs but some are better than others.

Noncovered levels of care. Usually applied to stays in extended-care facilities that do not meet the requirements for SNFs. Also applies to patients in SNFs who do not require daily skilled nursing and other similar services. Generally speaking, any type of care that could be defined as custodial is a noncovered level of care. Noncovered means that Medicare will not pay any part of the charges.

Nursing home. A broad term for a facility where you reside and receive various services. There are many types of nursing homes and Medicare covers only SNFs.

100% coverage. Medicare pays 100% of the bill.

Outpatient. What you are when you receive hospital services but do not stay in the hospital overnight. An emergency-room patient may start out as an outpatient and become an inpatient when his or her medical condition requires hospitalization.

Partial coverage. Medicare pays part of the bill; you pay the rest. Some Medicare bills are 100% covered; most Medicare bills are partially covered.

Participating hospital. A hospital that has fulfilled certain requirements for acceptance by Medicare and to whom Medicare will reimburse covered expenses according to the Medicare schedule.

Pathological services. These include services in connection with clinical and anatomical pathology, such as microbiological, chemical, hematological, cytological and immunohematological. The pathologist can tell you whether or not service is covered.

Personal comfort or convenience items. All the little extras, such as rental of a television set when you are in the hospital, that make life more comfortable. Since they are not essential to your treatment, Medicare does not pay for them. It will, however, allow typical hospital hand-outs, such as baby lotion, bath powder, mouthwash, sometimes comb and toothbrush, if such hand-outs are routinely furnished to all patients.

Private-duty nurses. Registered nurses hired by you either at home or in the hospital. Medicare does not pay for them even if they are furnished and paid by the hospital which then bills you. They are in addition to the regular hospital nursing staff and are presumed to give you more personal service, although in practice they often take care of more than one patient at a time.

Private room. A hospital room for a single occupant. Some hospitals have only private rooms, in which case Medicare will pay for it. If you have a choice, however, Medicare will pay only for a semiprivate room, unless your doctor says a private room is "medically necessary."

Professional standards review organization (PSRO). Organizations set up in various localities by the federal government to review the use of health-care services in an effort to reduce fraud and misuse of the Medicare program. They oversee hospitals primarily, and one of their functions is to determine whether a hospital admission and a hospital stay or an operation is "medically necessary." Decisions made by the PSRO supersede those made by your physician. It is possible, therefore, for you to be denied Medicare coverage for a hospital stay, even though your doctor says it is necessary.

Prosthetic device. A device that replaces all or part of a body organ, or all or part of the function of a permanently inoperative or malfunctioning body organ; for example, artificial legs, cataract lenses, pacemakers.

Provider. Any organization or facility or persons from whom you get covered Medicare services. This includes home health agencies, hospitals, skilled nursing facilities, rehab centers and physicians. The provider supplies services to the beneficiary.

Radiological services. These services include: X rays or rays from radioactive substances used for diagnostic or therapeutic purposes; radium therapy, radioisotopes (as used in nuclear medicine); various diagnostic tests, including angiograms, myelograms, ventriculograms, pyelograms and aortograms. The radiologist can tell you whether or not a service is covered.

Reasonable charge. The amount of a covered bill that Medicare accepts as a basis for coverage. Medicare will usually pay only 80% of what it determines is a reasonable charge no matter what the amount of the actual bill. See Chapter 19 for fuller explanation.

Residential-care facilities. You may think of this type of facility as a nursing home because it provides a certain amount of care and monitoring of patients who are basically "functionally" independent and can assume the responsibility for most daily needs. (It might not be entirely safe for you to live alone but you may not require actual day-to-day help in most activities.) This type of facility is commonly called a nursing home but is never covered by Medicare.

Routine physical. A routine physical or a "checkup" is an examination performed without an indication of a specific illness and unrelated to any symptom or injury. This includes the examinations sometimes required by insurance companies or prospective employers. An exception is the preadmission requirement by some hospitals for a chest X ray for detection of possible respiratory disease.

Semiprivate room. A hospital room with two or more occupants.

Skilled nursing facility. Usually referred to as an SNF, this is the only kind of nursing home that Medicare will pay for. To qualify as an SNF, a nursing home must have at least one full-time registered nurse and a supervising physician, and provide 24-hour skilled nursing services. Admission to an SNF does not, however, automatically guarantee that Medicare will partially cover your costs; your stay in an SNF must be approved by Medicare as medically necessary or coverage will be denied. Most nursing homes are *not* skilled nursing facilities.

Spell of illness. See **Benefit period.**

Supplementary medical insurance. Same as **Medicare Part B (SMI).**

United States. All the 50 states plus Puerto Rico, the American Virgin Islands, Guam, American Samoa and the Northern Mariana Islands.

Insurance Glossary:
Terms You Should Know
When Reading a Medigap Policy

Benefit maximum. No matter how good a policy is it won't pay an unlimited amount of money for a benefit. Usually a policy specifies the most it will pay for a given benefit—either a length of time (for example, 60 days in the hospital) or a dollar amount ($500, $1000). Compare these maximums carefully; here is one of the areas where you will find sizable differences between policies.

Coinsurance. The amount you share with the insurance company in paying bills. Just as Medicare pays 80% of your provider's "allowable charge" and you pay 20% coinsurance, Medigap policies often pay less than 100% of a bill and you pay the difference. Read the policy carefully; you probably are also paying anything above the "allowable charge," since most Medigap policies follow Medicare guidelines.

Daily benefit amount. The specific dollar payment an indemnity policy will give you under specified conditions.

Deductible. The amount of your covered bills that you must pay before your insurance company starts picking up the tab. The higher the deductible, the better for you (everything else being equal) because the premiums should decrease as the deductible increases. Get policies with the highest deductible you can manage.

Duration of benefits. Specifies how long an indemnity policy will continue to pay cash benefits for hospitalization and nursing-home stays.

Elimination period. This is a term common to indemnity policies. It acts like a deductible in that coverage doesn't start until the end of the elimination period. Some hospital policies, for instance, do not start to pay until you have been in the hospital for a week; since the average hospital stay is less than a week, the insurance company is not taking much of a risk in selling this type of policy. On the other hand, the longer the elimination period, the lower the premium (usually).

Exclusion. Usually used in connection with the pre-existing condition clause to make clear that the policy will not pay benefits for illness arising from that condition. Can be very broadly interpreted by the insurance company so that a condition such as diabetes or hypertension can rule out coverage for eye problems, kidney problems or any heart problems. Be careful with this one.

Guaranteed renewable. This type of policy guarantees that you can retain your premium up to the age specified (often 65) as long as you pay the premium. It usually also guarantees that it cannot raise your premium unless it also raises the premium of everyone else who has the same policy. Some policies are guaranteed renewable for life.

Hospital income policy. An indemnity policy that does not pay any part of your actual in-hospital bills but pays you a certain amount of dollars per covered days of hospitalization. Coverage usually starts after a waiting period (usually the first week of hospitalization) and ends after a specified number of days.

Lifetime maximum. This is an upper limit on the dollar amount the policy will pay no matter what claims you make—even if they are for legitimate covered items. It is usually quite high—some policies have a lifetime maximum of a million dollars—but you should take a look in case it's stingy. Keep in mind that a short hospital stay can cost $10,000 to $15,000 without half trying.

Major-medical policy. A policy designed to cover large medical bills for major illnesses and not to pick up the small charges you incur in a minor illness. Usually has a high deductible and a high lifetime maximum.

Pre-existing condition. A health problem that you have at the time the agent writes out the policy. Anything from hypertension to flat feet. The policy will usually say any condition for which you are "receiving treatment," so if you are taking aspirin for frequent headaches, the headaches could be counted as a pre-existing condition. Even if you haven't been to the doctor for ten years, if you are still taking a prescription he gave you ten years ago, whatever you are taking it for is a pre-existing condition. Read the section on this clause; it can make your policy practically worthless.

Renewable at company option. In other words, the company alone decides whether or not to renew your policy. Usually this decision is made on the anniversary of the date you originally took out the policy, but sometimes it has to do with dates or premium payments. It is not usually effective during a period of illness. This type of decision can be extremely arbitrary and you have no recourse.

Waiting period. Here again, usually used with the pre-existing condition clause to specify how long you will not be covered for pre-existing conditions. Any time is too long, but a year is ridiculous and you should look for a policy that is more reasonable.

Wrap-around policy. Insurance term for a certain type of Medigap insurance. Good ones pay for services not covered by Medicare as well as picking up Medicare deductibles and co-insurance. The name comes from the fact that they supposedly wrap around and fill in the gaps in Medicare coverage.

Where to Send Your
Medicare Claims

Your claims should be filed at the Medicare office in the state in which they were incurred. Here are the names and addresses to which claims in each state should be sent.

If you should make a mistake and send your claim to the wrong office, it will be forwarded to the correct office, but this will delay payment of your claim.

ALABAMA

Medicare
Blue Cross–Blue Shield of
Alabama
450 River Chase Parkway,
East
Birmingham, AL 35298

ALASKA

Medicare
Aetna Life & Casualty
Crown Plaza
P. O. Box 991
Portland, OR 97201

ARIZONA

Medicare
Aetna Life & Casualty
Medicare Claim
Administration
3010 West Fairmont Avenue
Phoenix, AZ 85017

CALIFORNIA

*Counties of Los Angeles,
Orange, San Diego, Ventura,
San Bernadino, Imperial, San
Luis Obispo, Riverside, Santa
Barbara:*

California: counties (*cont'd*)

Medicare
Occidental Life Insurance Co.
of California
Box 54905
Terminal Annex
Los Angeles, CA 90051

Rest of State:
Medicare
Blue Shield of California
P. O. Box 7968, Rincon
Annex
San Francisco, CA 94120

COLORADO
Medicare
Blue Shield of Colorado
700 Broadway
Denver, CO 80273

CONNECTICUT
Medicare
Connecticut General Life
Insurance Co.
100 Barnes Road
Wallingford, CT 06492

DELAWARE
Medicare
Blue Cross and Blue Shield of
Delaware
201 West 14th Street
Wilmington, DE 19899

DISTRICT OF COLUMBIA
Medicare
Medical Service of D.C.
550 12th St. S.W.
Washington, DC 20024

FLORIDA
Counties of Dade, Monroe:
Medicare
Group Health, Inc.
P. O. Box 981370
Miami, FL 33198

Rest of State:
Medicare
Blue Shield of Florida, Inc.
P. O. Box 2525
Jacksonville, FL 32203

GEORGIA
The Prudential Insurance Co.
of America
Medicare Part B
P. O. Box 95466
Executive Park Station
Atlanta, GA 30347

HAWAII
Medicare
Aetna Life & Casualty
P. O. Box 3947
Honolulu, HI 96812

IDAHO
Medicare
The Equitable Life Assurance Society
P. O. Box 8048
Boise, ID 83707

ILLINOIS
Cook County
E.D.S. Federal Corp.
Medicare Claims
P. O. Box 66906
Chicago, IL 60666

INDIANA
Medicare Part B
120 West Market Street
Indianapolis, IN 46204

IOWA
Medicare
Blue Shield of Iowa
636 Grand
Des Moines, IA 50307

KANSAS
*Counties of
Johnson, Wyandotte:*
Medicare
Blue Shield of Kansas City
P. O. Box 169
Kansas City, MO 64141

Rest of State:
Medicare
Blue Shield of Kansas
P. O. Box 239
Topeka, KS 66601

KENTUCKY
Medicare
Metropolitan Life Insurance Co.
1218 Harrodsburg Road
Lexington, KY 40504

LOUISIANA
Medicare
Pan-American Life Insurance Co.
P. O. Box 60450
New Orleans, LA 70160

MAINE
Medicare
Blue Shield of Massachusetts
P. O. Box 2410
Boston, MA 02208

MARYLAND
Counties of Montgomery, Prince Georges:
Medicare
Medical Service of D.C.
550 12th St. S.W.
Washington, DC 20024

Rest of State:
Maryland Blue Shield, Inc.
700 East Joppa Road
Towson, MD 21204

MASSACHUSETTS
Medicare
Blue Shield of Massachusetts, Inc.
P. O. Box 2194
Boston, MA 02106

MICHIGAN
Medicare
Blue of Shield of Michigan
P. O. Box 2201
Detroit, MI 48231

MINNESOTA
Counties of Anoka, Dakota,
Filmore, Goodhue, Hennepin,
Houston, Olmstead, Ramsey,
Wabasha, Washington,
Winona:
Medicare
The Travelers Insurance
Company
8120 Penn Avenue, South
Bloomington, MN 55431

Rest of State:
Medicare
Blue Shield of Minnesota
P. O. Box 8899
Minneapolis, MN 55404

MISSISSIPPI
Medicare
The Travelers Insurance Co.
P. O. Box 22545
Jackson, MS 39205

MISSOURI
Counties of Andrew,
Atchison, Bates, Benton,
Buchanan, Caldwell, Carroll,
Cass, Clay, Clinton, Daviess,
DeKalb, Gentry, Grundy,
Harrison, Henry, Holt,
Jackson, Johnson, Lafayette,

Livingston, Mercer, Nodaway,
Pettis, Platte, Ray, St. Clair,
Saline, Vernon, Worth:
Medicare
Blue Shield of Kansas City
P. O. Box 169
Kansas City, MO 64141

Rest of State:
Medicare
General American Life
Insurance Co.
P. O. Box 505
St. Louis, MO 63166

MONTANA
Medicare
Montana Physicians' Service
P. O. Box 2510
Helena, MT 59601

NEBRASKA
Medicare
Mutual of Omaha
Insurance Co.
P. O. Box 456, Downtown
Station
Omaha, NE 68101

NEVADA
Medicare
Aetna Life & Casualty
P. O. Box 7290
Reno, NV 89510

NEW HAMPSHIRE
Medicare
New Hampshire–Vermont
Health Service
2 Pillsbury Street
Concord, NH 03301

NEW JERSEY
Medicare
The Prudential Insurance Co.
of America
P. O. Box 4000
Linwood, NJ 08221

NEW MEXICO
Medicare
The Equitable Life Assurance
Society
P. O. Box 3070, Station D
Albuquerque, NM 87110

NEW YORK
*Counties of Bronx, Columbia,
Delaware, Dutchess, Greene,
Kings, Nassau, New York,
Orange, Putnam, Richmond,
Rockland, Suffolk, Sullivan,
Ulster, Westchester:*
Medicare
Blue Cross–Blue Shield of
Greater New York
P. O. Box 535
Murray Hill Station
New York, NY 10016

County of Queens:
Medicare
Group Health, Inc.
Box A, 966 Times Square
Station
New York, NY 10036

*Counties of Livingston,
Monroe, Ontario, Seneca,
Wayne, Yates:*
Medicare
Genesee Valley
Medical Care, Inc.
41 Chestnut Street
Rochester, NY 14647

*Counties of Allegany,
Cattaraugus, Erie, Genesee,
Niagara, Orleans, Wyoming:*
Medicare
Blue Shield of Western New
York, Inc.
298 Main Street
Buffalo, NY 14202

*Counties of Albany, Broome,
Cayuga, Chautauqua,
Chemung, Chenango, Clinton,
Cortland Essex, Franklin,
Fulton, Hamilton, Herkimer,
Jefferson, Lewis, Madison,
Montgomery, Oneida,
Onondaga, Oswego, Otsego,
Rensselaer, Saratoga,
Schenectady, Schoharie,
Schuyler, Steuben, St.
Lawrence, Tioga, Tompkins,
Warren, Washington:*

New York *(cont'd)*

Medicare
276 Genesee Street
P. O. Box 393
Utica, NY 13503

NORTH CAROLINA
The Prudential Insurance Co.
of America
Medicare B Division
P. O. Box 2126
High Point, NC 27261

NORTH DAKOTA
Medicare
Blue Shield of North Dakota
301 Eighth Street, South
Fargo, ND 58102

OHIO
Medicare
Nationwide Mutual
Insurance Co.
P. O. Box 57
Columbus, OH 43216

OKLAHOMA
Medicare
Aetna Life & Casualty
1140 N. W. 63rd Street
Oklahoma City, OK 73116

OREGON
Medicare
Aetna Life & Casualty
Crown Plaza
1500 S. W. First Avenue
Portland, OR 97201

PENNSYLVANIA
Medicare
Pennsylvania Blue Shield
Box 65 Blue Shield Bldg.
Camp Hill, PA 17011

RHODE ISLAND
Medicare
Blue Shield of Rhode Island
444 Westminster Mall
Providence, RI 02901

SOUTH CAROLINA
Medicare
Blue Shield of South Carolina
Drawer F., Forest Acres
Branch
Columbia, SC 29260

SOUTH DAKOTA
Medicare
South Dakota Medical
Service, Inc.
1601 W. Madison
Sioux Falls, SD 57104

TENNESSEE
Medicare
The Equitable Life Assurance
Society
P. O. Box 1465
Nashville, TN 37202

TEXAS
Medicare
Group Medical and Surgical
Service
P. O. Box 22147
Dallas, TX 75222

UTAH
Medicare
Blue Shield of Utah
P. O. Box 30270
2455 Parley's Way
Salt Lake City, UT 84125

VERMONT
Medicare
New Hampshire–Vermont
Health Service
2 Pillsbury Street
Concord, NH 03301

VIRGINIA
*Counties of Arlington,
Fairfax:
Cities of Alexandria, Falls
Church, Fairfax:*
Medicare
Medical Service of D.C.
550 12th St. S.W.
Washington, DC 20024

Rest of State:
Medicare
The Travelers Insurance Co.
P. O. Box 26463
Richmond, VA 23261

WASHINGTON
Medicare
Washington Physicians'
Service
Mail to your local Medical
Service Bureau

*If you do not know which
bureau handles your claim,
mail to:*
Medicare Washington
Physicians' Service
4th and Battery Bldg.
2401 4th Avenue
Seattle, WA 98121

WEST VIRGINIA
Medicare
Nationwide Mutual
Insurance Co.
P. O. Box 57
Columbus, OH 43216

WISCONSIN
County of Milwaukee:
Medicare
Surgical Care–Blue Shield
P. O. Box 2049
Milwaukee, WI 53201

Rest of State:
Medicare
Wisconsin Physicians' Service
Box 1787
Madison, WI 53701

WYOMING
Medicare
The Equitable Life Assurance
Society
P. O. Box 628
Cheyenne, WY 82001

PUERTO RICO

Medicare
Seguros de Servicio de Salud
de Puerto Rico
P. O. Box 3628
104 Ponce de Leon Avenue
Hato Rey, PR 00936

VIRGIN ISLANDS

Medicare
Seguros de Servicio de Salud
de Puerto Rico
P. O. Box 3628
104 Ponce de Leon Avenue
Hato Rey, PR 00936

AMERICAN SAMOA

Medicare
Hawaii Medical Service Assn.
P. O. Box 860
Honolulu, HI 96808

GUAM

Medicare
Aetna Life & Casualty
P. O. Box 3947
Honolulu, HI 96812

Medicare Part B (SMI)
Toll-free Telephone Numbers

These numbers can be used *only* when calling within the state or service area indicated. For example, 1-800-352-0411 can be used to phone the Medicare office in the state of Arizona, except if you are calling from Phoenix. To call from Phoenix, the number is 263-7722. To check an 800 number, call Information, 1-800-555-1212.

ALABAMA (except Birmingham)   800-292-8856
ALASKA   no toll-free number
ARIZONA (except Phoenix)   800-352-0411
    (In Phoenix area call 263-7722)
ARKANSAS (except Little Rock)   800-482-5525, 5526, 5529, 5531
    (In Little Rock call 378-2320)
CALIFORNIA
    (In Los Angeles area call 748-2311)
    Counties of: Los Angeles, Orange, San Diego, Ventura, San Bernardino, Imperial, San Luis Obispo, Riverside, Santa Barbara; i.e., Area Codes 213, 714, & 805   800-252-9020
        Rest of state:
        (In San Francisco area call 445-5781)
        Area Codes 916, 707, 415, 408, & 209   800-792-8040
        Area Codes 213, 714, & 805   800-792-2982
COLORADO (except Denver)   800-332-6681
    (In Denver area call 831-2661)
CONNECTICUT (except Hartford & Wallingford)   800-982-6819
    (In Hartford area call 728-6783)
    (In Wallingford area call 265-7651)

DELAWARE (except Wilmington)   800-292-7865
   (In Wilmington area call 575-0600)
DISTRICT OF COLUMBIA   no toll-free number,
   call collect (202)-484-9200
   (Local: 484-9200)
FLORIDA
   (In Jacksonville area call 355-3680)
   Counties of Dade, Monroe   800-442-1515
   Group Health, Inc., statewide number is   800-432-8250
GEORGIA (except Atlanta)   800-282-0957
   (In Atlanta area call 325-5668)
HAWAII (except Honolulu)   no toll-free number
   (In Honolulu area call 524-1240)
IDAHO (except Boise)   800-632-6574
   (In Boise area call 342-7763)
ILLINOIS (except Chicago)   800-942-5261
   (In Chicago call 635-6020)
INDIANA (except Indianapolis)   800-622-4792
   (In Indianapolis area call 634-8450)
IOWA (except Des Moines)   800-532-1285
   (In Des Moines area call 245-4911)
KANSAS (except Topeka)   800-432-3531
   (In Topeka area call 232-1000)
KENTUCKY (except Lexington)   800-432-9255
   (In Lexington area call 233-1436)
LOUISIANA (except New Orleans)   800-362-6740, 6741, 6749
   (In New Orleans area call 821-2530)
MAINE   800-225-2054
MARYLAND (see exceptions below)   800-492-4795
   (In Baltimore area call 825-8711)
   (In Montgomery and Prince Georges counties call 484-9200;
      if long distance, call collect 202-484-9200)
MASSACHUSETTS   800-882-1228
MICHIGAN
   Detroit area   800-482-4045, 4046
   Lansing area   800-322-2793
   Western or Grand Rapids area   800-442-8020
   Upper Peninsula   800-482-4049
MINNESOTA
   (In Bloomington area call 884-7171)
   (In Minneapolis/St. Paul area call 450-8682)
   Counties of Anoka, Dakota, Filmore, Goodhue, Hennepin,
      Houston, Olmstead, Ramsey, Wabasha, Washington,
      Winona   800-352-2762
   Rest of state   800-352-0343, 9344

MISSISSIPPI (except Jackson)   800-682-5417
   (In Jackson area call 982-9411)
MISSOURI
   Blue Shield of Kansas City, Missouri   800-892-5900
      (In Kansas City call 932-5410)
   General American Life Insurance Company   800-392-2070
      (In St. Louis area call 843-8880)
MONTANA (except Helena)   800-332-6146
   (In Helena area call 442-2355)
NEBRASKA (except Omaha)   800-642-8340, 8341
   (In Omaha area call 978-2240)
NEVADA   800-528-0311
NEW HAMPSHIRE (except Concord)   800-852-3472
   (In Concord area call 224-9511)
NEW JERSEY
   Questions on Medicare Coverage and Reimbursement for
      Medical Equipment   800-462-9305
   Counties of Middlesex, Monmouth, Hunterdon, Mercer, Sum-
      merset, Ocean   800-462-9312
   Counties of Camden, Union   800-462-9335
   Counties of Atlantic, Cape May, Cumberland, Gloucester,
      Salem   800-462-9351
   Counties of Essex, Burlington   800-462-9385
   Counties of Morris, Warren, Sussex   800-462-9397
   Counties of Bergen, Hudson   800-462-9306
   County of Passaic   800-462-9307
NEW MEXICO (except Albuquerque)   800-432-6660
   (In Albuquerque area call 265-7605)
NEW YORK
   Blue Shield of Greater New York   800-442-8430
   Counties of Columbia, Delaware, Dutchess, Greene, Orange,
      Putnam, Rockland, Suffolk, Sullivan, Ulster, and that part
      of Westchester north of Scarsdale
   In New York City and counties of Bronx, Kings, Nassau,
      New York, and Richmond call 490-4444
   Blue Shield of Western New York   800-252-6550
   Counties of Albany, Broome, Cayuga, Chautauqua, Chemung,
      Chenango, Clinton, Cortland, Essex, Franklin, Fulton, Ham-
      ilton, Herkimer, Jefferson, Lewis, Madison, Montgomery,
      Oneida, Onondaga, Oswego, Otsego, Rensselaer, Saratoga,
      Schenectady, Schoharie, Schuyler, Steuben, St. Lawrence,
      Tioga, Tompkins, Warren, Washington
   (In Queens call Group Health, Inc.)   760-6790, 6795, 6800
NORTH CAROLINA (except High Point)   800-672-3071
   (In High Point call 885-8171)

NORTH DAKOTA (except Fargo)   800-342-4718
    (In Fargo call 282-6241)
OHIO (except Columbus)   800-282-0530
    (In Columbus area call 227-7157)
OKLAHOMA (except Oklahoma City)   800-522-9079
    (In Oklahoma City call 848-7711)
OREGON (except Portland)   800-452-0125
    (In Portland call 222-6831)
PENNSYLVANIA (except Camp Hill)   800-382-1274
    (In Camp Hill call 763-3601)
RHODE ISLAND   no toll-free number
    (Consult directory under "Medicare Claims Information"
    or call 831-7300)
    (On Block Island ask Operator for Enterprise 5301)
SOUTH CAROLINA (except Columbia)   800-922-2340
    (In Columbia call 788-8100)
SOUTH DAKOTA (except Sioux Falls)   800-952-3902
    (In Sioux Falls call 336-1976)
.TENNESSEE (except Nashville)   800-342-8900
    (In Nashville call 244-5600)
TEXAS (except Dallas)   800-442-2620
    (In Dallas area call 647-2282)
UTAH (except Salt Lake City)   800-662-3398
    (In Salt Lake City area call 487-6441)
VERMONT   800-258-3480
VIRGINIA (see exceptions below)   800-552-3423
    (In Richmond call 359-9181)
    Counties of Arlington, Fairfax and cities of Alexandria, Falls
    Church, Fairfax call 484-9200; If long distance call 202-484-
    9200
WASHINGTON
    Spokane County   800-572-5256
    Kitsap County   800-552-7114
    (All other counties call local Medical Service Bureau or call
    collect to Seattle office 206-763-9222)
WEST VIRGINIA   800-848-0106
WISCONSIN (except Madison)   800-362-7221
    (In Madison call 221-4711)
WYOMING (except Cheyenne)   800-442-2371
    (In Cheyenne call 632-9381)
PUERTO RICO AND VIRGIN ISLANDS call collect   800-754-2263

Medicare Sample Forms and
Record-keeping Materials

HEALTH INSURANCE CLAIM FORM

READ INSTRUCTIONS BEFORE COMPLETING OR SIGNING THIS FORM

Form Approved
OMB No. 0938-0008

☐ MEDICARE ☐ MEDICAID ☐ CHAMPUS ☐ OTHER

PATIENT & INSURED (SUBSCRIBER) INFORMATION

1 PATIENT'S NAME *(first name, middle initial, last name)*

2 PATIENT'S DATE OF BIRTH

3 INSURED'S NAME *(First name, middle initial, last name)*

4 PATIENT'S ADDRESS *(Street, city, state, ZIP code)*

5 PATIENT'S SEX
MALE ☐ FEMALE ☐

6 INSURED'S I.D. MEDICARE AND/OR MEDICAID NO *(Include any letters)*

7 PATIENT'S RELATIONSHIP TO INSURED
SELF ☐ SPOUSE ☐ CHILD ☐ OTHER ☐

8 INSURED'S GROUP NO *(Or Group Name)*

TELEPHONE NUMBER

9 OTHER HEALTH INSURANCE COVERAGE Enter Name of
Policyholder and Plan Name and Address and Policy or Medical
Assistance Number

10 WAS CONDITION RELATED TO
A PATIENT'S EMPLOYMENT
YES ☐ NO ☐
B AN ACCIDENT
AUTO ☐ OTHER ☐

11 INSURED'S ADDRESS *(Street, city, state, ZIP code)*

12 PATIENT'S OR AUTHORIZED PERSON'S SIGNATURE *(Read back before signing)*
I Authorize the Release of any Medical Information Necessary to Process the Claim and Request Payment of MEDICARE Benefits
Either to Myself or to the Party Who Accepts Assignment Below

SIGNED _____ DATE _____

13 I AUTHORIZE PAYMENT OF MEDICAL BENEFITS TO UNDERSIGNED
PHYSICIAN OR SUPPLIER FOR SERVICE DESCRIBED BELOW

SIGNED *(Insured or Authorized Person)*

PHYSICIAN OR SUPPLIER INFORMATION

14 DATE OF ▶ ILLNESS (FIRST SYMPTOM) OR
INJURY (ACCIDENT OR
PREGNANCY (LMP)

15 DATE FIRST CONSULTED
YOU FOR THIS CONDITION

16 HAS PATIENT EVER HAD SAME
OR SIMILAR SYMPTOMS?
YES ☐ NO ☐

16a IF AN EMERGENCY
CHECK HERE ☐

17 DATE PATIENT ABLE TO
RETURN TO WORK

18 DATES OF TOTAL DISABILITY
FROM _____ THROUGH _____

DATES OF PARTIAL DISABILITY
FROM _____ THROUGH _____

19 NAME OF REFERRING PHYSICIAN OR OTHER SOURCE *(e.g. public health agency)*

20 FOR SERVICES RELATED TO HOSPITALIZATION
GIVE HOSPITALIZATION DATES
ADMITTED _____ DISCHARGED _____

21 NAME & ADDRESS OF FACILITY WHERE SERVICES RENDERED *(If other than home or office)*

22 WAS LABORATORY WORK PERFORMED OUTSIDE YOUR OFFICE?
YES ☐ NO ☐ CHARGES _____

23 DIAGNOSIS OR NATURE OF ILLNESS OR INJURY RELATE DIAGNOSIS TO PROCEDURE IN COLUMN D
BY REFERENCE NUMBERS 1, 2, 3 ETC OR DX CODE

1.
2.
3.
4.

B
EPSDT
YES ☐ NO ☐
FAMILY
PLANNING
YES ☐ NO ☐
PRIOR
AUTHORIZATION NO

24 A DATE OF SERVICE FROM — TO	B PLACE OF SERVICE	C FULLY DESCRIBE PROCEDURES, MEDICAL SERVICES OR SUPPLIES FURNISHED FOR EACH DATE GIVEN *(EXPLAIN UNUSUAL SERVICES OR CIRCUMSTANCES)* PROCEDURE CODE (IDENTIFY)	D DIAGNOSIS CODE	E CHARGES	DAYS OR UNITS	G* T O S	H LEAVE BLANK

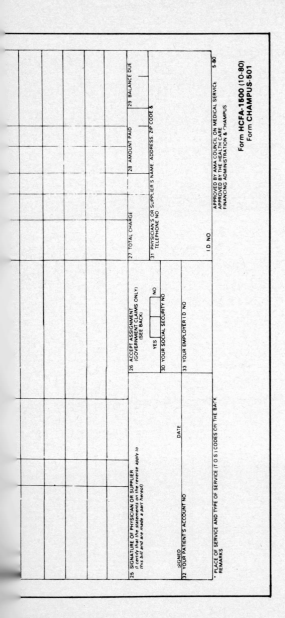

Form **HCFA-1500** (10-80)
Form **CHAMPUS-501**

Form HCFA-1500. This is the form that is filed by your doctor or other Part B provider. You will be asked to sign it, but you will not usually be expected to send it in to Medicare. The provider's office can file this for you even if the assignment is not accepted (line 26 indicates this information). If you have been receiving Medicare benefits for a number of years, you may have filled out this form yourself, but now Form HCFA-1490S is the only form you have to fill out and it is much simpler than this one.

FORM SSA-1533 (11-75)

U.S. DEPARTMENT OF HEALTH, EDUCATION, AND WELFARE / SOCIAL SECURITY ADMINISTRATION

MEDICARE HOSPITAL, EXTENDED CARE AND HOME HEALTH BENEFITS RECORD

DATE: 03/04/77

E994703470446022 076034

John Doe
MERWIN LN
WILTON CT

HEALTH INSURANCE CLAIM NUMBER

C44-C3-CL51A

◄ Always use this number when writing about your claim.

THIS IS NOT A BILL. This notice is to give you a record of the Medicare benefits you used during the period shown in Item 1. For important additional information please see the other side of this form.

1 OUR RECORDS SHOW THAT YOU RECEIVED THESE SERVICES

Type of Services	Services Were Provided By		Date
INPATIENT HOSPITAL	NORWALK HOSP 24 STEVENS ST NORWALK CONNECTICUT	06852	01/20/77 THRU 01/22/77

2 MEDICARE HAS PAID FOR ALL COVERED SERVICES EXCEPT

$124.00 FOR THE INPATIENT DEDUCTIBLE.

IF YOU HAVE ANY QUESTIONS
ABOUT THIS RECORD
PLEASE GET IN TOUCH WITH:

CONNECTICUT BLUE CROSS INC
370 BASSETT ROAD
NORTH HAVEN CONNECTICUT   06473

3 OUR RECORDS SHOW THE FOLLOWING BENEFITS WERE USED THIS TIME

Inpatient Hospital Days	Lifetime Reserve Days	Extended Care Days	Home Health Visits Hospital Insurance	Home Health Visits Medical Insurance
2				

This form is your record of your Part A coverage. It does not take the place of an itemized bill that you should insist on receiving, in addition, direct from the hospital. Although it is not a bill, it does show on line 2 whether you still owe anything. In this example, the bill is from a hospital and the inpatient deductible is the only amount owed. Be sure, however, that that amount is not covered by your Medigap insurance; do not pay it until you have checked. It may well be that you do not owe anything.

CONNECTICUT GENERAL LIFE INSURANCE COMPANY

200 PRATT ST. • MERIDEN, CONNECTICUT 06450

DATE OF NOTICE	HEALTH INSURANCE NUMBER	CONTROL NUMBER
04/01/79	000-11-2222A	9001-11112-00

BENEFICIARY

John Q. Public

*FOR HEALTH INSURANCE
SOCIAL SECURITY ACT

NOTICE OF NON PAYMENT

John Q. Public
21 Main Street
Anytown, Connecticut   06492

EXPLANATION OF MEDICARE BENEFITS

BENEFITS WERE MADE PAYABLE TO THE PROVIDER OF SERVICES

1 SERVICES WERE PROVIDED BY	2 WHEN FROM MO DAY	TO MO DAY YR	3 AMOUNT BILLED	4 AMOUNT APPROVED	5 EXPLANATION OF ANY DIFFERENCE BETWEEN COLUMNS 3 & 4 MEDICARE DOES NOT PAY FOR.	SERVICE CODES SEE BACK
John Fixum, M.D.	02 04	03 10 9	20.00	20.00		1 A
		02 05 9	5.00	5.00		1 E
		03 10 9	3.00	3.00		1 E
		03 11 9	25.00	20.00	See Item 5 on Back	3 A
	03 12	03 21 9	100.00	100.00		3 A

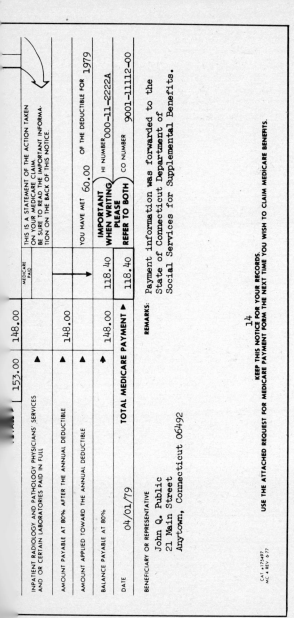

Here are examples of EOMB forms, showing some variations you may encounter. Included are forms from California, Massachusetts, Colorado and Connecticut. A filled-out form is explained in detail in Chapter 17. The differences among the forms are minor; all forms contain the same information—sometimes in a different part of the form. Two Massachusetts forms are illustrated: one shows where a check would be attached if you were entitled to one. The check will always be positioned so that you can easily detach it for cashing. In this event, you should retain the rest of the form for your records.

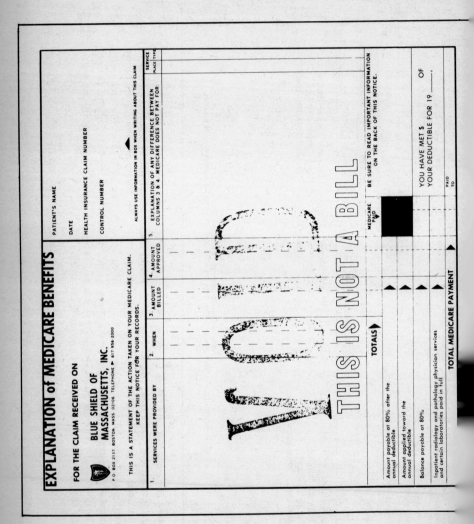

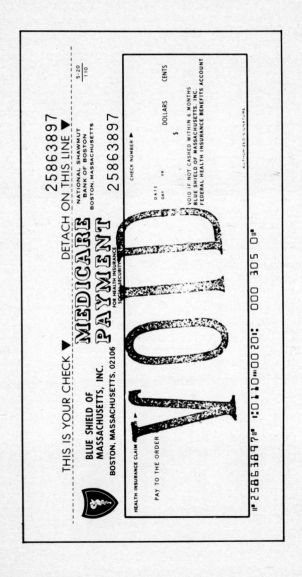

EXPLANATION OF MEDICARE BENEFITS

Blue Shield. of Colorado
700 BROADWAY
DENVER, COLORADO 80203
TELEPHONE (303) 231-2131

DATE	HEALTH INSURANCE CLAIM NUMBER	THIS PROCESSING NUMBER
06/16/76	123-45-6789	78-654321

BENEFICIARY
JOHN Q. PUBLIC

FOR HEALTH INSURANCE
SOCIAL SECURITY ACT

PAYMENTS MADE BELOW, IF ANY,
WERE MADE TO:
NAME AND ADDRESS

JOHN Q. PUBLIC
123 WEST STREET
MIDTOWN, AMERICA 10000

THIS IS A STATEMENT OF THE ACTION TAKEN ON YOUR MEDICARE CLAIM. KEEP THIS NOTICE FOR YOUR RECORDS

SERVICES WERE PROVIDED BY:	2. SERVICE DATES: FROM MO DAY YR	TO MO DAY YR	3. AMOUNT BILLED	4. AMOUNT APPROVED	5. EXPLANATION OF ANY DIFFERENCE BETWEEN COLUMNS 3 & 4 & SERVICE CARE DOES NOT PAY FOR	SERVICE CODES (SEE BACK)
DR. J. SMITH	03 15	04 15 6	70.00	70.00		A1
TOPPER LABS		03 30 6	35.00	35.00		06
DR. T. BROWN		04 05 6	500.00	450.00	SEE ITEM 5 ON BACK	B3
DR. T. JONES		05 15 6	25.00	00.00	ROUTINE EYE EXAM	I1

| | TOTALS ▲ | 630.00 | 555.00 | MEDICARE PAID | |

PLEASE BE SURE TO READ THE IMPORTANT INFORMATION ON THE BACK OF THIS NOTICE.

PHYSICIAN CHARGES FOR INPATIENT PATHOLOGY AND RADIOLOGY SERVICES AND CERTAIN LABORATORY SERVICES ARE PAID IN FULL BY MEDICARE. ▲ 00.00 00.00

AMOUNT PAYABLE AT 80% AFTER THE ANNUAL DEDUCTIBLE ▲ 555.00

AMOUNT APPLIED TOWARD ANNUAL DEDUCTIBLE ▲ 60.00

YOU HAVE MET $60 OF THE DEDUCTIBLE FOR 1976

BALANCE PAYABLE AT 80% ▲ 495.00 396.00

YOUR MEDICARE NUMBER 123-45-6789   HEALTH INS. CLAIM NO.

DATE 06/16/76   TOTAL MEDICARE PAYMENT ▲ 396.00

IMPORTANT WHEN WRITING   THIS PROCESSING NUMBER 78-654321

PLEASE REFER TO BOTH

REMARKS

Blue Shield of Colorado
700 BROADWAY
DENVER, COLORADO 80203
TELEPHONE (303) 831-2131

Use the Attached Request for Medicare Payment Form the Next Time You Wish to Claim Medicare Benefits

THIS IS NOT A BILL

USE THE ENCLOSED
REQUEST FOR
MEDICARE PAYMENT
FORM THE NEXT
TIME YOU WISH TO
CLAIM MEDICARE
PAYMENT.

SEE REVERSE SIDE
FOR ADDITIONAL
INFORMATION

EXPLANATION OF MEDICARE BENEFITS

THIS IS A STATEMENT OF ACTION TAKEN ON YOUR MEDICARE CLAIM

SERVICES WERE PROVIDED BY NAME / NUMBER	BLUE SHIELD CONTROL NO.	PROCEDURE NO.	UNITS	PLACE OF SERVICE	TYPE OF SERVICE	SERVICE DATES FROM MO DAY YR	TO MO DAY YR	CHARGES SUBMITTED	AMOUNT APPROVED BY MEDICARE	DEDUC TIBLE	REIMB RATE %	NET PAY
DR. J. SMITH	78-654321	90045	7	1	1	031576	041576	70 00	70 00	60 00	80%	8 00
TOPPER LABS	78-654321	50243	2	5	4	0330 76		35 00	35 00	00 00	80%	28 00
DR. T. BROWN	78-654321	24639	1	3	2	0405 76		500 00	450 00	00 00	80%	360 00
SEE ITEM 5 ON BACK												
	78-654321	42120	1	1	9	0515 76		25 00	00 00	00 00	00%	00 00

THIS SERVICE BY AN OPTOMETRIST, NOT A BENEFIT

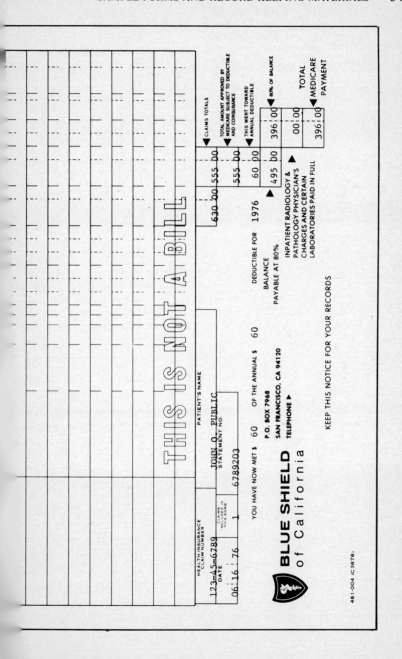

THIS IS NOT A BILL

HEALTH INSURANCE CLAIM NUMBER
123-45-6789

DATE   CLAIMS INCLUDED IN THIS ECMB
06 16 76   1

STATEMENT NO
6789203

PATIENT'S NAME
JOHN Q. PUBLIC

YOU HAVE NOW MET $ 60   OF THE ANNUAL $ 60

BLUE SHIELD of California
P.O. BOX 7968
SAN FRANCISCO, CA 94120
TELEPHONE ▶

KEEP THIS NOTICE FOR YOUR RECORDS

461-004 (C387B)

CLAIMS TOTALS   630 00

TOTAL AMOUNT APPROVED BY MEDICARE SUBJECT TO DEDUCTIBLE AND COINSURANCE   555 00

THIS WENT TOWARD ANNUAL DEDUCTIBLE   60 00

TOTAL AMOUNT SUBJECT TO DEDUCTIBLE   555 00

DEDUCTIBLE FOR 1976

BALANCE PAYABLE AT 80%   495 00

INPATIENT RADIOLOGY & PATHOLOGY PHYSICIAN'S CHARGES AND CERTAIN LABORATORIES PAID IN FULL

80% OF BALANCE   396 00

00 00

TOTAL MEDICARE PAYMENT   396 00

EXPLANATION of MEDICARE BENEFITS

FOR THE CLAIM RECEIVED ON

BLUE SHIELD OF MASSACHUSETTS, INC.
P.O. BOX 2137 BOSTON, MASS. 02106 TELEPHONE ▶ 617 956 4000

THIS IS A STATEMENT OF THE ACTION TAKEN ON YOUR MEDICARE CLAIM.
KEEP THIS NOTICE FOR YOUR RECORDS.

PATIENT'S NAME

DATE

HEALTH INSURANCE CLAIM NUMBER

CONTROL NUMBER

ALWAYS USE INFORMATION IN BOX WHEN WRITING ABOUT THIS CLAIM

1. SERVICES WERE PROVIDED BY	2. WHEN	3. AMOUNT BILLED	4. AMOUNT APPROVED	5. EXPLANATION OF ANY DIFFERENCE BETWEEN COLUMNS 3 & 4. MEDICARE DOES NOT PAY FOR:	SERVICE PLACE	TYPE

THIS IS NOT A BILL

TOTALS ▶				MEDICARE PAID	BE SURE TO READ IMPORTANT INFORMATION ON THE BACK OF THIS NOTICE.
Amount payable at 80% after the annual deductible	▶				
Amount applied toward the annual deductible	▶				
Balance payable at 80%	▶				YOU HAVE MET $ OF YOUR DEDUCTIBLE FOR 19____.
Inpatient radiology and pathology physician services and certain laboratories paid in full	▶				
TOTAL MEDICARE PAYMENT	▶			PAID TO	

REMARKS:

Medicare Medical Insurance Claims Record

Note: After payment is made on a claim, cross out the information you recorded in the columns below. This way, you will know the claim has been completed.

Date you mailed claim	Date of service or supply	Doctor or supplier who provided service or supply	Service or supply you received	Charge for service or supply

Form SSA-3596 (7 77)   ☆U.S. Government Printing Office: 1977—243-159

This compact Claims Record chart is available free from Medicare. It will fit in the same pocket of *Your Medicare Recordkeeper* as your EOMB forms.

Your
Medicare
Recordkeeper

Your Health Insurance Claim Number

Use the block above to keep a record of your health insurance claim
number. Copy the number, including the letter at the end, exactly as
it's shown on your Medicare card. Always carry your card with you. If
you ever lose your card, notify a social security office right away.

This handy three-pocket folder is available free from Medicare. It has
room to keep: (1) General information (including your *Medicare Handbook*); (2) Your claim forms (HCFA-1490S), both blanks and copies of
forms you have sent in; (3) Notices (such as your EOMB forms).

I.   **Medicare Supplement Policies**

NOT COVERED BY MEDICARE (1982 figures—Subject to Change in 1983)	COVERED BY PROPOSED POLICY? YES NO		WHAT DOES PROPOSED POLICY PAY?
$260 for the first 60 days of inpatient hospital services in a benefit period (the inpatient hospital deductible)			
$65 a day for the 61st to 90th day of inpatient hospital services in a benefit period			
$130 a day for inpatient hospital services for each "lifetime reserve" day used (can be used up to a total of 60 days in your lifetime, whenever you need more than 90 days in a benefit period)			
Over 150 days of inpatient hospital services in a benefit period (over 90 days if you have used all your "lifetime reserve" days)			
$32.50 a day for the 21st to 100th day in a benefit period for inpatient services in a skilled nursing facility			
Over 100 days of inpatient skilled nursing facility care in a benefit period.			
Nursing home care in *other* than a skilled nursing facility.			
Private room in a hospital or skilled nursing facility (except when medically necessary)			
Private duty nurses in a hospital or skilled nursing facility.			
The first 3 pints of blood under either Medicare hospital *or* medical insurance			
The first $75 of doctor bills and other medical services and supplies under Medicare medical insurance (the medical insurance annual deductible)			

Here is a checklist prepared by the Health Care Financing Administration to help you evaluate a Medigap policy. You can simply copy it or adapt it to suit yourself.

Medicare Supplement Policies (cont.)

NOT COVERED BY MEDICARE (1982 figures—Subject to Change in 1983)	COVERED BY PROPOSED POLICY? YES	NO	WHAT DOES PROPOSED POLICY PAY?
After the first $75, 20% of "reasonable charges" for doctor bills and other bills for covered medical services and supplies under Medicare medical insurance.			
Charges *above* the Medicare "reasonable charge" in non-assignment cases.			
Drugs and medicines you buy yourself			
Eyeglasses (except after cataract surgery)			
Hearing aids			
Dental care			
Medical care outside the United States			

Are there any additional benefits the proposed policy pays?   YES ☐ NO ☐

If yes, describe. _____

_____

_____

_____

a.   Is there a pre-existing condition exclusion?   YES ☐ NO ☐

     If yes, what conditions are excluded and for how long? _____

_____

_____

b.   Is there a waiting period before policy pays benefits?   YES ☐ NO ☐

     If yes, when does the policy begin paying benefits? _____

II. **Hospital Indemnity Policies**

    a. What is the daily payment rate? $ _____ per day

    b. On what day of a hospital stay do payments begin? _____

    c. What is the maximum number of days the policy will pay? _____

    d. Is there a maximum payment provision? If yes, what
        is the maximum amount? _____   YES ☐   NO ☐

    e. Are there any excluded illnesses? If yes, describe.   YES ☐   NO ☐

        _____

        _____

    f. Are there any benefits in addition to the daily payment rate?
       If yes, describe.   YES ☐   NO ☐

        _____

        _____

III. **Nursing Home Policies**

    a. Does the policy cover care in facilities other than skilled nursing facilities?   YES ☐   NO ☐

        If yes, what other kinds of nursing homes?

        _____

        _____

    b. Does the policy cover your stay in a skilled nursing facility or other
        nursing home when the care you need is primarily *custodial* care,
        that is, mainly personal care, such as help in feeding, dressing,
        getting in and out of bed, and taking medicine.   YES ☐   NO ☐

        If yes, under what conditions and for how long will the policy
        pay for such care?

        _____

        _____

    c. Are there any excluded illnesses. If yes, describe.   YES ☐   NO ☐

        _____

        _____

        _____

Index